The first in a series entitled
Man, His Community and Natural Resources

# Water and Community Development
Social and Economic Perspectives

Donald R. Field
James C. Barron
Burl F. Long

Andrew S. Thomas Memorial Library
MORRIS HARVEY COLLEGE, CHARLESTON, W. VA.

**ann arbor science** PUBLISHERS INC.
POST OFFICE BOX 1425 • ANN ARBOR, MICH. 48106

Copyright © 1974 by Ann Arbor Science Publishers, Inc.
P.O. Box 1425, Ann Arbor, Michigan   48106   USA

Library of Congress Catalog Card No. 73-86058
ISBN   0-250-40038-3

Manufactured in the United States of America
All Rights Reserved

# Preface

The basic purpose of this book is to explore the role of water resources in contributing to community development and, conversely, the role of specific institutional arrangements, *i.e.*, communities, in contributing to the utilization, alteration or conservation of water resources. The specific topic assigned each author ensured a direction of thought, although no attempt was made to force them into a mold of conformity. It should not be surprising that there are differences among the authors in their definitions of community development, what it should be, or what constitutes the relationship among community institutions and water within those institutions. Consequently, the papers are diverse in character but do represent current thrusts in both sociology and economics. We see this as an advantage to the reader.

This volume was made possible through support of a conference, "Water and the Community," by the State of Washington Water Research Center, Department of Agricultural Economics, Washington State University, and the College of Forest Resources, University of Washington. The conference was held at Lake Wilderness Continuing Education Center, a facility of the University of Washington. Preliminary drafts of papers emanated from that conference and due to the critical summarization by Jim Hildreth who attended the conference, the final products are much improved. The papers which appear in this volume have not appeared elsewhere.

We would like to express our appreciation to Shirley Scott, Pat Davis and Nola Koesel for assuming major responsibilities in planning, coordinating, and implementing the many details necessary for the success of the conference. It was not by chance that the participants arrived at the right place, at the right time, were fed and housed. These efforts ensured an atmosphere in which an intellectually stimulating and pleasant social experience was achieved. Shirley Scott assumed additional responsibilities by assisting in the initial editing of each manuscript.

To

M. E. John

for interdisciplinary motivation

# About the Editors

*Donald R. Field* is Research Sociologist, National Park Service, U.S. Department of Interior, and Associate Professor of Forest Resources, University of Washington. He earned his PhD at Pennsylvania State University. His research interests focus on interrelationships between social structure and natural resources. Professor Field's current work includes the study of recreation areas as human leisure settings.

*James C. Barron,* Extension Economist and Associate Agricultural Economist at Washington State University, received his PhD at Pennsylvania State University and has conducted extension and research projects on water resource planning, land use, and local government finance.

*Burl F. Long* is Assistant Professor, Department of Agricultural Economics, Virginia Polytechnic Institute and State University. His MS degree was received at Oklahoma State University and his doctorate at Pennsylvania State. Both research and teaching interests include the economics of natural resources, environmental quality, community development and public policy. Environmental quality and regional economic development are treated in his current publications. Professor Long has served as resource economist to the U.S. Department of Agriculture.

# Contents

## I. THEORETICAL PERSPECTIVES

1. Toward an Integration of Economics and Sociology
   *Burl F. Long and Donald R. Field* ...................... 11
2. The Economic Meaning of Water: Patterns in Variation
   *Paul W. Barkley* ........................................ 27
3. Social Meanings of Water: Patterns of Variation
   *William R. Burch, Jr. and Neil H. Cheek, Jr.* ............ 41

## II. WATER RESOURCES AND REGIONAL DEVELOPMENT

4. The Role of Water Resources in Community Development
   *Walter R. Butcher* ...................................... 59
5. The Changing Nature of Water Resource Investments: Implications for Community Development
   *Daniel W. Bromley and Richard L. Barrows* ............ 81
6. Institutional Reorganization for Water Resources Management
   *Steven C. Smith* ........................................107

## III. WATER RESOURCE DEVELOPMENT AND HUMAN RESPONSE

7. Dynamics of Agency-Public Relations in Water Resource Planning
8. Self-Interest Groups and Human Emotion as Adaptive
   *Gordon L. Bultena* .....................................125
   Mechanisms
   *Courtland L. Smith* ....................................151

9. An Analysis of Community and Individual Reactions to Forced Migration Due to Reservoir Construction
    *Sue Johnson and Rabel J. Burdge* .........................169

## IV. COMMUNITY AND LEISURE

10. Social Groups and Water Activity Clusters: An Exploration of Interchangeability and Substitution
    *Joseph T. O'Leary, Donald R. Field and Gerard F. Schreuder* ...............................195
11. Impact of New Water-Based Facilities: Behavior and Management Implications
    *Dean R. Yoesting* ..........................................217
12. Economic Impact of Outdoor Recreation: What Have We Learned?
    *Herbert H. Stoevener, Bruce Rettig and Steve Reiling* ....235

## V. ENVIRONMENTAL DEMANDS ON WATER

13. Water and the Economics of Implementing Environmental Objectives
    *Thomas D. Crocker* ........................................261
14. The Three Fixes: Technological, Cognitive, and Structural
    *Thomas A. Heberlein* ......................................279

# Introduction

Community development is the process by which a community is strengthened or maintained to create an enlargement or diffusion of choices, opportunities and experiences for people as they seek to satisfy their personal and group goals, while sustaining the physical and biological system on which life depends. Development occurs as people acting individually or collectively are able to widen the range of their experiences and satisfactions. While there are different perceptions of what community development is among professionals and the general public, much of the confusion arises from attempts to define it too narrowly or specifically in terms of the outcome of particular projects. For example, the successful introduction of a manufacturing firm which will enhance an otherwise stagnant economy might be viewed as community development. Additionally, sending children from a town or city on an exchange to a foreign country, removal of a pollutant source from river systems and establishment of ecological preserves adjacent to community parks may be considered community development, or as aspects of community development.

Today, however, events affecting the vitality of the community emanate from the region and society in which it is located as well as the immediate locality. Decisions made there which influence community life alter the social and economic base and reduce options for growth or survival. These factors also might be considered as inputs in any community development matrix.

Economists think of community development in terms of increases in aggregate or per capita income, employment and shopping or service facilities. Sociologists may look to specific changes as noted above for consequences for the total institutional structure in which people and groups interact with each other. Political scientists tend to emphasize public decision-making processes and the responsiveness of public officials to community needs. An anthropologist may conceive of community development as changes in cultural patterns affecting human behavior positively. This is not to say that any given person will define development only in terms of a narrow disciplinary approach, but it illustrates different concepts of community development.

The important point is that communities are complex collections of people with a mixture of wants, preferences and habits. Changes which lead to greater satisfaction or human welfare constitute community development, whether those changes are economic, social, political or cultural.

Natural resources have played an important role in the location, function and growth of communities, but the nature of that role and peoples' perceptions of it are changing. The literature on development is replete with theoretical and empirical examples of various stages of growth through which a community, region or nation may proceed.

The first step is to exploit one or more natural resources for the production of primary products such as food, lumber or minerals. If the community continues to grow, it may also develop secondary production—manufacturing, processing and fabrication of products. Even further maturation of society leads to a relative increase in tertiary activities, *i.e.*, the service economy. Each succeeding stage grows in relative importance to the entire community, and the rate of change or the mix of activities may be influenced by the natural resource base. In earlier stages it is assumed the community is most heavily influenced by available resources, but at later stages the community begins to exert its own impact on the resource base. Technology, a changing mix of people and values, economic interdependencies, and new demands can lead to a redefinition of resources and a realignment of institutional structures.

Water has a certain mystique associated with community development because man obviously cannot survive in its absence. He has demonstrated, however, an amazing capacity to alter both the quantity and quality of water over time and space and for a variety of purposes. Water "development" has been pursued for any number of actual reasons, but leading the pack has been the objective of community development in one guise or another and with varying geographical boundaries of the community. Many federal, state and local agencies are exclusively or primarily concerned with water resource planning, development or management.

Given our definition of community development, it is obvious that hydropower, irrigation, flood control, water transport, recreational facilities and municipal supplies can lead to an expansion in the range of choice or opportunities for people in a community. It was on this basis that waterways were built or dredged, dams were erected, and dry land was converted to green fields. In recent years, however, new concerns have brought into question some of the traditional assumptions under which water development has occurred. A major conclusion of the National Water Commission is that while existing national water policy was once appropriate, it is no longer responsive to the needs of the present.

The papers in this book are not intended to evaluate overall water policy, but focus instead on the changing relationships between water and community development. Concern for this issue results from the addition of new demands being placed on the environment by communities. Recreational uses and improved water quality appear to be receiving higher priority than the older demands for irrigation, power production, and other water uses. Proponents of population control and a stable economy are gaining prominence in the array of water-related interest groups. The nature of public investments in water is beginning to reflect these shifts and the implications for community development are important both for growing areas and for communities in declining situations.

At this juncture a word should be said about the contributors and the perspectives they bring to the subject under discussion. They represent the disciplines of sociology and economics. While incomplete representation of the various social sciences is apparent in the volume, the desire for mutual exchange certainly is present. Commitment to interdisciplinary research is growing among all social scientists, for the answers sought will be derived from questions they ask.

Unfortunately, many answers are currently sought where few yet exist. Social scientists are moving more rapidly to establish research programs concerning natural resource questions. The mandate is firmly established. Man is part of the environment. His capacity to alter, adapt and react to the environment necessitates sound research answers in order to understand this dynamic relationship. Research which eventually transcends traditional disciplinary boundaries will provide the most comprehensive information for eventual problem-solving situations. We hope that the joint involvement by these sociologists and economists in the present effort is such a beginning.

# Part I
# Theoretical Perspectives

# About the Contributors

*Paul W. Barkley* is Professor of Agricultural Economics, Washington State University. His PhD was earned at Kansas State University. Major research interests include socio-economic developments in rural Washington State. Dr. Barkley has served as a member of Governor Evans' Urban Affairs Council and Rural Affairs Task Force. His publications include *Economic Growth and Environmental Decay* and *Introductory Economics*.

*William R. Burch, Jr.* is Associate Professor in Sociology and Forestry at Yale University. He earned his PhD at the University of Minnesota. His publications include numerous articles on social change, leisure, regional planning, and natural resources. Dr. Burch is the author of *Daydreams and Nightmares: A Sociological Essay on the American Environment* and editor with Neil H. Cheek, Jr. and Lee Taylor of *Social Behavior, Natural Resources and the Environment*. He has acted as consultant to the Urban Ecosystems Advisory Council and the Connecticut Department of Environmental Protection.

*Neil H. Cheek, Jr.* is Professor of Recreation and Parks, Texas A & M University and Adjunct Professor of Sociology, University of Denver. Formerly he was Senior Scientist (Sociology) with the National Park Service. His research interests lie in the social organization of leisure in human societies and in the sociology of natural resources. Dr. Cheek received his PhD in sociology from Washington University, St. Louis.

# Part I
# Theoretical Perspectives

Resources are constantly changing in response to man and his utilization of them. Among social scientists there is general acceptance of the dynamic interpretation of resources whereby the application of knowledge may expand or contract the resource base. Resources are important for the functions they may serve to satisfy human wants. This view is not altered by the recent emergence of an environmental ethic which consistently places higher values upon preservation than consumption of resources. It merely means that some shifting has taken place in human priorities as they relate to the satisfactions which may be derived from resources. While preservation is equated with unproductive non-use by some, it is to others a highest and best use. This conflict in values is important in analyzing the issues confronting society over resource use and its relation to community development.

Economists and sociologists have long been concerned with the use of natural resources. With regard to economics this interest has tended to follow three general themes. The first has to do with production of commodities—food and fiber—from the available resource base. Second has been the emphasis on conservation or the intertemporal use of resources. Third is the question of allocating resources among different uses to satisfy human wants. Each of these themes has some implications for community .development, although it has seldom been treated explicitly by researchers or practitioners.

Two theoretical issues that have emerged from economics are particularly important in thinking about water and community development—benefit/cost analysis and externalities. Although they were refined by economists, these issues are by no means limited to that discipline and their ultimate development will depend on the interaction of a variety of professions.

Cost/benefit analysis originated with concern over water resource development and has been most successfully applied to water problems. Neither the benefits nor the costs of a project are entirely economic; some may argue that economic effects are not even the major ones. In any case, the full impact on community development cannot be stated until the other social effects are also included.

Externality theory dates back to Alfred Marshall but in the last decade has been refined and applied in many ways to water. In its early formulation, the notion of an externality dealt with external effects on firms or individuals rather than upon communities. Recent conceptual developments have emphasized the very broad community impacts which again demonstrate the need for an integrated look at the total community rather than a narrow disciplinary approach.

Sociologists have emphasized the inherent social meaning or definition of resources in terms of the social structure man creates to deal with varying environmental conditions. Man is part of the ecosystem; his communities are real and dynamic and subject to change as the man-resource relationship is altered. Theories of modernization have captured economic growth and corresponding transition in societies from traditional to industrial in terms of man-community-resource relationships. In contrast, community analysis today must consider the joint interdependence of resources and communities in terms of societal stability and maintenance as well as exploitation. Given resource constraints, structural adaptation of communities may be more pronounced in its impact upon community life than that which occurred in an unlimited growth era.

The mutual dependence of communities and natural resources has always been a fact. The dominance of social structure or resources may vary. At times resources like water may constrain institutional development. At other times social structure alters or redefines the resource base, but in any event resources *are* because of man's definition. Regardless of the stage of social and economic development, resources and man's consideration of them are depicted within culture.

The initial chapter in this section deals with a different aspect of water and community development. While Burch and Cheek and Barkley outline from disciplinary perspective the context within which water may be examined, Long and Field suggest ways that both economic and sociological concepts may be considered jointly in the examination of water. Their approach emerges from a belief that interdisciplinary efforts can provide a more complete analysis and solutions to resource problems. Barkley places in perspective the history of U.S. water policy for economic development. He emphasizes the need to consider the broader relationship between water developments and the community to avoid the hazards of unanticipated consequences of narrowly focusing on short-run economic effects. The chapter by Burch and Cheek is a broad conceptual examination placing the discussion of water in such a context. Their focus on institutions and status systems clearly identifies water as an aspect of social structure. Comparison among communities from different ecological zones draws attention to the commonalities found in all communities as they adapt to existing resource conditions.

# 1. Toward an Integration of Economics and Sociology

**BURL F. LONG AND DONALD R. FIELD**

> The noble concept of the unification of science has always attracted the imaginative thinker. It is a concept, however, which has proved disappointing, and perhaps even positively dangerous in practice.
> —K. Boulding

We are not naive enough to consider ourselves imaginative thinkers and yet perhaps we should be bold enough to ignore the disappointments and dangers of which Boulding warns. It is all too obvious that many grandiose integrative systems have led at best to unimpressive results. Boulding cites two major reasons for failure of premature syntheses of different sciences—(1) the system may remain empty because knowledge fails to fit the model of the systems builder, or (2) we design pseudo-systems that are intellectually appealing without being true to reality (Boulding, 1968).

In the disciplines of economics and sociology much dissatisfaction and self-examination of our theoretical basis and our empirical analysis is afloat (Ward, 1972; Heilbroner and Ford, 1971). This is not new and seems to be somewhat peculiar to the social sciences. A recurring theme of most of these critiques is that economists have not been sociological enough in their theory and models and sociologists have ignored too many economic variables. We accept this general conclusion and hope to suggest a few ideas that may lead us toward a more integrative approach. Faster progress may be made by following separate disciplinary paths, but the quality of the results may be less than could be achieved through integration. The path of least resistance may be fastest, but it could lead us down the path of the man in San Francisco who wanted to go to Seattle but took a plane to New York instead because it was faster.

The purpose of this paper is to call attention again to the need and opportunities for more coordinated research efforts by social scientists and to suggest some avenues where this might take place.

## INTERDISCIPLINARY RESEARCH—PROBLEMS AND POTENTIAL

There is no magic way of organizing or conducting research. (At best, research outcomes are not fully predictable.) Whether water resources research be conducted in groups, by individual scientists, or along narrowly defined disciplinary lines, the skills, intuition, and dedication of the researcher are major determinants in the success of the effort.

The desirability of considering various disciplinary orientations in an integrated manner when dealing with natural resource environmental topics is apparent. Complex problems require comprehensive investigation. The nature of the subject field encompasses both social and physical phenomena. Consideration of sociological, economic, political and physical science factors is a prerequisite for obtaining meaningful answers. As a complex interdisciplinary problem, traditional disciplinary answers fail in and of themselves to provide sufficiently inclusive perspectives for understanding and resolving environmental problems. Academic parochialism is less entrenched in these areas than others; hence, no discipline has a strong historical precedent from which to infer academic invasion by another discipline. Consequently, the potential for cooperation is enhanced.

Potentially results from interdisciplinary research offer broad insights into the many aspects of a given problem. Awareness of the inherent interconnectedness provides policymakers with a set of tools by which they can comprehend the magnitude of the problem. Equally as important are the consequences of a decision for other sectors of the society. Therefore, the policymaker must assess the broad ramifications of a decision before it is made.

Likewise, the insights gained from interdisciplinary efforts can provide policymakers with a more comprehensive understanding of barriers that may prevent eventual implementation of policy. This is an especially important facet of decision-making undertaken within the democratic process. Ultimately such a thorough understanding can shorten the time lag between research results and final implementation and acceptance of a given policy.

We are not suggesting, however, that interdisciplinary research replace disciplinary research. There appears to be little argument regarding the need for integrated research as well as a continuation of traditional disciplinary investigations. Individual research programs are necessary and perhaps preparatory to any substantial interdisciplinary investigation, and the contributions of individual scientists should not be minimized. A great deal is yet unknown regarding human behavior and the environment that requires independent disciplinary attention. Each discipline can contribute through its own body of theory and method to an understanding of natural resource and community development concerns, but as with any disciplinary approach, explanation is more often partial than complete. Disciplinary research should not be treated as a substitute but rather as an essential effort at building a data bank upon which interdisciplinary efforts may emerge.[1]

This does not mean, however, that all interdisciplinary research efforts have been encompassing rather than segmented. Much of it has been something less than a complete success. Disciplinary research operating from a specific theoretical-methodological framework often has been more rigorous and explanatory. Interdisciplinary research has more often been viewed as an umbrella under which individualistic inquiry is pursued as a means of adding appeal to grant proposals. More often than not a loose collection of independent efforts pursuing a common but vaguely defined problem has been considered interdisciplinary research. Even though several disciplines may be working together, the specific research problem and approach employed are established independently. Efforts are piecemeal and the overall value of the end product may be questionable.

A second common approach parallels the above with the exception that a project leader may attempt to assign aspects of a problem to researchers. Again disciplinary perspectives prevail but efficient coordination of the task may allow for a more realis-

---

1. Some social scientists would argue that the data bank is already present. What is required is for social scientists to discontinue a wild search for new theory to explain or account for human behavior in natural resources-environmental problems and utilize the theoretical and methodological sophistication previously established in their discipline. The arena in which the action takes place may be different but human behavior, regardless of the arena, contains regularized patterns of behavior. Some would not agree.

tic problem-solving situation. (Community development research need not follow these characteristic patterns. Instead a more coordinated approach is recommended, one combining the advantages of both substantive sophistication and interdisciplinary breadth.)

We might draw an analogy with inter-agency water resources planning, which is supposed to result in an integrated, comprehensive and thorough plan formulation. These efforts have been largely unsuccessful in bringing about the desired product because each agency still pushes its own particular interests and the end result is often little more than a conglomeration of various agencies' programs. Priorities and objectives are never really established as a coordinated effort. What is lacking here, and in some attempts at interdisciplinary research, is an integration of the purposes and the inputs. It becomes obvious that interdisciplinary research cannot be organized as an agglomeration of researchers, each pursuing a specific interest while assuming that whatever emerges represents the best of all possible worlds. Methods of resolving conflicts and establishing objectives and priorities must be built into the effort in order to assure a truly integrative treatment.

Two misconceptions regarding research dealing with natural resource issues should be noted here. The first misconception concerns the need for new theory to explain or account for natural resource problems at the expense of existing theory. When reviewing selected social science literature concerning the environment and natural resources, one notes immediately how often the need is expressed for new theory to explain new phenomena. This can be misleading and perhaps is an excuse for engaging in descriptive research activities without due consideration to theoretical or methodological matters. What must emerge is *not* an orientation to the discovery of new theory, but a desire to expand existing sociological, geographic or economic theory.[2] Knowledge gained from incorporation of joint work focusing on human behavior and water resources has implications for human behavior in some other areas where social interaction occurs. Variations or modifications in theoretical frameworks are perhaps desirable. But the abandon-

---

2. "The indictment against it (economics) should read not that economics is irrelevant but that its very relevant tools have been too sparingly applied to the kinds of problems now confronting us." Charles L. Schultze, "Is Economics Obsolete? No, Underemployed," *Saturday Review*, January 22, 1972, p. **50**.

ment of core disciplinary theory is unrealistic and can only lead to placing water and community studies on the periphery of disciplinary efforts.

The second misconception is the passive way in which natural resources such as water have been treated within a research problem. Social scientists have treated natural resources at best as a passive variable. Quantitative measures of pollution, water quality, and other environmental characteristics can be generated. Very seldom do we find an operationally defined measure of an environmental variable where this measure can be employed as an independent or dependent variable in research. Certainly an empirical definition would be a better approximation than no measure at all.

## ECONOMIC AND SOCIOLOGICAL CONSIDERATIONS

Unfortunately, there is still a widespread belief that economics is concerned only with maximizing profits and financial returns. Economists themselves are partially responsible for this view because a large share of the most visible "economic analysis" has been just this sort. It is well to remember, however, that economics is basically a theory of, or approach to, social choice. Economics, and especially welfare economics, seeks to take into account not only market prices and values, but also those values that are not reflected in market prices. It is our view that the most useful part of economics is not in its subject matter, but in its approach to the theory of choice. We agree with Mason Gaffney on the functions of economic analysis:

> One of the most important functions of economic analysis is to evaluate public policy. Economics, contrary to common usage, begins with the postulate that man is the measure of all things. Direct damage to human health and happiness is more directly "economic," therefore, than damage to property, which is simply an intermediate means to health and happiness. Neither do economists regard "economic" as a synonym for "pecuniary." Rather money is but one of many means to ends, as well as a useful measure of value. "Economic damage," therefore, includes damages to human functions and pleasure (Gaffney, 1965).

Economists have been criticized justifiably for ignoring all nonmonetary values. As Smith has pointed out, there are times when monetary values are insufficient. Whether we like it or not, both our disciplines are concerned with values—and values do not arise from things but only through the process by which things become useful to man, the social animal.

Man is indeed an animal responding to environmental conditions in ways not dissimilar to the ways other animals respond to their environments. He lives in communities. He is continuously adapting to his environment, just as other animals are adapting to theirs. Man enhances his adaptation through cultural and social organization, which in one sense is the essence of community.

Human communities are dynamic and, like man himself, alter and respond to varying environmental conditions. If we seek an understanding of behavior in response to the use of water, we need to consider the community in which man lives. As Burch has stated: "Natural resources are a product of the society, not the earth" (Burch, 1971). His meaning is clear: man determines what is to be a resource.

One shudders at the task of defining sociology because the theoretical approaches to behavior vary with the school of thought. However, recent research efforts by sociologists into natural resources have demonstrated the efficacy of the social group as one variable that can enhance the understanding of human behavior and natural resources (Burch, 1969; Cheek, 1971; Meyerson, 1969; Field and O'Leary, 1973). In many ways the social group can be considered the elemental unit around which communities arise.

It appears logical to focus upon the social group as a unit of analysis for an exploration of human behavior and the social meaning attached to water within a community context. The consideration of human groups as an entity within which action originates or is defined by members is not new. The development and refinement of this concept as an operational measure has a long history. Warringer (1956) suggests that in one sense groups are real. They influence individual action and are capable of altering individual action (Davis, Spaeth, and Hudson, 1961). In short, groups represent something more than the summation of the individual constituent parts (Burch, 1971).

Groups attach social meanings to water by defining for themselves what the resource is and how it is to be utilized. Whether it is the use of water for leisure, where differential use is noted between kinship and friendship groups, or household consumption where upper class families have a higher consumption rate and a wider variety of uses for water, or where public involvement impedes the construction of a reservoir, a social group forms the basis within which choice is determined.

## SOME COMPLEMENTARY AREAS

Several concepts and techniques lend themselves to joint research approach because of their complementary natures. In fact, deriving operational definitions and improving explanatory power may be enhanced. For example, the assumption of human rationality in action often employed in economics is perhaps not valid. It is not that man acts nonrationally but rather that he acts and reacts toward a set of facts from a perspective internalized in terms of general values and attitudes held as well as those representative of the social group to which he belongs. Modification of the rationality concept to include variability among individual actors and social groups is an important joint contribution to be made by sociologists and economists.

Concepts such as opportunity costs, externalities, interindustry analysis, group decision-making and statistical methods, all of which are important in the study of water and community, have joint socioeconomic dimensions. In order to arrive at comprehensive understanding, sociological as well as economic dimensions must be ascertained. The knowledge contributed by one discipline has benefits for the other.

### The Concept of Externality

The concept of externality has been a part of economic theory for many years, although throughout much of its history it was treated as little more than a footnote. In the past few years, the concept has received unprecedented attention. Widespread concern with air and water pollution, urban congestion, land and water use, and other environmental effects of economic growth has caused economists to realize that externalities are pervasive in our economy, rather than exceptional and minor imperfections in an otherwise smoothly functioning market mechanism.

An externality may be said to be present when the action of one party (group) creates uncompensated or unpaid for effects on a party (group) outside the decision-making unit, or external to the transaction. The external effects could include physical, social, or technological effects and may exist in either consumption or production activities. There are two key elements in the definition. The first of these is *interdependence* among production, consumption, or utility functions. This relationship may assert that A's welfare is dependent upon the level of one of B's activities, which may be solely controlled by B. The other important element in the definition is the failure to pay or receive payment for a service or disservice that someone provides to others. In essence, both interdependence and lack of compensation are necessary for the existence of externality.

Air and water pollution are classic examples of the existence of externalities. In economic terms, pollution occurs because of divergence between private and social costs. Such divergence occurs because an externality permits the shifting of costs of harmful side effects to parties other than those producing the effects. The policy implications of this are clear. A need exists for causing the offsite damages to be taken into account in the decision-making process, or as economists are fond of saying, we need to "internalize the externalities." The existence of externality suggests that the market mechanism is not working in a manner to maximize social welfare. Existence of externalities does not necessarily imply the necessity of governmental action to bring into balance private and social costs. However, it does imply the necessity of collective action in most cases where water pollution imposes damages on widespread and diverse groups. Where externalities are widespread, as in water pollution, the unfettered market system is not likely to allocate resources in such a way as to maximize social welfare, as was postulated by the *laissez-faire* economists. The values that people hold in no small measure determine the extent of damages imposed by uncompensated externalities.

The existence of externality compounds our problem in defining decision-making groups. As Smith (1971) and others have pointed out, the issue is in defining and identifying new communities of interest. This process of community definition and identification seems to be a natural ground on which economists and sociologists can come together. We seem to be in the process of continually forming new communities of interest. It will take our best combined efforts to sort these out, to determine the values and boundaries that define them, and to discover how they organize themselves to formulate decisions and actions. Pervasive externalities associated with water resources make this task a difficult one.

**Opportunity Costs**

Because resources are limited in their availability, their use in the production of a certain class of goods or services diminishes their use in production of alternative goods or services. For too long, we have tended to view air and water as unlimited resources, freely available for all uses. The real cost of producing any good or service is the value of resources used in the process had they been devoted to alternative uses. This is referred to by economists as the opportunity cost, which does not always coincide with the nominal or money cost of the resource. The difficulty arises in accurately measuring the real cost, or opportunity cost. When we neglect the offsite damages that a polluting firm has on other uses of the water, the nominal cost of the resource used by the firm is lower than the real cost of the resource in terms of alternative uses. For some social groups the reverse also applies. Evaluation of opportunity costs of society depends on a number of factors, many of which are not the domain of economics. One of these variables is the social group. Assessment of opportunity costs is enhanced when social groups are introduced into the analysis.

Variation arises among social groups in their perception of what is or is not pollution or a quality environment, or what constitutes valuable use of water. When is an alteration of the environment a pollution problem? A definition of pollution in a recent publication perhaps best exemplifies social group variability in ascertaining if an alteration is a problem. The definition states "that pollution is the unfavorable alteration of our surrounding, wholly or largely as a by-product of man's action. . . ." In general pollution originates with man, but until man defines an alteration as a pollution problem it is not a problem to him.

Many groups argue water pollution in the perspective of a quality environment. In order to understand reasons for variation in human response toward pollution as a problem, knowledge about social groups and culture is mandatory. Culture transmitted through the socialization process shapes attitudes and values. Many urban inner city residents do not articulate air or water pollution as a problem even though these conditions are present in fact in most of our large metropolitan centers. Pollution abatement for them may be the correction of poor housing or poor diet rather than cleaning up the water. Likewise, when confronted with problems of rat infestation and inadequate garbage disposal, they see treatment of these problems as having a higher priority than any other pollution problem.

Workers threatened with unemployment when a plant is ordered by a state pollution control agency to clean up effluent discharges may react contrary to the desires of environmentalists. Pollution from the firm may not have been viewed as a serious problem. In towns where lumbering, steel or coal represent a major or only source of employment, this reaction has been commonplace. Work and its associated side effects (including income) is more important than the improved water quality resulting from closing the plant. In their pollution argument many conservation groups emphasize the need to solve air and water pollution problems so that a quality environment may be attained. This view of a pollution problem is uppermost in the minds of only certain segments of the population. If we are going to make meaningful analysis of policy prescriptions, we need to know the values attached to alternatives, how they arise and how social as well as economic variables affect them. The concept of community becomes crucial in defining and articulating these values.

**Interindustry Models (Interconnectedness)**

Input-output models are based on the assumption that economic activity can be divided into various, relatively homogeneous sectors that have direct and indirect linkages to each other. In its simplest form, the model is used to measure the interrelationships between the various sectors of economic activity. We know that what happens in one sector has effects on other sectors. The models can be constructed in physical or economic terms. They have been used to measure the economic impact on all sectors of the economy of certain exogenous changes occurring in a specific sector.

Application of an interdisciplinary type model to an examination of various alternative approaches to water quality improvement would provide a great deal of empirical information to decision makers. The local economy could be divided into sectors indicating the output structure of the economy and input use patterns. Such a model would provide information on both the direct and indirect effects associated with alternative courses of action. Flexible models that combine techniques, such as linear programming and input-output, facilitate the setting of constraints on resource inputs and measuring the effects of exogenous changes on the economy. In this way, estimates of the distributional effects as well as the magnitude of the effects of alternative courses of action can be estimated. For example, various legal and economic constraints of alternative approaches could be imposed on such a model and the impacts of economic growth could be measured.

There is some relation between the input-output model and the sociological concept of social system. The levels of abstraction or analysis are complementary. The notion of a social system, with concomitant social processes and inherent interdependences among constituent parts, approximates the intent of the input-output model. Quantitative estimates of economic relationships coupled with measures of social processes offer opportunities for delineating specific systematic properties and the assignment of weights in the social realm as is done in the economic realm.

Application of the input-output and related quantitative techniques suggests intriguing possibilities for identifying relationships among social groups within a given social system. Measurement of the nature and extent of interaction among groups with divergent environmental philosophy has meaning for assessing dimensions of the environmental issue in a broader context.

Some groups interact on resource problems within a given social system. Many groups are primarily consumers of the environment while others interact on a broader scale, such as with national environmental concerns. This is analogous to exchange outside the system and approximates output. Many questions arise from such considerations. Do environmental groups who contribute most of their efforts to problems outside a given social system concern themselves with the local situation? In other words, is there an imbalance in exchange favoring an output? What is the relationship among social groups who concentrate on environmental problems within the system to those whose efforts are tied to the outside?

**Collective Choice or Group Decision-Making**

New frontiers are being opened in the rapidly developing area of public choice. It is a move that seems particularly appropriate as more and more of the problems we define as crucial depend on and can only be solved through collective choices. Nowhere is the process of collective decision-making more important than in water and community development. Much discipline-bridging has occurred in the study of public choice, especially economics, political science and law. For the most part, sociologists have been less involved in this work. This should not be so. Sociologists have much to offer regarding human behavior as we move through the spectrum from the individual actor to a group to inter- and intra-group actions. All social science is concerned with the *individual* (person, firm, group) and the *interactions* among individuals in a biological, social, physical and political environment. The sociologist needs to tell the economist that he has a naive view of behavior. As Boulding points out, the economist's individual just starts out knowing everything—he is never permitted to learn anything through the process of interactions with other individuals. Economists need to recognize that behavior takes place in an environment in which the individual, in concert with others, shapes the environment and the environment shapes him—man interacts in an environment of which he is a part. On the other hand, sociologists need to appreciate the economist's concept of preferences and values and that the economizing motive is a strong one. Somewhere, and perhaps in our collective decision models, we need to improve our understanding of each other's concept of the existence and use of social power.

We believe the area of public choice and collective decisions as it relates to the problems of water and community development is one in which we need to join forces. There is need for caution as this field develops. Already there are signs that we may become so obsessed with mathematical sophistication that we lose sight of the most important (but messy) human institutional problems. Nowhere is Schmid's plea for more "analytical institutionalism" more relevant. Some of the recent attempts to apply probability models to public choice assumes a sort of random behavior, somewhat similar to coin flipping. The efforts of sociologists and economists are needed to determine how and why choices occur.

**Statistical Methods**

Differential costs are involved in reducing pollution damage and other water resource decisions. Realistic cost figures depend on physical, economic and sociological variables. When assessing pollution damages, economists have been continually confronted with partial answers because the sociological variables were missing. Values and attitudes held by individuals and groups were unavailable. Measures of social values and/or attitudes have been created elsewhere. Attitudes toward pollution or pollution abatement costs can be established in such a way as to provide quantitative measure of those sociological variables. Statistical examination then becomes a technique whereby social and economic variables are considered in an integrated context. Statistics is one of the more direct ways in which a "variable interchange" can occur. Such an approach including social as well as economic variables would enhance predictability and reduce unexplained variance further than might be possible operating independently. Various techniques are suitable. Analysis of variance and multiple regression are two such examples.

A discussion of concepts and techniques should not preclude initial interchange at another level of conceptualization theory. This might be pursued in several ways. The potential arises whereby sociological variables could be incorporated within an existing theoretical orientation of another discipline such as economics. The opposite is also true.

Theoretical studies in which hypothesis testing is pursued are the ultimate goals for researchers. Indeed, the accumulation of or contribution to knowledge progresses in this manner. Natural resource issues are part of a broader context. The manner in which individuals relate to given problems has meaning elsewhere. Theoretically based studies exploring such relationships have contributory importance for understanding human behavior in the environment as well as for human behavior in general. Insights gained by sociologists and economists in joint work have potentially rewarding insights for individual disciplinary theory. We do not recommend merging the disciplines. At this state, we feel that is neither necessary nor desirable. We do feel strongly that in analyzing and understanding water resources in a community framework, we must remember that each discipline has something to offer, and a cooperative undertaking will enhance research output.

## CONCLUSION

The linkages between water and community are many and often hazy. As society shifts its concerns to include broader goals than mere accumulation of more affluence, community boundaries and linkages continue to change. Social scientists have long been concerned with the use and development of water resources. Too often their efforts have been narrowly oriented and of a piecemeal variety, pursuing disciplinary-oriented efforts while ignoring many of the most important aspects that cut across disciplinary lines. It is our contention that this has reduced the usefulness of much of the social science research in solving the very real problems of water resources and community development.

We suggest that a problem-oriented research, which takes into account the theories, methods and disciplinary efforts required by the particular situation, be used. Interdisciplinary research is not an end itself. It should not be inferred that all problems lend themselves to interdisciplinary efforts. It is our view, however, that many of the problems of water and community are multifaceted, and that more meaningful solutions are likely to be found in the joint efforts of economists and sociologists.

We have discussed a few concepts important in water and community research on which it appears there could be convergence of interests of economists and sociologists. Our examples do not come close to exhausting the list, and one could argue over our choice of concepts. Certainly, we have omitted many equally important areas in which the grounds for common pursuit may be even easier. The institution of property and property rights relating to water and community may be one such area. As discussed in other chapters, the set of property rights largely determines the exchange possibilities and sets the framework within which a community makes decisions concerning the use of water resources. The way in which a community distributes property rights, both private and public, to its water resources is not only or even primarily a legal question, but rather a socio-economic-political matter.

Our plea for integration should not be taken as a call to abandon disciplinary efforts, nor as an attempt to exclude other sciences. By exploring a few areas important in the study of water and community problems, the basis for cooperative efforts may be seen more clearly. It is possible that we will eventually learn to talk to each other, and if we really work at it we may even learn to hear each other if we practice some "active listening."

## REFERENCES

Boulding, K. "A Conceptual Framework for Social Science," in *Beyond Economics* (Ann Arbor, Michigan: University of Michigan Press, 1968).

Burch, W. R., Jr. *Daydreams and Nightmares: A Sociological Essay on the American Environment* (New York: Harper and Row, 1971).

Burch, W. R., Jr. "The Social Circles of Leisure: Competing Explanations," *J. Leisure R.* 1, 125 (1969).

Cheek, N. H., Jr. "Toward a Sociology of Not-Work," *Pacific Soc. Rev.* 1, 245 (1971).

Davis, J. A., J. L. Spaeth, and C. Huson. "A Technique for Analyzing the Effects of Group Composition," *Amer. Soc. Rev.* 26, 215 (1961).

Field, D. R., and J. T. O'Leary. "Social Groups as a Basis for Assessing Participation in Selected Water Activities," *J. Leisure Research* 5, 16-26 (1973).

Gaffney, M. "Applying Economic Controls," *Bull. Atomic Sci.* 6, 20 (1965).

Heilbroner, R., and A. M. Ford, Eds. *Is Economics Relevant* (Pacific Palisades, Calif.: Goodyear Publishing Co., 1971).
Meyersohn, R. "The Sociology of Leisure in the United States: Introduction and Bibliography, 1945-1965," *J. Leisure Res.* **1**, 53 (1969).
President's Science Advisory Committee, "Restoring the Quality of Our Environment," Report of the Environmental Panel, Washington, D.C. (1965).
Smith, S. C. "Institutionalism as an Analytical Approach to the Analysis of Economic and Sociological Problems," Conference Proc., Committee on Community and Human Resource Development of the Western Agricultural Economics Research Council, San Francisco (1971).
Ward, B. *What's Wrong with Economics* (New York: Basic Books, Inc., 1972).
Warringer, C. K. "Groups are Real: A Reaffirmation," *Amer. Soc. Rev.* **21**, 549 (1956).

# 2. The Economic Meaning of Water: Patterns in Variation

## PAUL W. BARKLEY

In the past quarter century, dozens of economists have launched their careers by researching and writing in the field of water economics. A smaller number of established scholars have—in the same time frame—picked their way through the complex subject of economics to point out circumstances under which economics can contribute to the solution of water-related problems. All these efforts plus the volumes of reports of empirical research yield a water economics literature nearly as vast as the literature in the fields of economic growth or economic stability. It is legitimate to ask why so many economists have bent their attentions to studying this resource.

Two possible hypotheses emerge. The first is based on the conviction that water is only a medium used by economists to explore problems such as resource valuation, efficiency, income distribution and equity. Water performs well in this capacity.[1] A second hypothesis is rooted in the economic problems associated with water and the changing relationship between water and man. While the real reason for economists' interest likely stems from elements of both hypotheses, this paper concentrates on the latter. The nature of water problems and the relationship between water and man are changing so demonstrably that the economic meaning of

---

1. During the sessions at which this paper was first aired, R. J. Hildreth remarked that academics ordinarily spent a good deal of time "solving riddles." This hypothesis is germane to the water economics theme. Academics hope that solving water riddles will provide answers to a more general set of riddles or problems.

water has had to undergo significant variation through time. In many respects, the history, scope, and practice of water resource economics can be found in the 18 annual reports published by the Committee on the Economics of Water Resource Development of the Western Agricultural Economics Research Council. These reports include papers by all the major figures in the water economics field and form an interesting chronology from early statements dealing with theory and institutions to later volumes devoted to results of empirical efforts.

Regardless of motivation, water research effort has been extensive and diverse but, like much research, frequently it has been directed toward trivial problems, and seldom has it been used in incisive ways in the formation of policy related to either the resource or the people who use it. Economists could have avoided much of this fate had they spent more time with Walter Firey, *Man, Mind and Land: A Theory of Resource Use,* (Glencoe, Illinois: The Free Press, 1960). Firey builds an impressive argument about the interrelatedness existing among resources and between resources and man. He writes as a sociologist but builds heavily on a tradition similar to institutionalism in economics. One particularly neglected portion of water economics research is the relationship between water and man—the relationship between water and community. This paper is directed toward that theme but is arranged in a curious way, one followed strictly for ease of exposition. The discussion includes comments on an early era when the water/community relationship was not subjected to economic analysis, comments on the early years of intense economic analysis, some reflections on contemporary problems and some unfinished business. The discussion is heavily weighted toward activities in this century and toward those that have occurred in the West.

## THE NECESSARY WATER/COMMUNITY RELATIONSHIP

This nation's involvement with the water resource began in 1802 when the U.S. Army Corps of Engineers (probably because they were the only engineers available) were given responsibility for clearing channels, developing port facilities and stabilizing the flows of rivers along the Eastern seaboard. These functions produced services that would now be called public goods since they are not sold in usual, well-behaved markets. There is no readily accessible record to indicate that these early activities were accompanied by any economic analysis. The values of the output of defense and commerce were probably assumed to be (1) necessary and (2) widely dispersed, so these functions were developed without extreme concern for economic evaluation.

In the early years of nationhood and during the periods of rapid development, cities, counties and states each faced special water problems. Local economies could not grow without water and the capital values of land and other permanent investments depended upon finding water for municipal or industrial purposes. Because of the importance attached to water development, there seems to have been little effort expended in economic analysis. The benefits were obvious and the costs were those a community had to bear if it were to survive. In this situation, the economists' suggestions and recommendations took a position second to public sentiment: If the area wanted water badly enough, it would incur the costs. The growth of Los Angeles was stymied in the early years of this century but was resumed (albeit at very high costs) when the waters of Owens Valley were tapped and transported nearly 300 miles to the southern California urban area. San Francisco was in similar straits until the Hetch-Hetchy complex was developed on the edge of Yosemite National Park.

In both of these cases, the connection between water and the community is a difficult one. The scarcity of water in Los Angeles created a strong sense of community in that city. This sense of community permitted (or required) a search for water sources that eventually led to a small agricultural valley in the Sierra Nevada's 300 miles away. There was no sense of a water/community relationship between the demand community (Los Angeles) and the supply community (Owens Valley). Los Angeles incurred great cost to purchase the water of Owens Valley and to develop a conveyance system. Transporting the water resulted in continued growth, maintenance of capital values and a stronger community in Los Angeles but it ended economic activity, reduced capital values and decimated a community in Owens Valley.

Figure 1 displays the changed relationship. In the upper panel, a comfortable relationship exists with the Owens Valley community utilizing its ground water aquifer. Los Angeles is bounded by a lack of water. In the lower panel, the situation is reversed with the Owens Valley economy essentially collapsed while Los Angeles is shown as having grown tremendously. There is no record that the deleterious external effects of the water transfer were ever considered by Los Angeles.[2] The water/community relationship is strictly one-way (Baugh, 1937, and Nadean, 1962).

*Before the purchase by Los Angeles:*

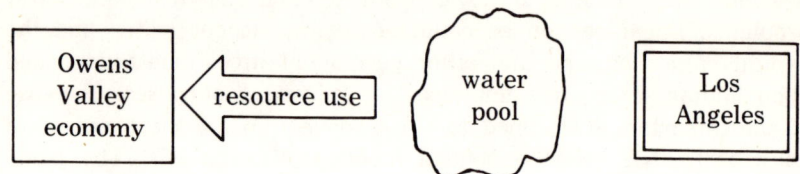

*After purchase by Los Angeles:*

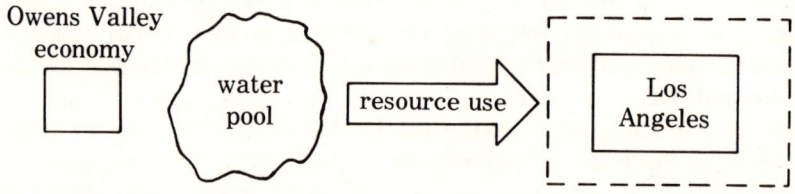

*Figure 1.* Ties between resource pools and local communities.

A similar phenomenon emerges in the case of flood control. Most major efforts at controlling floods depend on huge structures many or even hundreds of miles from the cities to be protected. Nowhere is this more evident than in the Mississippi/Missouri drainage where Kansas City, St. Louis, and New Orleans are protected by a series of massive dams stretching through the Dakotas and into Montana. It is hard to imagine that people who lived in the valley now flooded by Fort Peck were a part of the "community" upon which the Corps of Engineers lavished its attentions while that facility was being built.

The branch of economics that bases its prescriptions on efficiency has a comfortable solution to the problem faced by residents of Owens Valley or the upper reaches of the Missouri: If the resources can be paid for, justice has been served. That branch of

---

2. This judgment may be too harsh. Los Angeles paid handsome prices for rights to water in Owens Valley. These prices may have been thought to reflect some external benefits being taken from the area.

economics tracing its roots to Bentham and the Utilitarians is concerned with equity, and is not comforted by this solution. Unfortunately, this school of economics can not offer a systematic alternative other than the suggestion that compensation "ought" to be paid or that, over time, the inequities would vary in some random but compensating fashion. Different communities would have different claims on the same waters but no mechanisms could be arranged to make the disparate claims equitable. In these questions, the only economics of water problems is market economics and the market economics may bypass the problem of water and community.

**A Special Economics: The Case of Irrigation**

The water and community relationship takes on real meaning in the case of irrigation. It is conducted by many independent irrigators in ground water basins or it is conducted by groups of persons who have formed irrigation districts to exploit the surface flows frequently found in the West. In either instance, water, the irrigator, the irrigation-dependent industry and the local community form a complex economic organism that deserves close study.

As settlement moved across the high plains and into the West, individuals and small groups of individuals made efforts to exploit the water resource. The reason was straight-forward. Applying water to lands of the high plains, the intermountain areas, the desert Southwest and the valleys of the South Pacific coastal regions demonstrably shifted the production function for many crops and greatly expanded the range of crops that could be successfully grown in arid regions. Depending on locale, the availability of water permitted shifts from grasses to field crops or from small grains to fruits, or from no agricultural output to rather handsome outputs of high-valued fruits and vegetables or cotton. Early irrigators were able to singularly appropriate values of water that appeared as increased profits and were ultimately capitalized into the value of land. This practice set off a series of events that had significant consequences for communities. Increased agricultural productivity brought with it increased profits to those handling either inputs or outputs for the agricultural industry. A two-way relationship developed in which strength in town and strength on the farms combined to form viable and interdependent communities.

A whole new era of water development activity and responsibility emerged in 1902 with the passage of the Reclamation Act. This Act was prompted by two major forces and a host of lesser ones.

One major force emerged with the closing of the frontier. According to many the frontier had provided a social safety valve in the United States but (more appropriate to the present argument) it provided for rapid expansion of the acreage used for agricultural production. With its closing, the fear spread that the still increasing population would press against available agricultural land and food prices would rise, ending only when the limits of subsistence had been reached. This fear had strong precedent since this had been the experience of both developed and underdeveloped nations through most of history. It was reasoned that all effort would have to be made to avert this fate. One way to avert it was to apply water to arid lands to make them suitable for cultivation. The Reclamation Act was to aid in expanding the quantity of water available for irrigation.

A second argument in favor of passing reclamation laws was related to the interconnectedness between agricultural output and secondary and tertiary economic activity, the water and community theme. With growth in agriculture came growth in processing and in towns and community functions. Legislators sponsoring increased irrigation development stressed the capacity of irrigation effort to induce new investment. New projects in the West were to provide increased agricultural output; they were to provide the economic base for strong rural communities; they were to provide opportunities for new entrants into the ranks of farm operators; they were to serve as inducements to spread the population into every suitable nook and cranny of the nation (see Folz, 1951).

Even with the vast numbers of private irrigators, irrigation companies, and the newly established Bureau of Reclamation irrigation projects, the economist's role was minimal and remained so until the Flood Control Act of 1936 and Public Law 566 (1954) insisted that economic analysis accompany public investment in water resource projects.

The 1936 Act required involvement in benefit/cost analysis and its accompanying difficulties (direct and indirect benefits, associated costs, the discount rate, and joint allocation to name but a few). The later act emphasized all of these things and added the upstream/downstream controversy and the three way interagency dispute that has varied in intensity over the years.[3]

These numerous themes have each provided fuel for the econo-

---

3. Although it is somewhat dated, Otto Eckstein, *Water Resource Development,* (Cambridge: Harvard University Press, 1961) still gives excellent accounts of these problems. See especially Chapters 1, 2, 5, 6, 7, and 8.

mist's fires but have neglected the main thread running through this collection of papers: water and community. Discussions among economists and decision-makers have raged over the appropriateness of the decision criterion, the role of the discount rate, the proper assessment of secondary benefits and, sometimes, the opportunity costs associated with development. Only a trivial amount of effort has been expended on water and the community and most of this effort has been local. No general results have appeared. Attention must turn to that topic.

## WATER AND THE COMMUNITY—SOME DIRECT TIES

The Bureau of Reclamation has spent a great deal of effort trying to ascertain the nature of the unique tie between water and the community. The Bureau's efforts understandably have been restricted to irrigation efforts in the West and have been limited to discussions of ratios existing between primary agricultural activity and secondary and tertiary activities taking place in nearby towns. Prior to 1947, the Bureau used very primitive methods to show the relationship between productive activity in a newly irrigated area and economic activity in a nearby town. The methods were based on such items as school attendance, bank clearings, tax collections and other generally available but weak indicators of economic activity. After 1947, the Marion Marts studies became available and were corroborated in every essential by a small number of independent investigators examining other geographic areas (Marts, 1956). In crude terms, the Marts studies showed that each dollar of added net income received by farm operators would (through the multiplier effect) yield approximately $1.25 in added net income in nonfarm sectors of the local economy. Schmitt, studying in central California, found ratios of farm to nonfarm net incomes to be between 1.0 and 1.25, close enough to suggest that the ratios *in that period of time* and *in isolated agricultural communities* may have been somewhat regular.[4]

In 1950, the Bureau made a third attempt to understand the relationship between water and community by asking a panel of

---

4. The importance of the underlined phrases cannot be underestimated. Ratios between types of economic activity have been the object of extensive research since the 1930's. Richard B. Andrews, the most prolific writer on economic base ratios, used a series of articles to show that (1) ratios are not transferable, (2) ratios are not stable and (3) there is no *a priori* reason to suspect that a given ratio will change in an upward rather than a downward direction. The Andrews' articles appear in successive issues of *Land Economics* beginning in May, 1954 and continuing through February, 1956.

qualified economists to examine the effects of water development on local economies. The examination was to be carried out on a crop-by-crop basis. The panel found the use of rules of thumb somewhat abhorrent but recommended their continued use. The rules of thumb stated that, depending on the crop, the local community could expect profits ranging from 6 to 83 per cent of the crop's value to accrue to local businessmen (Eckstein, 1961).

In more recent years, especially since 1950, a number of scholars have tried to quantify the relationship between water development and community development (Holje, et al., 1956; Kelso 1953). The more impressive documents stress that (1) quantification is very difficult, (2) results are not likely to be transferable from one area to another, and (3) even if the relationship can be determined, neither the distribution of benefits nor the distribution of effects within a town can be identified. Perhaps the most comprehensive study of this kind is one conducted a decade ago at Oklahoma State University that showed local net incomes would ultimately reach an amount approximately 1.62 times the increase in primary farm income resulting from watershed improvement (Jansma and Back, 1964).

To summarize, it is safe to say that in the case of some water uses, especially irrigation, there is a direct connection between water and community. This direct connection is hard to measure, and even when it is, there is no way to rely on the results as accurate, stable, or transferable. All that has been accomplished is the explicit recognition of a water-community relationship.

## WATER AND COMMUNITY: THE QUESTIONS THAT HAVE NOT BEEN ASKED

Economists generally have been totally committed in theory and in practice to economic growth. This statement is made in full recognition of the currently fashionable deemphasis on recommending increases in GNP or NNP. Even those economists who are arguing for zero growth or for reduction in productivity are doing so using economic models designed for the explicit study of growth. They have merely changed definitions so that "growth" has a qualitative as well as a quantitative component. Perhaps this commitment to growth has been responsible for the economist's propensity to overlook the decline in community activity that has occurred in many water/community settings. At this moment, it is quite likely that most of the towns that developed on the basis of a unique connection between water and growth are losing population. The reasons are not hard to find. In some cases, especially in the Texas High Plains and throughout the area covered by the High Plains Lens, the water table has fallen to levels so deep that pumping is no longer economical and the land has been forced back to grass or certainly to less productive forms of agricultural output (Grubb, 1966). In other areas, improvements in technology and in communications have caused the size of the economic farming unit to increase, thus disrupting the balance between water and community (Haurin and Tolley, 1972). In other cases, increased output stemming from the application of irrigation water has increased supply enough to depress prices of agricultural products. In these instances, consolidation or dissolution of farm units is called for and the water/community relationship is again altered. These last three reasons, or combinations of them, have been responsible for structural changes in the agricultural economies of central California, the Columbia Basin and large parts of Arizona.

Two lessons emerge. First, the water/community relationship must be ascertained even if it requires intensive (and expensive) inquiry in each individual area where water development is proposed. This is essential so that communities in developing areas can arrange capital investment patterns that will provide necessary collections of social overhead capital but will also be compatible with resource availability and will be flexible enough to withstand the shock of changes in technology, prices, communications, or resource availability. Once the physiologic and geologic characteristics of the High Plains aquifer became known, there was no reason for any community in that region to build a permanent school, a new hospital or add another inch of thickness to the street paving. The problem of overbuilding communities is just as severe as the problem of over-appropriating resources. The only difference is one of distribution of capital losses. In over-appropriating a resource, the owners of resource-related capital bear losses associated with depletion. In over-building a town, direct and indirect users of resource or resource-related products stand to lose capital value as the resource is depleted.[5]

---

5. Those studying the relationship between water and community may be well served to examine the behavior of developers of timber and mineral resources. Admittedly, exploitation of these resources has led to the appearance of hundreds of ghost towns in the west. While the ghost town can be viewed as a reduction in the quantity of social capital, it may be more appropriate to view it as a case of planned obsolescence. Persons in the water field have apparently overlooked this possibility.

Second, planners must spare no effort in pointing out that even in areas served by a generous water supply, the business establishments and institutions developed to serve the resource-based industry may be short-lived. Nowhere is this more likely than in the state of Washington where many isolated areas are now being irrigated and additions to the Columbia Basin Project are geographically dispersed. True, these developments will bring increased income but, as Haurin and Tolley have pointed out, the increased income will more than likely allow the individual irrigators to drive through the local community to some neighboring area to do their trading. Increased wealth for irrigators may bring increased misery for local communities—the water/community relationship must be better understood and economists working with small groups of irrigators must develop some responsibility for pointing out the possibility of a negative relationship developing between water and the towns close to it.

## SOME UNFINISHED BUSINESS

In the early paragraphs of this paper, a number of water uses and possible developments were dismissed as being unimportant in a discussion of water and the community. This was done because in most cases, vast distances exist between the area expected to be the net beneficiary of the development and the area that must pay the physical cost in terms of being flooded, having its water rights purchased, or having its availability of water changed in some demonstrable fashion. That question must be reopened because in many places, the sheer existence of a major area of slack water provides the opportunity for a different kind of water/community relationship to develop. This is the water-based recreation town—one that is likely to increase in importance as the nation's affluence increases. Many towns situated close to water may develop simply to take advantage of man's quest for variety.

Again, the economist has some chores to do; again, the economist has already done some of these. There are numerous studies available reporting the results of research geared to ascertaining the business volume generated by recreational use of water. (See Chapter 12). The techniques have varied but most rely on some variation of input/output studies in the Leontief tradition or the economic base studies in the Hoyt tradition. Some studies, too, rely on changes in land value as indicators of the "worth" of an investment in recreation (Schutjer and Hallberg, 1968). This latter method has some advantages from the point of view of the economic theorist but it does depend upon the existence of a land market that functions in a nearly perfect way.

In the recreational type of water/community setting, the economist must struggle to learn something of the threshold variables crucial to the development of a suitable and well-used recreation facility. It is generally known that large bodies of slack water will be used by recreationists but the timing and extent of use are still open questions. Moreover, they are likely to remain open as the nation proceeds through a period of high interest in maintaining a high quality environment.

## DISCUSSION

Economics is a systematic study of the process of production (transformation), exchange and consumption. The field is so complicated that no one economist can expect to master it in its entirety. An integral part of all aspects of economics, though, is the idea of equilibrium or of the *quid pro quo* relationship. This relationship insures that economics remains a study of a system and it insures that all economic problems can ultimately be described in terms of a deviation from some equilibrium situation. The individual economist specializes by choosing a point at which to break into this equilibrium-oriented system and by choosing a small part of the feedback mechanism for close study. One economist might choose to study factor markets, one to study air pollution, and one to study the market for No. 2 yellow corn.

A large number of economists have chosen to exercise their skills in studying problems associated with water. The possible reasons for this have been mentioned. In their studies of water, economists have addressed all manner of questions and have attempted to solve all manner of riddles. However, few have examined the critical linkages that exist between water and the community. Those who have chosen to do so have done it in a most superficial and entirely descriptive way. This is unfortunate since the economist behaving in this fashion is not exercising his skills to full advantage. Knowledge of the equilibrium concept, the *quid pro quo* relationship and/or the circular nature of economic activity could provide important clues to understanding water and community.

A water development appears and induces primary users to exploit the resource and appropriate any values that might arise in connection with the resource use. Secondary users then arrive to serve primary users and perhaps, if the resource is present in large enough quantities, tertiary users appear to provide still another level of economic activity. All users act in a complex system of two-way relationships in which irrigator buys seed from town, town buys corn from irrigator. This relationship can be summarized and simplified by using a circular flow diagram straight from economics textbooks or it can be described using the complex system of interconnected industry relationships used in a Leontief type model. Each of the two methods depends on interdependence in equilibrium.

Economists who have plied their trade in the water field have been happy to point out that towns exist because of irrigation or recreation; they have been somewhat remiss in addressing the fact that, while irrigators can have a profound effect on towns, towns can have very little effect on irrigators. What appears as a closed and self-perpetuating system is actually a microeconomy with strong linkages in one direction but very weak linkages in another. The consequences of this are scarcely trivial. Rapid development of a ground water basin may lead to strengthened economic ties between farm and city but there is no way in which nonfarm elements of the local economy can influence behavior of water users. (A reviewer of this paper aptly pointed out that, in some cases, irrigators are being influenced by nearby communities because the act of irrigating has reduced the quality of a surface stream that is also used for recreation. This is a valid point but it brings a third factor—pollution—into the interdependence system. The main point remains the same. If no outside influence emerges, the farms can alter the town but the town cannot alter the farms.) If such influences were possible, it could understandably be the intention of nonfarm, dependent actors to slow development so as to extend the useful life of the town's long range investments in social overhead capital.

This may be one of the more fruitful arenas for future research in the economics of water development. Society needs to know how rapidly development will occur, how widely its results will be distributed and how long it will last. Society needs to know the community's response to such development and, most of all, society needs to learn if the feedback loop from communities to irrigators can find a suitable method of closure.

If society continues to make decisions from a limited base of information, the mistakes of the past will surely continue in the future. Since the economy of the future will be more complex and more interconnected than the present one, there is some real assurance that future errors will be more costly and will affect more people.

"The Economics of Water: Patterns in Variation": there is a haunting lesson in this title because the economics of water has varied from decade to decade. Now, after 175 years of involvement with water problems, a pattern seems to be emerging. Concern in the water field has developed as more problems have appeared and as more tools of economic analysis have become available to solve the problems. The pattern in the variation has been a rather noticeable drift toward specific problems—the discount rate, the appropriateness of the decision criterion, the measurement of secondary effects. Behind this, though, has been a grander pattern, one perhaps best described as a 200-year cycle in water development. In this nation's early efforts at dealing with its water problems, it was forced to work with purposes whose benefits were widely dispersed and for which no market could be effectively developed. As time passed, interest narrowed to concentrate on those parts of water development that permitted private appropriation of value and/or private use. The public goods producing functions were somehow ignored. In the last decade, interest in public goods, especially recreation, has mounted, and perhaps such things as the public interest in private development may become important themes. This is not a casual issue because people's life styles, their net worth, their daily behavior, and their self images are at stake. Water and community is indeed a legitimate question and the pattern of variation in water economics is a crucial part of the legitimacy of the question.

## REFERENCES

Baugh, R. E. "Land Use Changes in the Bishop Area of Owens Valley, California," *Land Geog.* **13**, 17 (1937).

Eckstein, O. *Water Resource Development* (Cambridge, Mass.: Harvard University Press, 1961).

Folz, W. E. "The Economics of Water Development: A Theoretical Analysis," CEWRD-WAERC, Water Report No. 0 (December, 1951).

Grubb, H. W. "Optimum Utilization of Ground Water Resources," CEWRC-WAERC Report No. 15 (December, 1966).

## 40 WATER AND COMMUNITY DEVELOPMENT

Haurin, D. R., and G. S. Tolley. "The Rural Town and the Scale Question," Proc. Western Agric. Econ. Assoc. (July 26, 1972).

Holje, H. C., R. E. Huffman and C. F. Kraenzel. "Indirect Benefits of Irrigation Development," Montana State College AES Technical Bulletin 517, March, 1956; Department of the Interior, Report of Panel Consultants on Secondary or Indirect Benefits of Water Use Projects, Bureau of Reclamation, 1952.

Jansma, J. D., and W. B. Back. "Local Secondary Effects of Watershed Projects," U.S. Dept. Agric., Econ. Res. Service Publ. 174 (May, 1964).

Kelso, M. M. "Evaluation of Secondary Benefits of Water Use Projects," Report No. 1 of CEWRD-WAERC, Berkeley, 1953.

Kimball, N. D., and E. N. Castle. "Secondary Benefits and Irrigation Project Planning," Oregon AES Technical Bulletin 69, May, 1963.

Marts, M. E. "Use of Indirect Benefit Analysis in Establishing Repayment Responsibility for Irrigation Projects," *Econ. Geog.* 32, 132 (1956).

Nadean, R. "The Water War," *Amer. Heritage* 13, 30 (1962).

Rohdy, D. D., D. B. Tanner and P. W. Barkley. "Secondary Effects of Irrigation on the Colorado High Plains," Colorado AES Bulletin 5455, June, 1971.

Schutjer, W. H., and M. C. Hallberg. "Impact of Water Recreational Development on Rural Property Values," *Am. J. Agric. Econ.* 50, 572 (1968).

Struthers, R. E. "The Role of Irrigation Development in Community Economic Structure," Grand Valley Trade Area, Colorado, (Bureau of Reclamation, GPO, 1962).

# 3. Social Meanings of Water: Patterns of Variation

## WILLIAM R. BURCH, JR. AND NEIL H. CHEEK, JR.

Sociology examines geophysical variables in terms of the social meanings embodied in the social institutions that make up the community. The relationship between water, a geophysical variable, and community development will be considered by examining the influences of institutions and their corresponding effect on the distribution of social honor, or status. Such an examination must include the identification of the degree or level of congruence between social institutions and the subsequent assignment of social status. Lenski's (1966) discussion of the dynamics of this process is pertinent.

Communities in which kinship, political, and religious institutions function to distribute social honor consistently to the same individuals are described as ascriptive, thus indicating a high degree of congruency among institutional sources of status. Conversely, in communities in which there is less agreement among institutions as to the conferring of social honor, social status must be achieved.

Communities in which social status must be achieved exhibit a low level of congruency among institutional sources, thus posing questions concerning methods used for evaluating social status. One study in this area theorizes that the dominant institutional source of status is utilized, either ignoring all others or treating them as equivalents (Benoit-Smullyan, 1944). However, for the purposes of this discussion, the important factor about communities of low congruency levels is the comparative ease with which status systems can be permeated.

Thus when we begin to examine the meanings attached to a

resource (such as water) and its place in the community, we do so by recognizing its location within an institutional matrix and identifying the nature of congruence characteristic of the community. It is comparatively rare for water *per se* to become an end in itself. Even in ecological zones where water is scarce, it tends to be defined as follows:
1. A *means of subsistence, i.e.,* narrowly construed as necessary to sustain human life, a foodstuff
2. A *method of communication, i.e.,* trade, warfare, booty, etc. are received from its use
3. A *production technique, i.e.,* both extractively and as necessary for other economic activities
4. A *symbolic expression,* such as the mother Nile, the sacred Ganges, where water bodies are part of religious expression; and hot springs and spas where mythical curative powers are involved

Before examining these definitions more extensively some selected aspects of community and development should be considered.

## COMMUNITY AND ECONOMY

Most life scientists deal in one way or another with relations between habitat, economy and community. Habitat usually refers to a particular configuration of geology, climate, biomass, and topography that permits certain energy and nutrient flows to characterize a given locale. A community is a collection of animals and/or plants with a given regularity, structure, and frequency of interaction making them distinguishable from other such groupings. The term "economy" is one that has caused unintended confusion because it defines both a discipline of study and a process to be studied. Thus ecologists, sociologists, and other life scientists focus on *interspecific* trophic exchanges, whereas most economists concentrate on exchanges within a particular species and indeed a particular culture and time frame, for example, Western Europe within the past 200 years.

Because their central metaphor—the market—is seen as the regulator of all necessary exchanges, economists often have a more benign view of environmental issues than do life scientists. In nomadic pastoral economies or hunting-gathering economies, signals of adjustment come from a relevant trophic level; thus shifts to new grazing areas or water holes are directly perceived meanings that maintain a certain ecologic balance. In market economies such signals are indirect and seldom within the normative meanings of the system; thus, healthy markets can thrive on deteriorating ecosystems.

This distinction is important when we talk of community development because such a notion is most often identified in terms that fit the measurements of modern economists. A "developing community" is one that has consistent growth in production and consumption of those goods that command a monetary price and that can be summed in some arbitrary index, such as the per capita income, trade balance, or gross product. Community development, in this sense, means the destruction of an existing community's myths and the substitution of another set of myths. A hunter-gatherer group in the Khalahari desert, a nomadic pastoral group in the Sahara, a pueblo group in Arizona, or Spanish-American group in New Mexico must convert its web of natural and social relations into "commodities" that command a price.

## WATER AND ITS OCCURRENCE

In order to place the question of water and community development into its broadest perspective, some human communities that exist in ecological zones where water seems crucial to social organization will be examined. Of particular interest will be the institutional matrices and the degree of congruency characteristic of these communities.

At first glance it would seem that water has been *the* defining influence on the size and distribution of human populations. Certainly the tropical, arid, and arctic regions are three geographic bands of persistently low human density, where water has either been too much, too little, or too hard. However, arid regions have supported highly dense and complex civilizations and the tropical regions of Southeast Asia, Central America, and Central Africa continue to reveal the artifacts of great civilizations. This has not been the case in frigid areas where the highest level of cultural density and complexity is represented by the nomadic Laplander or the sedentary Eskimo communities.

Therefore, it is evident that a water resource alone does not determine community development. Rather, the more complex development often found in tropical and arid zones seems to be due to the greater concentration of solar energy available. This will be our assumption as we direct our attention to the arid zones.

Meigs's (1953) classification and mapping of arid regions indicates that every continent except Europe has a sizable expanse of extremely-arid, arid, and semiarid lands. Though historically the boundaries of these arid regions have fluctuated along the margins, their general placements have remained constant. Further, there are interesting patterns of continuity and variation in the social structures that have occurred within and at the edges of these consistent desert environments.

Thus, arid regions are useful study locales for examining the ways in which environmental factors affect continuity and change in human societies. Such regions combine a set of potentially rich resources with harsh environments of sufficient magnitude to test the adaptive capacity of past and present social forms. Personal greed must be balanced by social altruism if the individual is to survive. In the desert, the essential balances maintained by all enduring social forms are clarified.

There are four general and often coexisting social forms that provide distinctive adaptive strategies in arid environments. There are the small hunter-gatherer bands, such as the !Kung Bushmen of the Khalahari or the Shoshone of the Great Basin; the tribal organizations, such as the Rwala Bedouin; the sedentary villages around oases and water courses, such as those of the Zuni or Hopi of the Colorado Plateau; and, finally, the state organizations of hydraulic civilizations such as the Aztec or Sumerians.

These different "communities" exhibit characteristic mechanisms for maintaining social solidarity. Hunter-gatherer groups are bound together largely on the basis of blood ties and extended family organization. Nomadic tribal groups have certain broad territorial ranges and combinations of ranked lineages often sharing a distinct language. Villages have a more elaborate division of labor and a dense propinquity for functional and residential interactions. Hydraulic civilizations represent the interplay and reinforcement between religious syncretism and bureaucratic organizations in such a way that villages and tribesmen become class and ethnic components of the new order.

Hydraulic civilizations seem to have emerged at significant ecological edges. Thus the edges between the Thar Desert and the Indus River, the Gobi Desert and the Huang River, the Iranian and Turkestan Deserts and the Tigris and Euphrates Rivers, the Saharan and the Arabian Deserts and the Nile River were the earliest sites of hydraulic civilization. Spreading out from such important points of energy concentration are the agrarian villages, the nomadic tribes, and the hunter-gatherer bands.

Initially these seem either points along a linear scale of social evolution or eddies spun off from the great thrust of social progress. Such visions are the stuff of grand theory but it seems more likely that each of the forms has simply found the appropriate structure for its given habitat.

Given the kind of biosocial animal they are, humans from any hunter-gatherer band, nomadic tribe or village unit, if placed in the particular ecological niche of a Nile Valley, would evolve the only organizational form appropriate for dealing with a great desert river system. Such systems, with their regular cycles of drought and flood and corresponding demand for extensive irrigation and diking systems, would seek a greater division of labor than that of age and sex; the new specializations and coordinating authority would require organizational forms that, step by step, would soon assume a survival life of their own so that society would come to be seen as existing primarily for their benefit.

As Wittfogel notes:

> Development in political structure is most consequential when the primitive governments of hydraulic tribes, managed largely by part-time functionaries, evolve into statelike organizations, managed by a body of full-time officials. The hydraulic state provides more comprehensive opportunities for imposing hydraulic installations upon the natural environment, but it also gives the men of the state apparatus the opportunity to neglect water works which will benefit the people, in order to build huge palaces and tombs and process precious organic and inorganic materials which will benefit the rulers.
>
> ... The organizational methods of hydraulic despotism (such as record-keeping, census-taking, centralized armies, a state system of post and intelligence) as well as its acquisitive methods (such as general labor service, general and heavy taxation, and periodic confiscations) and its legal and political methods (such as fragmentative laws of inheritance and the suppression of independent political organizations) [worked] to keep private property weak and the nonbureaucratic forces of society politically impotent (Wittfogel, 1956).

The highly complex social organization that long predated technological developments in hydraulic civilizations permitted large, concentrated populations and, more importantly, permitted several such social forms to persist from three to five millenniums. Yet it is wise to recall Farb's description of the hunting-gathering Shoshone of the Great Basin as the "most leisured people" (Farb, 1968). Sahlins (1968), Lee (1966), and others have also reported a reasonable life of ease for peoples surviving in most harsh environments. Lee (1966) reports that for the !Kung Bushmen:

## 46 WATER AND COMMUNITY DEVELOPMENT

The work week varies from 1, 2 and 3.2 work days per adult. In other words, each productive individual supports herself or himself and dependents and still has 3½ to 5½ days available for other activities. The index of Subsistence Efforts varies from 0.11 to 0.31, which is 11 and 31 work days per 100 consumption days (Lee, 1966).

It is important to note that scarcity in the usual economic sense is *not* a grinding reality into which all of mankind is born. Indeed, peoples sharing the fruits of western culture seem to be those most blessed by the rewards of scarcity. As Lee notes: "One of the most striking cross-cultural regularities yet discovered is the almost universal practice of voluntary food sharing among small-scale hunter-gatherers" (Lee, 1966). He argues that such a norm maintains the subsistence organizational pattern as it tends to keep food inventories at a minimum and maintains minimal differences in wealth between persons.

Survival under the harshest environments for hunter-gatherers seems due to flexibility in social structure so that clans can band together during periods when there are high concentrations of desired foods and then divide into smaller units during dry periods. Thus, water supplies are sustained and energy expenditure in gathering food away from waterholes remains less than the energy consumed. This organizational pattern is reinforced by an absence of need or ability to "save" and a culture of sharing.

Studies of nomadic groups indicate similar, if more complex, organizational patterns of survival. Sweet (1965) and others describe how camp units can fluctuate from *sections* of ranked lineages numbering 800 or more tents (2500 people) to small kinship units of an adult male, his camels, wife, and dependent children. Regardless of the size of the group and its mode of maintaining social solidarity, all nomadic pastoralists must flow with the routines of nature. The transhumance cycle described by Brémaud and Pagot is typical.

> The basic transhumance cycle can be broken down diagrammatically into five normal phases and a sixth is exceptional.
>
> Phase 1. The first of the rains and the turning out of the herds from around the major waterpoints into the pasturage beyond the dry season grazing limits, to be watered at the pools left by the first rains.
>
> Phase 2. The advent of the full wet season conditions (small meres full of water, and green grass) and treks to saltings or grazings unusable in the dry season for lack of watering points.

Phase 3. Towards the end of the wet season, the drift back from the saltings, using the pasturage thrown open temporarily by the existence of the small meres; the exhaustion of small surface water reserves.

Phase 4. Grazing the same pastures as in phase 3, using water holes for the stock, insofar as the location of the permeable stratum and amount of rain in the year make it possible to find supplies.

Phase 5. Progressive concentration first round the larger watering points and finally round the great dry-season wells.

Phase 6. In specially dry years, the abandonment of the wells fed by alluvial groundwater and the retreat to those where watering of stock is still possible. This last migration, occurring at the end of the hot season, usually takes a heavy toll of livestock, since the drying of the wells means that beasts start off inadequately watered, to travel exceptionally long stages which take them over tracts already overcrowded with stock (Brémaud and Pagot, 1962).

Flowing with the cycles of nature, fierce and independent, the nomad has always been a problem to sedentary civilizations because he is difficult to census, to tax, to regulate. (And, one suspects, because he seems to carry out our romantic fantasies.) Thus most developing societies in the arid regions have sought various means of making him more sedentary so that he will share—and support—community progress and development.

Barth has noted: "There are no competing and more effective means of utilizing the seasonal pastures on which the nomadic adaptation is based" (Barth, 1962). He then goes on to identify three reasons why attempts to fix nomads in place so that "community development" can begin are not likely to work. These are:

1. A comparison of nomadic and settled communities in their present forms reveals a clear difference in the average standard of living in favour of the nomad camp. Even in spite of recent great advances in public health in the villages of the region, the diet, hygiene, and health of all but the poorest nomad communities is better than that of most villages.

2. Through much of the region, the present social structure of villages, particularly the patterns of land-ownership and tenancy, are such that wholesale assimilation of nomads into the sedentary population can only be achieved through economic and social proletarianization: the nomads can find a place only near the bottom of sedentary society, since they lack the capital to become landowners, or the skills to become craftsmen and other specialists. This tendency towards sedentarization through impoverization, which can be observed in most parts of South West Asia today, serves only to swell the already

large and politically volatile rural proletariat and create new and more serious problems for the future. . . .

3. In areas with an established nomadic minority, a strong economic interdependence tends to develop between the village communities and the nomads, and one finds a situation of symbiosis where they mutually depend on each other's products, and where the whole economy of the area is based on the presence of both groups. The removal from such a system of all the specialized pastoral producers can only result in economic decline for the area as a whole (Barth, 1962).

It is doubtful if Barth's concern will slow the press of "progress" for the nomad. Certainly the 1970's drought in the Southern Sahara, which is driving the nomads into urban centers such as Tombouctou, is likely to speed-up the proletarianization and ultimate demise of the nomadic organizational form. Perhaps, this form will ultimately be replaced by social systems that demand tremendous inputs of external energy to sustain themselves, a condition that can be observed in Salt Lake City, Los Angeles, Phoenix and Denver. Or nomadism may continue, but by different means, as Mather (1972) sees occurring on the American Great Plains where mass movement through the region has always been the characteristic influence upon regional social forms from the Amerindian pathway to the modern pickup camper on an interstate highway. Certainly the continuities and varieties of social structures characteristic of arid lands remind us of some potentials and some likely consequences to be considered while relating water to community development. Perhaps the most important of these will be recognition of the limits to the market system.

Cottrell's (1972) study of the modern American desert community, "Caliente," demonstrates that the middle strata will hold to their myths as tightly as the allegedly conservative developing peoples. Caliente was a convenient stop for steam engines crossing the desert from Salt Lake City to Los Angeles. With the introduction of the diesel, the corporate structure no longer had a use for the community and had abandoned it when Cottrell first studied it in the early 1950's. In a follow-up study Cottrell found that business and professional people who paid the greatest costs in terms of economic change retained all the myths of the market system—the price of one's labor is the appropriate measure of his worth; hard work and deferred gratification bring rewards; welfare and cooperation are morally wrong. Ironically, given the ecological and resource base of the town, the only means for its persistence has been a form of long-distance welfarism. As Cottrell describes it:

> The income of most Caliente people comes from outside sources who pay Caliente people for doing things mostly for each other. They care for the sick. They educate their own children. They work to rehabilitate juvenile girls. They house and provide amenities for older people. They provide parks and other free services for the traveler. They maintain law and order. They keep dependent people from falling below a standard which is set, not in Caliente, but in the state capital or in Washington. So it is only as people elsewhere maintain their own values and the social structure that this requires that Caliente is provided with an income. But with that income it can continue to teach and maintain a set of values that are in many respects contradictory to the values that make the community viable (Cottrell, 1972).

Such contradictions between myths and realities abound in human societies because issues in the stability and survival of ecosystems are given substance to the degree to which they affect the distribution of social honor. Thus, our southwestern states have grown to expect the rest of the states to subsidize the shrinking of a limited water table and the exporting of a saline solution downstream, and then to subsidize the surplus cotton resulting from the previous subsidization. In these same arid regions grazing rights on public lands are part of private mortgage capital, while the fees for those rights are set at artificially low rates and overgrazing is endemic. However, since these are public lands, taxpayers in other states are expected to pay for restoring the lands. Apparently indirect "community development" in the western "Calientes" becomes "welfarism" only when applied to eastern urban ethnic communities.

"Community development" in the western arid lands has seldom considered the realities presented in John Wesley Powell's *1878 Report on the Arid Lands of the United States*. But then, Powell was determined to prevail over the myths of early western optimists such as William Gilpin who promised that " . . . rain follows the plow." Powell argued that water, not land, was the resource in the arid west, and laid out a blueprint for a new kind of social democracy to be formed if societies in the western states were to survive. It is interesting that he developed his model from the practices of the then existing Mormon and Amerindian communities. Water was a communal resource to be owned, organized, distributed, and husbanded in a communal fashion.

Powell argued:

> It is best to permit the people to divide their lands for themselves—not in a way by which each man may take what he pleases for himself, but by providing methods by which these settlers may organize and mutually

protect each other from the rapacity of individuals. The lands, as lands, are of but slight value, as they cannot be used for ordinary agricultural purposes, *i.e.*, the cultivation of crops; but their value consists in the scant grasses which they spontaneously produce, and these values can be made available only by the use of the waters necessary for the subsistence of stock, and that necessary for the small amount of irrigable land which should be attached to the several pasturage farms. Thus, practically, all values inhere in the water, and an equitable division of the waters can be made only by a wise system of parceling the lands, and the people in organized bodies can well be trusted with this right, while individuals could not thus be trusted (Powell, 1962).

Powell's plan never gained acceptance. Indeed, recent study of the Bear Lake Region of Utah and Idaho by Andrews and Geersten (1970) indicates a continuing rejection of the Powell vision by residents of the arid lands. Large proportions of their sample seem to have images of boundless quantities of water in the region. They insist on providing these resources at considerably less than cost for the private gain of agriculturists, emphasize priority of mining and commodity uses over other uses, assign to the general public costs of environmental restoration after private gain has been extracted, and almost unanimously favor obtaining more industry even if this puts more pressure on the supply of water in the area. As a modern Gilpin might say: "Water follows the factory stack."

Though such notions are ecologically absurd, they are sociologically accurate. Expansion of the major sources of social honor in a market society—economic growth, rising land prices, increasing populations—promises significant gains for present residents. They are unlikely to consider ecologically grey tomorrows when today glows bright with new deference to be gained.

Communities located in arid zones tend to exhibit a high degree of congruency among institutional sources of social honor. In areas where water is more prevalent, communities tend to demonstrate a lower degree of congruency. Low congruency seems to occur only where water is abundant in a cycle that can be identified and observed. Apparently, water as a flow resource broadens the definition of water beyond that associated with subsistence. Once the definition of water includes production and communication, the community tends to exhibit lower degrees of congruency among institutional sources of social honor. What remains to be considered is whether the presence of water, particularly as a flow resource, is a necessary condition in order for communities with lower degrees of institutional congruency to arise. The scope of such an inquiry lies beyond this discussion, but a few suggestions can be made.

## COMMUNITIES AND WATER

In the contemporary world, social geographers such as Gilbert White and his colleagues have estimated that 70% of the human population draws water for household use and personal consumption from outside the dwelling place (White, *et al.*, 1972). This observation immediately suggests that social meanings of water are unlikely to be the same in those communities where water is available in the dwelling as compared with those where it is not.

A certain amount of everyday activity will be concerned with obtaining water for household use. Which social persons are to be the drawers of water differs in communities. In some, only the young are, in others, only females are, and elsewhere only older males are. The number of daily trips to the common supply influences rates of interaction in other institutional patterns for these same individuals.

Containers and their manufacture differ between the two classes of communities. Consumption levels per capita differ substantially between the two categories. In no known case do communities consume as much water where it is not available in the dwelling as in those where water is available from taps in the households. Obviously, communities that possess a collective water supply available within dwelling places will show a somewhat different occupational configuration than communities that do not. A similar conclusion can be drawn for sedentary and nomadic communities, for agricultural and industrial, and for extractive and nonextractive.

Regardless of the substantive differences existing among communities with respect to these matters, all are aspects of the resolution of the system problem of allocation of social resources. These questions remain: do those communities with more elaborate occupational complexes associated with water distribute social honor differently than other communities? Are occupational rewards greater to water-related occupations or not? What determines distribution of such social honor? There appear to be few communities in which occupations associated with water and its provisioning are ranked highly.

Another question concerns the presence or absence of comparatively large bodies of water, whether they are flowing or stock, fresh or saline, and their relationship to community development. In general, it appears that those communities located near such bodies of water tend to have more complex social stratification systems (*i.e.*, more and finer gradations of social honor), though water-related social statuses do not by themselves rank especially high. Hence, large, natural bodies of water tend to be associated with particular types of communities and influence rates of change within those communities. Inland communities appear more conservative than sea communities. The cultures of the latter are often more complex due to the ease of cross-cultural diffusion.

There is also the matter of historical and ahistorical water. Wherever men are capable of establishing supplies from groundwater or surface water through wells, dams, etc., there arise potentials for change in community structure not previously present. Let us hasten to add that the changes are unlikely to be as great as observers once thought. Most significant social changes require at least a generation to work through their consequences. Initial consequences may seldom be persisting ones to which institutional adjustments are made. For example, the creation of a reservoir on lands previously farmed or used for other purposes does not necessarily mean that recreational use will be substituted by the same inhabitants as a means of livelihood. As with other cultural innovations, a considerable period of time may have to elapse before acceptance occurs within a community. Thus while many claims for short run economic benefits may be made, and some realized, a more challenging aspect for consideration is how economic variations are constrained by other institutional factors, and what these joint effects are.

## CONCLUDING OBSERVATIONS

Our analysis suggests that the relationship between water and community development can be seen as an aspect of larger sociological processes: (1) changes in the degree of congruency among institutional sources of social honor in a community, (2) variations in the flexibility of social organizational forms to respond to ecosystem signals, and (3) adaptability in the mechanisms for maintaining social solidarity. For the majority of communities, water is defined largely within terms related to subsistence *per se*. Interestingly, these communities also tend to exhibit a high degree of congruency among institutional sources of social honor, relatively flexible patterns of social organization, and highly adaptive mechanisms for maintaining social solidarity.

## REFERENCES

Andrews, W. H. and D. C. Geersten. *The Function of Social Behavior in Water Resource Development* (Logan, Utah: Institute for Social Research on Natural Resources, 1970) p. 353.
Barth, F. "Nomadism in the Mountain and Plateau Areas of South West Asia." *The Problems of the Arid Zone* (Paris: UNESCO, 1962).
Brémaud, O. and J. Pagot. "Grazing Lands, Nomadism and Transhumance in Sahel." *The Problems of the Arid Zone* (Paris: UNESCO, 1962).
Cottrell, W. F. *Technology, Man and Progress* (Columbus, Ohio: Charles E. Merrill, 1972) p. 84.
Farb, P. *Man's Rise to Civilization* (New York: E.P. Dutton, 1968).
Lee, R. " !Kung Bushmen Subsistence: An Input-Output Analysis." in *Environmental and Cultural Behaviour*, A. P. Vayda, Ed. (Garden City, New York: The Natural History Press, 1966) pp. 67, 75.
Lenski, G. *Power and Privilege* (New York: McGraw-Hill, 1966).
Meigs, P. "World Distribution of Arid and Semi-arid Zone Hydrology." *Arid Zone Programme* 1:203-210, 1953.
Sahlins, M. O. "Notes on the Original Affluent Society," in *Man the Hunter*, R. B. Lee and I. DeVope, Eds. (Chicago: Aldine, 1968).
Mather, E. C. "The American Great Plains." *Annals of Association of American Geographers* 62 (June), 1972.
Powell, J. W. *Reports on the Lands of the Arid Region of the United States*, Wallace Stegner, Ed. (Cambridge, Massachusetts: The Balknap Press of Harvard University Press, 1962) p. 50.
Sweet, L. E. "Camel Pastoralism in North Arabia and the Minimal Camping Unit," in *Man, Culture, and Animals: The Role of Animals in Human Ecological Adjustment*, A. Leeds and A. P. Vayda, Eds., American Association for the Advancement of Science, 78, 1965.
Wittfogel, K. A. "The Hydraulic Civilizations," in *Man's Role in Changing the Face of the Earth*, W. L. Thomas, Jr., Ed. (Chicago: University of Chicago Press, 1965) pp. 152-64.
White, G., et al. *Drawers of Water* (Chicago: University of Chicago Press, 1972).
Benoit-Smullyan, E. "Status Types and Status Interrelations," *Amer. Soc. Rev.* **IX**:151-161, 1944.

# Part II
# Water Resources and Regional Development

# About the Contributors

*Walter R. Butcher* is an Agricultural Economist and Professor of Agricultural Economics at Washington State University. His PhD is from Iowa State University. His research interests include the economics of natural resource utilization and regional economic development. Recent publications treat methodologies of resource evaluation and planning, and evaluation of specific development problems or opportunities. Dr. Butcher has served as consultant to the National Water Commission.

*Daniel W. Bromley* is Associate Professor, Department of Agricultural Economics and Associate Director of the Center for Resource Policy Studies at the University of Wisconsin, Madison. He received his PhD at Oregon State University in 1969. Dr. Bromley has been consultant to the U.S. Water Resources Council, Army Corps of Engineers, Texas Water Development Board and Natural Resource Economics Division of U.S.D.A. Recent publications deal with evaluating public sector activity in natural resource development, and a forthcoming textbook, *Applied Economics*.

*Richard L. Barrows* is Assistant Professor, Department of Agricultural Economics, University of Wisconsin, Madison, and Natural Resources Specialist, University of Wisconsin-Extension. The role of natural resources in economic development and public policy for natural resource utilization and control are included in his research interests. Recent publications concern land use in agriculture and forestry, and rural economic development. His PhD was earned at the University of Wisconsin.

*Stephen C. Smith* received his PhD from the University of Wisconsin where he is now Professor of Agricultural Economics and Associate Dean, School of Natural Resources, College of Agricultural and Life Sciences. Dr. Smith's books are *Economics and Public Policy in Water Resource Development* and *Water Resources Research*. His major research interests are in natural resources economics with special attention to land and water resources and their relationship to social organizations and institutions.

# Part II
# Water Resources and Regional Development

Elementary textbooks in economics often contrast water with diamonds to illustrate the contribution scarcity makes to price or value. Water is necessary for many human activities, but it is relatively cheap even in regions where large investments have been made to alter the geographical and time distribution of water availability. The distinction between price and value has been debated by philosophers as well as economists. Water presents an excellent example of this continuing debate.

Water development has often been thought of as synonymous with economic growth or a necessary condition for growth, leading people to place a very high value upon water as a factor in regional development. Some confusion arises because of the different perspectives from which this issue is joined. The availability of adequate water versus no water at all is seldom the choice, although much discussion of water implies this to be so. To economists who employ the basic principle of marginality, the question is different and much simpler. What is the value of each successive increment of water? If there is zero water availability initially, then the value of the first unit may be exceptionally high, but each successive addition will be less valuable. Therefore, there is no single measure to assess the joint interdependency of water and regional development.

Butcher reviews in detail the relationship between water and economic development for small and large regions. He also relates water to more general models of community growth and presents the results of a simulation model for a river system in-

## 58 WATER AND COMMUNITY DEVELOPMENT

corporating economic structural analysis with the water system. Bromley and Barrows show that water resource investments are undergoing some review and are likely to change significantly due to changing demands for water. Smith argues persuasively that despite previous research and the monumental work of the National Water Commission we still lack an integrated water resources management policy. Some institutional adjustments are necessary to move toward such a policy.

# 4. The Role of Water Resources in Community Development

## WALTER R. BUTCHER

The notion that water resources can be the key for community growth and prosperity is a popular and long-enduring part of U.S., especially western, lore about water. It is prescribed procedure for a community's booster bulletins to refer to abundant supplies of pure water and favorable location on or near the shores of river X or lake Y. Rural areas and small communities seem to be especially inclined to tout their water resources, giving the appearance that they are relying heavily on their water resources for hope of growth and development.

The belief in water's importance extends to water projects. After all, water projects are designed to make water more useful by correcting some of nature's unfortunate quirks of bad timing and inconvenient location. It seems reasonable to expect that such improvements on nature would contribute to community growth and development, much as would a natural supply of water.

The push for depending upon or crediting water and water projects with a key role in community development comes from several sources. Land developers are often centrally involved. Politicians, especially members of Congress, have a well-earned reputation for regarding highly the impact of water projects on their communities. Even the most frugal of Congressmen can appreciate that "economy in government" should not be extended to the extreme of overlooking a chance for a water project in their home state or district. Congressmen seem to be more interested in development aspects than in efficiency. Water resource agencies can also be counted among those who believe that water resource development projects can do much to transform lagging communities into prosperous and happy growth centers.

Economists have a tradition of skepticism about these developmental benefits from water and water projects. For years their skeptical view tended to prevail with the agencies. Now, the tide of sentiment for water projects as development tools seems to be on the rise. The Water Resources Council has proposed new "Principles and Standards for Planning and Evaluation of Water and Related Land Resources Developments" that include explicit credit for the "regional development benefits." This concept has encountered some tough going among government budget watchers, but it is a popular idea. Congress has indicated an impatience to see these principles enacted so that they can proceed to authorize and fund projects planned, at least partly, on the basis of their expected role in bringing about community growth and development.

In the face of this popular sentiment for water as a development tool there is renewed need for understanding the role of water resources in community development. Does water really determine growth? Should communities depend upon their water resources for bringing about development? Should the justification for water projects be on an expectation of development benefits that offset at least some of the costs poured into the projects?

## OBSERVATIONS ON RELATIONSHIPS BETWEEN WATER AND ECONOMIC GROWTH

A few simple observations on water and past economic growth are enough to convince some that there is a close correlation between water and growth, or more particularly, between water projects and growth. I will briefly recount the basis for these views and review some attempts to subject them to systematic analysis.

### Water Availability Explains Economic Growth

One popular view is that water availability explains growth. Accordingly, localities with access to major bodies of water or streams grow to become great cities. Communities stranded on dry land languish.

It is not hard to find a basis for this view. There is an obvious tendency for principal cities throughout the U.S. to be located along major streams or bodies of water. Along the coast one finds Boston, New York, Philadelphia, Washington, D.C., New Orleans, Houston, Los Angeles, San Francisco, and Seattle. Then there are the Great Lake cities of Buffalo, Cleveland, Detroit, Chicago, Milwaukee, and the "big river cities" of Memphis, St. Louis, Minneapolis-St. Paul, Pittsburgh, Cincinnati, Louisville, and Kansas City. Even in the areas with no great water resources, one can find a tendency for correlation between size of city and size of streams. There are exceptions, to be sure, but it certainly appears that water availability has played a key role in the development of population centers. The friendly observer easily sees a principle at work here. Big cities are on big rivers and "backwater" towns are on little creeks.

This innocent but unexciting observation tends to be followed by the further inferences that, if River City's advantage is her superior water resources, why not improve Mudville's creek and bring her the same advantages and opportunities for growth as River City. Now, Mudville's proposal, repeated many times over, suggests a big program of growth stimulation by water resources development. More careful consideration is called for before such a program is launched on the basis of the simple observation that water and growth are found together.

*Tests of the Hypothesis that Water Brings Growth*

A few studies have tried the straightforward approach of investigating the relationship between water and community growth. The best known of these is by Charles Howe (Howe, 1967) in which he considered whether regions, classified as to water availability, exhibited significantly different rates of economic growth during the decade 1950-60. His tests did not support the hypothesis and he concluded that water availability was not sufficient, by itself, to account for differences in regional growth rates. He cited several cases counter to the hypothesis, such as the rapidly growing but arid southwest and the slowly growing but heavily watered lower Mississippi region. He concluded that other factors must have been of greater importance than water availability in determining regional rates of growth during the 1950-60 decade.

There is a possibility that water might be important in determining microlocations within regions even though it showed no effect on region-wide rates of growth. The relatively large regions studied by Howe do not permit a test of this hypothesis, but other men have investigated it. Garrison, in a study of counties within the Tennessee Valley region (Garrison, 1971), concluded that employment levels, growth and the competitive shift of employment in water-oriented industries were significantly related to the supply of water as measured by minimum flow levels. Ben-David (1970), in a study of water-oriented employment by counties in the eastern half of the U.S., also found that higher levels of employment were associated with higher levels of minimum stream flows. Ben-David's model is somewhat superior to Garrison's in that it includes explanatory variables other than water availability. Ben-David's results indicate that a 1 per cent increase in water availability (low flow) was associated with a 0.17 per cent increase in employment by water-oriented industries. While the indicated response is statistically significant, it is not large. Rather substantial increases in low flows would be required to bring about noticeable shifts in local employment, especially if water-oriented employment was only a small fraction of total employment.

The opposite conclusions reached regarding the effects of water supply on growth at subregional versus growth at regional levels hint at an interesting paradox. If local areas receiving expanded water supplies do in fact grow but the region's growth is not increased, then the local growth is being obtained within the constraint of a total output that is unresponsive to the increased water availability. The more rapidly growing localities with better water supplies must be balanced by localities that are declining or at least lagging behind the overall regional growth rate. If so, then the local gains in growth from an improved water supply will be only transfers balanced by declines or reduced rates of growth at other localities in the same region.

A similar tradeoff situation was considered by Howe and Easter in a study of interbasin transfer of water (Howe and Easter, 1971). They argue that the inelasticity of demand for farm products and the price support/production control programs place effective constraints on national outputs of farm products. Thus, output expansions obtained in one locality or region by increased water supply to irrigated agriculture are offset by decreases in output somewhere else. Evidence is brought to show that this has in fact happened with the U.S. Bureau of Reclamation's irrigation program. Growth in the area of Bureau projects has come, ultimately, at the cost of decline in competing agricultural areas.

These few empirical investigations indicate that availability of water is not a simple or overwhelming explainer of economic growth. Perhaps at an earlier time in our history it was more important. Perhaps, also, it can be useful to explain the division of growth among otherwise equal competing sites.

# WATER RESOURCES AND REGIONAL DEVELOPMENT 63

## Water Projects Bring Economic Growth

Another commonly held point of view is that water projects bring about economic growth. In part, this follows naturally from the preceding since water projects either increase the supply of water or make it more available for use. In addition, projects involve construction, which means employment and investment that can have its own stimulating effect on local economies.

Again, there are many instances where water resource projects have been closely followed by impressive growth of population and economic activity in the project area. Irrigation projects, such as the 500,000-acre Columbia Basin Project in eastern Washington and the Snake River Valley projects in southern Idaho, are notable examples of local community growth directly traceable to the existence of a water project. Navigation projects also have a reputation for inducing developments along improved waterways, such as the Ohio and the Illinois Rivers. It seems reasonable, many people maintain, to request a project for "our" area so that we can grow also.

### Tests of the Hypothesis that Water Projects Bring Growth

The only investigations of the relation between water projects and economic growth are case studies. There are, to my knowledge, no general studies of the probability that projects will be followed by growth or of the correlation of growth with characteristics of the project or the project area. The reason for this shying away from general studies is the complexity of forces leading to growth and the tendency for factors other than the project to affect growth, thereby confounding and confusing the analysis of project effects.

Most of the case studies of water projects and growth have been applied to irrigation projects. Irrigation projects differ significantly in that it is relatively easy to establish the amount of local growth attributable to the project. In many project areas it can be presumed that growth without the project would have been zero, just as it was before the project. Thus even a simple before and after comparison may serve as a valid measure of the regional and local growth attributable to the project. The results of studies dealing with this type of growth show a considerable degree of regularity from study to study. Total economic growth in the project area often is two to three times that of the value of products

## 64 WATER AND COMMUNITY DEVELOPMENT

produced on the project. Comparison with nonirrigated areas may show growth to be tenfold or more in the project area.

In conclusion, investigations completed to date give some evidence that water availability may be a factor in distributing growth among localities and that certain types of projects, in some situations, bring it about. But, there is no "law" that water or water projects assuredly bring about community growth. Water may play *a* role in it but it is certainly not always important enough to be *the* overwhelming determinant of growth.

## THE ROLE OF WATER INDICATED BY GENERAL MODELS OF COMMUNITY GROWTH

To find a better basis for determining water's role in economic growth, analysts have been turning to more general theories of growth (Leven, 1970; Lewis, *et al.*, 1972). Excursions into this field soon find that regional science shares with economics the quandary of choosing between powerful but impractical general equilibrium theories and practical but oversimplified operational models of adjustment and growth. Both are useful. The general equilibrium models can give a qualitative understanding of the nature and direction of changes and the operational models can provide a bridge to quantification and application.

### The General Equilibrium Approach

A good place to begin to understand the role of water resources in community development is to go back to impractical but general theories of adjustment and growth. In the concept of a general equilibrium, consumers and producers adjust their activities in response to their own situation and the price signals received through the markets that link them. Consideration of the fact that communities are complex economic units (producers and consumers) linked through markets to other communities opens up a thorough, although somewhat impractical, model for tracing through the effects of water and community growth.

### Community as Producer and Consumer

One way of describing community economic processes is to portray the community as a producing unit—a firm or aggregation of firms. As such, it is engaged in the production of goods and services to supply local and external markets, which it shares com-

# WATER RESOURCES AND REGIONAL DEVELOPMENT 65

petitively with many other producing units. The community's output depends on the amounts and types of resources employed and the technology used. The community has a stock of resources, natural, human and man-made, that may be increased or decreased by trade with other areas. The community firm is assumed to adjust its production activities in order to maximize the value of output (net of purchased inputs).

The community also is a consumer choosing a set of goods for consumption in accord with their relative ability to provide satisfaction and their relative prices. Purchases of goods for consumption are constrained by income, which is determined by the payments factor owners receive from the production entity.

## Markets

Treating the community as an entity means that the markets of interest are those involved in trade with other communities. Prices that a community faces will be determined by national supply and demand relationships, considering all potential producers and consumers. Most community/producers are like small firms, price takers in a competitive market, but some have a large enough share of the market to make them very aware of their own output's influence on price. Location is a definite factor because of the transportation costs involved in producing a good in one place for consumption in another.

An equilibrium from which no further adjustments are desirable will be reached when the marginal rates of substitution (product-to-product, resource-to-product and resource-to-resource) are each equal to the appropriate price ratios for producers and consumers in all locations.

## Disequilibrium and Adjustment

Once equilibrium is reached there will be no tendency to change unless something happens to upset the equilibrium. Thus, growth occurs only in response to some change that disturbs the system, moving it out of equilibrium in a way that results in growth in the community's size. "Disturbing" changes leading to growth might be: a shift in the aggregate market demand for one of the community's products, increased availability of resources, improved (lower cost) technology of production, and cost increases or productivity decreases by competing suppliers. Sometimes the change can be internal with the direct effect falling on producers and consumers within the region, for example, changed consumption patterns by the local consumers, work force growth rates, and savings/investment patterns.

The adjustments in production, consumption and trade with other units that would follow from changes of the above sort in turn push the system out of equilibrium elsewhere. Marginal productivities of resources are affected, the demand for inputs changes, factor prices may be bid up, distribution of income and hence, local consumption patterns change, etc. These in turn call for the other adjustments until the system finally reaches a new equilibrium. If the new equilibrium has greater output or employment than the old, we say that the region is growing.

**A General Equilibrium View of Water's Role**

Water is used for input in production processes, for transportation services, or for direct consumer purposes such as water for households or for recreation. A region's supply of water is one of the basic resources it has available for production and consumption activities. If the supply of available water is a limit to production activities (there is not a surplus of water), then more water can provide the means for growth. But for this to be true, other necessary conditions must be present. Other needed resources must be available at favorable costs and markets for the product must be able to absorb increased output without unfavorable price effects. If these conditions are met, growth in the water-using industry can be expected to follow an increase in water supply.

Water projects generally do not increase the total supply available to a community. Projects do make the given supply of water more readily available, perhaps at lesser cost. The effect is much the same. The supply function for an input to the community's production and consumption activities is shifted downward and to the right. Firms can then produce at lower cost than would otherwise be possible and may be able to expand output along a less rapidly rising cost function.

Beyond the initial adjustments in response to a "shock" to the system, such as a water project, there will be many other changes in response to the first-round adjustments. Sectors supplying inputs to the water-using industries will now face an expanded local demand for their output and likely will increase production in response. A similar change occurs in industries that transport or provide further processing for the output of the water-using industry. If the initial adjustments include expanding employment and incomes for former or new residents, then demand for consumer-serving sectors will also increase, leading them to expand their production.

These first, second, and subsequent round adjustments may also lead to significant changes in the cost structure of local industries. Much attention has been given to economies of scale and of agglomeration. Where these are important, growth induced by an exogenous change such as a water project can have the effect of lowering the local costs of producing goods and services. This in turn may make it feasible to initiate local production of goods and services that had formerly cost more to produce locally than to import from the nearest center large enough to produce at efficient scale. Scale economies generated for local sectors may also lower the cost of inputs for other sectors purchasing from them, thus improving their competitive position vis-a-vis other communities vying for position in the same national market.

Water projects have another initial effect on a community. They generally involve a substantial capital investment. Resources must be drawn away from other employments (unless they would be otherwise unemployed) to build the project structures and the associated private and public facilities needed to make use of the project output. These can be quite a boon to a local economy, with increased demands for goods and services of local firms and increased employment opportunities. Growth can be phenomenal when project funds come from outside the community and investments are large relative to the economic base of the community. But, the effect also terminates with the completion of project construction, which can create problems later. Furthermore, project construction might bid resources away from other production activities, leaving them in a weakened state when construction is completed.

## Practical Models of Growth

Regional analysts have sought to develop models that will reasonably approximate the processes of growth in local economies. These represent attempts at a compromise between the generality of equilibrium models and the realistic constraints of practical model building.

### *Competition-Location Models*

Early efforts at regional analysis concentrated on the question of why economic activities are located in one place or another. They concentrated on the costs of production and of transportation to markets as the major explanations for the location of economic activities. Communities favorably located for resource acquisition, production or transport to market are able to compete and establish production in their community. Hence, growth results. Different factors are important to different products. Thus, there is diversity, with some regions growing for one reason and some for another.

The location theory, competition view of regional activities, gets at the first kind of question about community response to a change in an input, such as water: how does it change cost and output potential for the sectors that employ it as a significant input in their production processes?

*Economic Structure Models*

A second class of models emphasizes the economic structure within regions. These models seek to estimate the total growth that will occur after an initial change in a region's economy has worked itself out in all the changes in associated and related sectors. Interest in these models has been especially fueled by a desire to portray growth in the complexly interdependent economies of large urban centers of manufacturing, trade and services. In these situations the related growth can be quite large relative to growth due to competition and location advantages in the industrial sectors.

The most widely used of these economic structure models is the popular export-base model. In its simplest form, it merely asserts that growth in export or basic sectors will be accompanied by proportional growth in nonbasic sectors at a rate specific to a community and depending upon the structure of the local economy. A more complex model following the same principle is the regional input-output model, which was first developed by Isard (Isard, 1953) and has since been increasingly applied to regional analyses. Regional input-output models could be thought of as disaggregated export-base models with the additional consideration of exogenous changes to demand from other sources as well as from increased exports.

The economic structure model focuses attention on the interrelationship among sectors within a regional economy. Generally, an assumption of constant rates of linkage is made to simplify the analysis. Unfortunately, this is not always a realistic assumption. A substantial change in output of some key sectors in the economy may cause not only changes in the quantity of a related sector's output but also in the relation among sectors. In particular, the economy may become more self-sufficient as it grows due to realization of economies of scale. On the other hand, "bottlenecks" or resource constraints encountered in supporting sectors may force the economy to become more import dependent.

Economic structure models typically treat questions about what initiates the growth process in a rather off-hand manner. Essentially, they say that if something happens to start the process, then this is what the final overall effect will be. This is a very useful answer but it is not in itself sufficient to answer questions such as what is the effect of a water resource project on economic growth? The initial effect of the project on production in the sectors that it directly affects must be known. What is needed is an analysis of the effect of water on competitive position and location advantage to precede the analysis of economic structure effects.

## THE ROLE OF WATER RESOURCES IN THE YAKIMA RIVER BASIN ECONOMY

In the fall of 1970, the Washington Water Research Center began a study of Yakima River Basin's water resources and the relationships between water management and various activities in the basin. Present findings do indicate something of the role of water resources in development of this particular community.

### The Basin

The Yakima River Basin is a fairly typical western river basin. The river originates in snowfields high in the rugged Cascade Mountains, falls rapidly through mountain canyons and then flows at a slower pace through a broad valley. The lower slopes of the mountains are timbered, but the valley floor is too arid to produce more than sparse grass and shrubs. But, as early settlers soon discovered, the valley land could be very productive if irrigated.

Irrigation has been extended to more and more basin lands. By 1970, over 500,000 acres of land in the valley were being irrigated. Agriculture provides most of the base for the economy. Mineral resources are not important. The basin has no location advantage for manufacturing—it is generally remote from both raw material sources and national markets for manufactured goods. Timber production and wood products manufacturing does provide a modest amount of employment and industrial activity, and the recreation industry is growing. But, for the most part, the economy that now exists in the basin is there by virtue of direct or indirect reliance upon irrigated agriculture.

**Potential for Water Supply Induced Growth**

There is definite interest within the basin in achieving economic growth, but there is also an undercurrent of antigrowth sentiment. The desire for growth stems from typical farm community concerns about outmigration of young people who cannot find attractive employment and the desire for the big city accouterments that could be obtained with an expanded trade area. The antigrowth sentiment stems mostly from concern about crowding and the environmental impacts of expanded industry and population.

Observing past growth patterns, it is natural to consider the possibilities for growth by expansion of irrigated agriculture. There are some indications that possibilities for attracting manufacturing and service industries not related to agriculture may be greater than in the past. Still, growth in these other sectors has not been dramatic and is far from assured.

A study by the Washington State University Agricultural Research Center (WSU, 1972) focused on the potential for growth of irrigated agriculture by expansion onto lands not currently irrigated. The study determined that there is a significant acreage of land (some 110,000 acres) suitable for irrigation development that could produce crops at costs competitive with other supply areas. A review of markets for the most promising crops indicated a potential for marketing this added output without encountering either drastic price declines or absolute barriers to expanded marketings.

Our analysis indicates that if these lands were supplied with water, growth of the basin's agricultural industry would result. But, supplying the water is no small matter. Natural flows in the river are ample but not at the time needed. If irrigation is going to be extended to more lands, the water supply will have to be "developed." There are four major options:

1. Increase upstream capacity to store spring runoff and make releases during the irrigation season.
2. Import water from the nearby, amply-supplied Columbia River.
3. Bring about a reallocation of water from current low return uses to anticipated higher return uses on new developments.

4. Expand commitments but not the supply, operating the existing system but with a higher probability of failing to supply all commitments.

Each option has its own problems and ramifications for water's role in economic growth. Options 1 and 2 involve large construction costs that would lower the profit margin for developers. Our calculations indicate that there would still be a positive margin for around 100,000 acres but it would be a narrow and by no means assured margin. The fact that the development has not occurred already can be attributed to a lack of sufficient risk capital rather than to any lack of water itself. There simply are not enough potential investors who have enough confidence in the development's prospects to be willing to risk their funds on it. A selling job might change their mind or a subsidy from public funds might cover some of the costs, leaving a wider profit margin that would be attractive enough to entice the remaining private funds required.

Options calling for reallocation of water (3 and 4) could be carried out at relatively low financial cost to developers, although even the cost of transporting water from the river to the development is no small amount. Expected profit margins would be wider, and hence more likely to attract risk capital. There would be some losses to present irrigators if they shared their existing water supplies with newcomers. These losses would have a negative growth effect and create problems in distributive justice. However, there are indications that much water could be reallocated with minor effects on output and incomes of existing irrigators. The missing element is the institutional mechanisms for reallocation without uncompensated confiscation of rights.

**The Basin's Economic Structure**

The economy of the Yakima River Basin[1] had an output in 1969 estimated at $1,076 million. Employment totaled 46,153 persons and the population of the basin was 192,470 persons. The composition of output from the basin's economy reflects reliance upon the basin's land and water resources. Output from extractive industries

---

1. The area used for functional economic analysis excludes the Richland/Hanford nuclear complex, which technically lies partially within the hydrologic basin but has an economy that is quite dissimilar and detached from the remainder of the basin economy.

of $227 million ($211 million agricultural output and the remaining $16 million forestry) made up more than 20% of total value output from the basin economy. Manufacturing industries had an output of $462 million, with $397 million of that attributable to processing and packing of agricultural and timber products. The output of $65 million from "other" manufacturing was mostly composed of equipment or materials used by the major industries of the basin. The trades and services sector accounted for the remaining $387 million in gross regional output.

The structure of the basin's economy can be more completely described by reference to Table I, which shows a gross flows matrix for an aggregated, five-sector model of the basin economy. One particularly significant element is the $130 million purchase from agriculture by the food processing and packing sector (row 1, column 3). This is by far the largest intersectoral flow. It provides an essential input to the food processing and packing sector, which accounts for one-third of total output from the basin's industries and 15 per cent of all payments to factor owners.

Other internal trade flows are quite small except for $27- and $37-million purchases from trades and services by agriculture and by food processing (row 5, columns 1 and 3). In fact, the agriculture, other manufacturing, and trades and services sectors all supply more of their needs by importing from other areas than by purchases from other Yakima Valley industries. The demands of consumers, government and capital investment likewise are supplied in substantial measure by importing an estimated $172 million in products of industries from outside the basin.

Exports from the basin consist mostly of agricultural products, either directly from the agriculture sector or after processing and packaging. Our estimates indicate a $28 million "balance of payments" surplus for the region. Estimates of imports are particularly difficult and we may have underestimated, or there may in fact be a surplus and compensating flow of funds moving from the valley to investments in other areas.

**Estimated Induced Growth**

The input-output model can be used to estimate the total economic changes that would result from an increase in irrigated agriculture. The procedure is as follows:
1. Estimate the increased agricultural output that would result from the anticipated expansion.
2. Estimate the portion of increased agricultural output that

## Table I
### Total Gross Flows for the Yakima Basin Economy, 1969

| From \ To | Agriculture (1) | Forestry & Wood Prod. (2) | Food Processing & Packing (3) | Other Manufacturing (4) | Trades & Services (5) | Total Sales to Local Industries (6) | Exports (7) | Local* (8) | Total (9) | Total Gross Sales |
|---|---|---|---|---|---|---|---|---|---|---|
| 1. Agriculture | 19.2 | 0.1 | 129.8 | — | — | 149.1 | 56.1 | 5.6 | 61.7 | 210.8 |
| 2. Forestry and wood products | — | 19.4 | 2.3 | 1.2 | 3.6 | 26.5 | 39.2 | 1.2 | 40.4 | 67.0 |
| 3. Food processing and packing | 3.4 | 0.1 | 15.5 | — | 2.5 | 21.5 | 312.0 | 12.7 | 324.7 | 346.3 |
| 4. Other manufacturing | 6.8 | 1.3 | 8.6 | 1.6 | 21.3 | 39.6 | 24.7 | 1.2 | 25.9 | 65.5 |
| 5. Trades and services | 26.8 | 5.9 | 37.5 | 3.2 | 49.7 | 123.1 | −10.3 | 274.1 | 263.8 | 386.9 |
| Total purchases from local industries | 56.2 | 26.8 | 193.7 | 6.0 | 77.1 | 359.8 | 421.7 | 294.8 | 716.5 | 1,076.5 |
| Imports | 50.8 | 6.2 | 77.0 | 22.0 | 66.0 | 222.1 | — | 171.7 | 171.7 | 393.8 |
| Factor owners | 103.7 | 33.9 | 75.5 | 37.5 | 243.8 | 494.4 | — | 173.6 | 173.6 | 668.0 |
| Total gross purchases | 210.8 | 67.0 | 346.3 | 65.5 | 386.9 | 1,076.5 | 421.7 | 640.1 | 1,061.8 | 2,138.3 |

*Local demands include purchases for personal consumption, government and private capital investment.

would be sold directly to final demand sectors (mostly out-of-the-region exports) and the portion that would be sold indirectly through the food processing and packing sector.
3. Utilize the inverse matrix $(I-A)^{-1}$ to calculate the changes in output of all sectors that would result from the changed level of deliveries to final demand.
4. Utilize estimated payments to factors per dollar of output to estimate the effect of output changes on regional income.

We used this approach to trace through the effects of a development on 70,000 acres of land for irrigation. The expected annual gross farm value of output would be $14 million. From this, we estimated that increased export sales from the region would amount to approximately $3 million of agricultural products shipped directly and $32 million of products sold by the local food processing and packing sector based on use of crops from the land. The resulting total changes to the basin economy due directly to the increases in agriculture and food processing and indirectly to changes in other related sectors are shown in Table II.

### Table II
Estimated Changes in Output, Purchases and Employment Due to 70,000 Acre Irrigation Development

|  | Increase in Output | Increase in Local Purchases | Increase in Imports | Increase in Payments to Factors | Increase in Employment Man Years |
|---|---|---|---|---|---|
|  | Millions of Dollars |  |  |  |  |
| Agriculture | 16.9 | 4.6 | 4.0 | 8.3 | 946 |
| Forestry & wood products | 0.4 | 0.2 | 0 | 0.2 | 12 |
| Food processing and packing | 33.8 | 18.9 | 7.5 | 7.4 | 3,718 |
| Other manufacturing | 1.8 | 0.2 | 0.6 | 1.0 | 99 |
| Trades and services | 6.9 | 1.4 | 1.2 | 4.3 | 449 |
| Total | 59.8 | 25.3 | 13.3 | 21.2 | 5,224 |

The increased payments to factors employed in the production of the expanded outputs suggest that there will be increased local purchases of goods and services used by the factor suppliers in their role as consumers. One could estimate this with a "closed" input-output model, containing an internalized production link between final demand purchases by households and employment of factors in the production activities of the region. We chose instead to incorporate this element in a general simulation model of water and development in the Yakima Basin.

## SIMULATION OF WATER AND ECONOMIC GROWTH IN THE YAKIMA RIVER BASIN

Our purpose in preparing a simulation of the Yakima River Basin was to provide a tool for quickly assessing differences in future trends that might arise from different water development policies and programs. We first conducted studies of key components (hydrology, water quality, irrigation, fish, and economics) and prepared detailed models to describe each. Then we formulated a general, aggregated and simplified model, following the approach recently developed by Forrester at MIT (Forrester, 1969). Such simulations are designed to incorporate in one dynamic model several interactive elements that bear upon outcomes such as growth, resource scarcity and environmental quality. Forrester has emphasized that social systems are often too complex to model adequately with the theories of individual disciplines. He suggests that dynamic simulation models that cut across several discipline boundaries will often yield results revealing critical junctures that would be overlooked by investigators from individual disciplines.

The Yakima River Basin simulation model focuses on water and the economy. A flow chart is included as Figure 1. Water available for irrigation is determined by natural flows (which vary stochastically), by storage capacity for release during low-flow periods, and by priority demands for water for municipal supplies, waste dilution to meet quality standards and to assure minimum flows for fish habitat. In turn, water demands depend mostly upon basin population levels and recreation demands. Storage capacity can be increased by investment in new or expanded reservoirs. The acreage of land irrigated and output of irrigated crops is determined by a profit-maximizing routine that allocates water among irrigable lands.

The effect of changing agricultural output upon the economy is estimated by applying changed export levels to an input-output model of the economy. The resulting estimates of output levels by

# 76 WATER AND COMMUNITY DEVELOPMENT

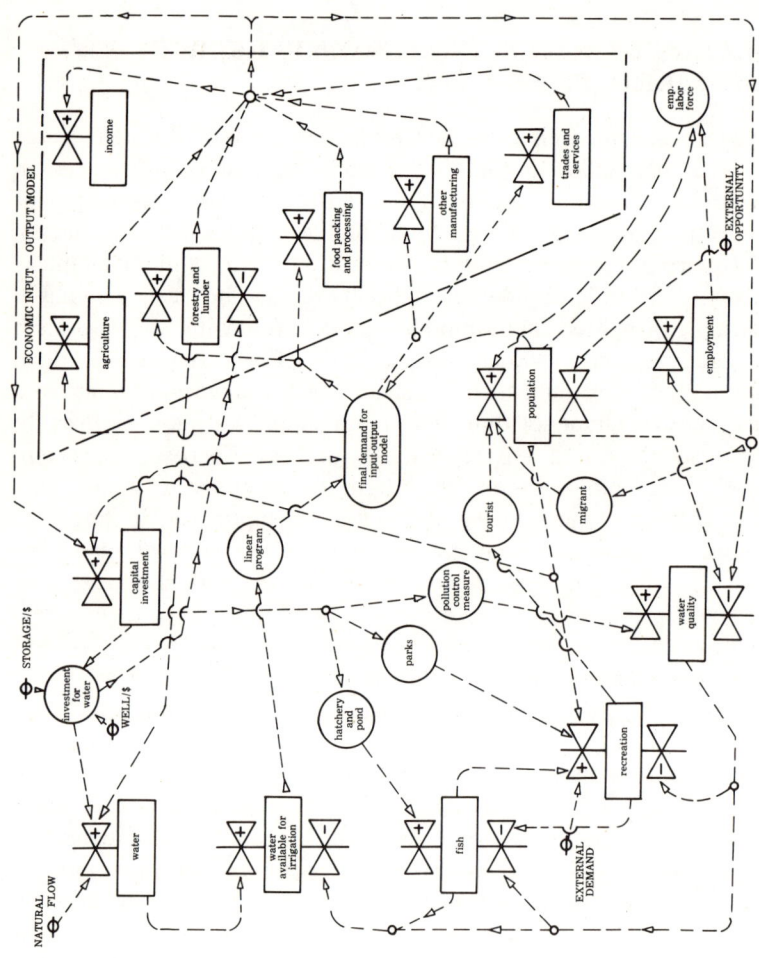

Figure 1. Flow chart of Yakima River Basin.

sector are used to estimate employment in the region's industries and trades and requirements for new investments if any sectors are expanded to new higher output levels. Changes in employment determine population levels since population in this area is believed to be determined by migration in response to relative rates of unemployment in the basin and in the rest of the country. Demands for personal consumption and for government purposes are assumed to be population determined so the model is effectively closed since population is ultimately determined by output and is also a determiner of output.

In a pilot run of the simulation model we assumed an unchanging sector purchasing pattern [constant $(I-A)^{-1}$], a steady 1.5 per cent-per-year growth in value of farm output per acre and in manufacturing exports, and a one-time development of 70,000 acres of new irrigation in the tenth year. Water for the new land could be most economically supplied by enlargement of the Bumping Lake reservoir. The results from this pilot run are shown in Table III for every fifth year. The economy begins a surge in the year 10 when the hypothesized irrigation development is initiated. Agricultural output, total output, net new investment and employment are all increased sharply in that year. The surge is carried on through to year 15 by the requirements for new investments in industrial, government and household sectors to handle expanded economic activity and increased work force. Year 15 is the peak and from that point the economy contracts as new investment needs are largely passed. Employment declines and people migrate from the area until about year 25, when stability is reached and steady growth occurs due to built-in increases in agriculture and manufacturing.

Results from the simulation model show two additional aspects of water-induced growth. First, the additional growth due to serving households and making necessary expanded capital investments is reflected in an overall gain in output that is nearly three times as large as the increase needed for meeting industry requirements alone. Second, the time path of growth shows a definite pattern of boom followed by mini-recessions when the development occurs in a short time span.

This model does not tell the full story about development. It indicates growth, but growth can occur without development, that is, without increasing the range of choice open to individuals in the community. There is a very real possibility that water development that induces water-intensive industries to the area will, in

## Table III
### Results of Yakima River Basin Simulation

| | Unit | Year | | | | |
|---|---|---|---|---|---|---|
| | | 5 | 10 | 15 | 20 | 25 |
| Area irrigated | (A,000) | 500 | 570 | 570 | 570 | 570 |
| Ag output | $ mil. | 220 | 294 | 322 | 338 | 370 |
| Total output | $ mil. | 1,157 | 1,478 | 1,777 | 1,726 | 1,801 |
| Net new invest. | $ mil. | 9 | 89 | 64 | 13 | 16 |
| Employment | 000 | 50 | 63 | 79 | 74 | 76 |
| Av. unemployment | % | 4 | −10* | 4 | 7 | 5 |
| Population | 000 | 186 | 202 | 294 | 282 | 283 |
| Net migration | workers | +500 | 0 | +2,800 | −2,400 | +800 |

*Negative indicates temporary overtime work; higher than normal labor force participation rates and temporary employment on nonresidents to meet sharp change in demand for workers.

fact, cause much more growth than development. To differentiate between the two, a model should measure not only output and employment, but also the type of employment and expected income levels that would be enjoyed by the employees.

## REFERENCES

Ben-David, S. "Effects of Water Development on Location of Water-Oriented Manufacturing," in George S. Tolley, Ed. *Estimation of First Round and Selected Subsequent Income Effects of Water Resources Investments* (Springfield, Va.: U.S. Army Engineering Institute for Water Resources, National Tech. Inf. Serv., 1970).

Forrester, J. W. *Urban Dynamics* (Cambridge, Mass.: M.I.T. Press, 1969).

Garrison, C. B. "Effects of Water Resources on Economic Growth in Tennessee Valley Regions," Dept. Economics, College of Business Administration, University of Tennessee, Knoxville (Jan. 1971).

Highland, S. "Yakima Simulation." A paper presented in partial fulfillment of Master of Science degree in Computer Science, Washington State University (1973).

Howe, C. W. "Water and Regional Economic Growth in the United States, 1950-1960." *Southern Econ. J.* 34(4):477-499 (1968).

Howe, C. W. and K. W. Easter. *Interbasin Transfers of Water: Economic Issues and Impacts* (Baltimore, Md.: Johns Hopkins, 1971).

Isard, W. "Regional Commodities Balances and Interregional Commodity Flow," *Amer. Econ. Rev. Suppl.* 43:167-180 (1953).

Leven, C. L., Ed. "Development Benefits of Water Resource Investments," U.S. Army Engineering Institute for Water Resources, National Tech. Inf. Serv., Springfield, Va. (1970).

Lewis, W. C., J. C. Anderson, H. H. Fullerton, and B. D. Gardner. "The Role of Water in Regional Economic Development," Report prepared for the National Water Commission PB 206-372, National Tech. Inf. Serv., Springfield, Va. (1972).

Washington State University Agricultural Research Center. "Land Development and Water Use, Yakima River Basin, Washington," Washington State University Ag. Res. Ctr., Pullman (1972).

# 5. The Changing Nature of Water Resource Investments: Implications for Community Development

**DANIEL W. BROMLEY AND RICHARD L. BARROWS**

The central purpose of this chapter is to discuss the nature of probable changes in the scope and purpose of water development projects, and to analyze the possible implications of these changes for community development. To speak definitively of the impacts of changes in water resource investments on community development requires the existence of good empirical research on the social and economic impacts of past water development projects. Though a few such studies do exist (Hogg, 1970; Wilkinson, 1969), there is insufficient evidence to permit unequivocal allegations. Hence, community development impacts will be discussed in a conjectural manner, with the hope of stimulating thought and further discussion. Even a very general treatment of the subject presupposes at least three areas of common knowledge: (1) an understanding of the political and economic issues traditionally important in project initiation, formulation, and justification, (2) a basic agreement as to what constitutes community development, and (3) an overview of the probable changes in the nature and scope of future water resource projects. Only in light of this common knowledge is it possible to speak meaningfully of the implications for community development of a change in water resource projects. This discussion is divided into four main sections: (1) the political and economic aspects of "traditional" water resource projects as they relate to community development, (2) definitions of community development resulting from differential emphasis of those with different disciplinary backgrounds, (3) the ways in which the water resource program of the federal government will probably change over the next 20 years, and (4) the ways in which these likely changes in the nature of water resource projects and programs might be expected to affect community development.

## WATER RESOURCE PROJECTS: THE TRADITIONAL APPROACH

### Politics of Water Resource Projects

Water resource investments result from the political process of decision making and resource allocation. Ingram's (1971) excellent article on the political nature of water resource investments summarizes many of the important elements that contribute to the "success" of a project, with success defined as the acceptance of the project by decision makers at various levels.

Interest groups are important in the process of public decision making for two reasons. First, they play a significant role in the initiation of a water project, and second, they are critical in the political bargaining that necessarily accompanies every proposed project. The role of interest groups in general can be better understood within the framework of "analytic pluralism," a political theory of interest group actions. Analytic pluralism is a political theory that argues as follows: (1) society is composed of groups of individuals that are unified around common values and goals, (2) as society becomes more complex, these groups take on added importance, (3) public policy results from the balancing of force among opposing groups, (4) groups are successful if they can muster not only numbers, but good tactics, (5) political stability results from the exercise of mutual restraint by all groups, and (6) there is no such thing as *the* public interest (Baskin, 1971).

Analytic pluralism further argues that, in addition to numbers and tactics, several important factors critical to a group's success in the policy arena are: (1) group respectability and status, (2) the coincidence between interests of the group and community norms, (3) control over information, and (4) the ability of a group to "localize" conflict (Baskin, 1971). Most water resource investments are initiated by local interest groups who stand to reap relatively large net benefits from proposed projects. These groups, in coalition with local offices of the major water resource agencies, work to obtain project approval from higher levels of the federal bureaucracy and, ultimately, from Congress (Lord and Smith, 1969).

Project initiation and approval illustrate the points set forth above as critical to a group's success in the policy arena. First, local businessmen who saw opportunities to increase sales as a result of federal investments were traditionally those promoting projects. The support of these businessmen gave credibility and respectability to efforts to gain development projects. Second, those promoting water resource projects were "in tune" with community norms, which place a high value on economic growth and development. Third, agencies and certain interest groups were able to effectively control generation and dissemination of information on proposed projects, since the technical complexity of planning and evaluation discouraged the involvement of nonagency personnel. In addition, the way in which information on a project was presented to the public was not only highly selective, but also often abstruse or misleading. Lack of information posed a serious handicap to groups or individuals opposed to a project. Finally, in the past, local interest groups and agencies were able to confine conflict over project approval to small geographic areas. The recent National Environmental Policy Act has broadened the geographical basis for conflict since local development-oriented interests may now be challenged by local or nonlocal groups on the basis of adverse environmental impacts.

In summary, although local interest groups, particularly businessmen, may have been important in initiating action on a project, there were no institutionalized procedures for eliciting broad-based public participation in project planning, or for controlling the resulting development. Local participation was limited to the initiation of agency action by interest groups and the provision of political support for federal agency requests. In general, the process of project authorization and appropriation was more concerned with displaying purported economic benefits than with public participation.

### Economics of Water Resource Projects

In addition to the local political activities stimulated by project potentials, water resource projects have also had important economic impacts on communities. These impacts result from flood control, irrigation, hydroelectric power, municipal and industrial water supply, and recreation. In order to understand the community development implications of changes in the nature and scope of water resource investments, it is necessary to briefly review the economic impacts of traditional water resource projects.

*Flood Control*

Both the Corps of Engineers and the Soil Conservation Service provide flood control services, with the latter agency being confined to smaller undertakings. The major benefits that arise from a flood control structure fall into one of four categories: (1) reduction of crop damage from flooding, (2) reduction of property damage from flooding, (3) reduction of noncrop output losses due to flooding, and (4) land and property productivity improvements possible without flooding. Although the prevention of flood damage can be important to a community, very little new economic activity is generated from flood control projects. In fact, it is possible that construction companies and other types of "repair" services might suffer economic losses from the prevention of flooding.

At the national level, it has been recognized for some time that without some form of flood plain regulation, there is an undesirable circularity in flood prevention programs. Benefits are computed and projects justified on the basis of damages avoided by building a structure. Unless development in the flood plain is controlled after the structure is built, another larger structure is soon "justified."

*Irrigation*

The traditional water project in the West is irrigation development. The direct benefit is an increase in the net income of the farming sector. Since the demand for food and fiber does not necessarily increase, there is considerable debate over how much of the new income is a legitimate "benefit" from a national point of view.

Although irrigation in the arid Southwest has had a profound impact on the economy of that area, there has also been a significant negative impact on the former cotton-producing areas of the Southeast. While some of these negative impacts have directly affected the farmers through lower prices, many of them have been more indirect. It is conventional to classify the indirect benefits as either "induced by" or "stemming from." "Induced by" benefits are increases in the net income of those engaged in the business of supplying inputs to the project farmers. An example would be those who sell gasoline, fertilizer, and equipment to the project farmers. "Stemming from" benefits include the increased net income of those engaged in processing, wholesaling, retailing, or transporting the product that is grown by the project farmers. Just as increases in the above categories are benefits of an irrigation project (usually concentrated in the project region), decreases are properly counted as costs (usually dispersed in other regions).

*Hydroelectric Power*

With the advent of extensive regional interties for the transmission of electric power, relatively slight local impacts have been realized from the location of a hydroelectric facility near a community. However, a locality could still promote industrial influx by boasting of such a facility. In some instances, local utilities were able to market electrical energy at rates lower than those elsewhere. The resulting implications for community development will be discussed below.

*Municipal and Industrial Water Supply*

The traditional water resource project has generally contained a provision for municipal and industrial water supply or for water quality alteration through low-flow augmentation. Communities in close proximity to a project were often able to argue successfully that the project should include a water-supply purpose, sometimes with a favorable repayment obligation compared to the alternative cost of providing water. With this new water supply, it would then be possible to mobilize efforts to attract industry, although the probability of success in such efforts may have been quite low. The mere presence of a project with water supply provisions does not necessarily create any impact on employment and income, although it is possible for the community to use the project to entice industry from other areas.

*Recreation*

To an isolated rural community, the existence of a nearby recreation facility can be significant indeed. The prospect of thousands of tourists flocking into communities throughout the summer is an inviting one to local chambers of commerce and the businessmen they represent. Indeed, the addition of recreation as a "purpose" in water projects has had a significant impact on the marshalling of local support for projects that, without recreation, might have had the support of only farmers and a few property owners.

Although the benefits from a recreational project may be of

# 86 WATER AND COMMUNITY DEVELOPMENT

great significance to the community, not all impacts of the project are positive. The beneficial effects would include increased service trade from those visiting the site and the increased purchases of recreational equipment by local residents. However, outside residents may spend very little in the area, often bringing even food and gasoline with them. In addition, unless a project results in higher incomes for local residents, their additional recreational expenditures must come at the expense of other types of local expenditures. Thus, it is often the case that water-based recreation increases in popularity, while other forms of recreation become less popular. Proprietors of movie theaters, bowling alleys, golf courses, and other recreational facilities may suffer income losses as a result of water-based recreation projects, while motel operators, restaurant owners, and gas station managers may benefit substantially.

**Conclusions**

Local interest groups have traditionally played a significant role in project initiation and justification. Such local involvement and support has generally been based on the supposition that significant economic benefits would accrue to the local area. The extent to which this expectation is realized depends on many factors —some of which are under the control of individuals on the local level, and some of which are entirely exogenous. The significance of past water resource projects for "community development" depends on the definition of that term. In order to assess the community development implications of traditional water resource projects, it is necessary to explore several definitions of community development.

**SOME DEFINITIONS OF COMMUNITY DEVELOPMENT**

Historically, there has been considerable ambiguity in the use of the term "community development." Bilinski (1969) points out that the term has been used to denote a process, method, program, social movement, and set of ideas. Sociologists have emphasized community development as a process of creating and strengthening relationships between local leaders while mobilizing community resources to accomplish various tasks (Warren, 1963). Economists have emphasized the task-accomplishment aspects of community development. Even within the task-oriented approach there are different emphases—equity *vs.* efficiency, or economic development *vs.* "social" development. The "process" and "task-oriented" approaches to community development will be examined in more detail.

**The Process Approach**

The "process approach" to community development emphasizes creation of a problem-solving concern by local leaders working together, using local resources to attack community problems. Warren (1963) defines community development as "... a deliberate and sustained attempt to strengthen the horizontal pattern of a community." The horizontal pattern is the structural and functional relation of various local individuals and groups to one another. Community development may be said to occur through the strengthening of horizontal ties, even if local leaders are not successful in affecting change in the physical or economic environment. Warren views community development as a process that may or may not result in reaching "extraneous objectives," such as new schools or industrial development. He argues that the "older, largely informal ties which held community units in an effective functional relationship are no longer found adequate. As a result, various deliberate attempts are made to achieve at least the minimum necessary functional interrelationship which formerly existed...."

Bilinski (1969) offers essentially the same definition:

> Community development is a conscious and deliberate effort aimed at helping communities to recognize their needs and to assume increasing responsibility for solving their problems.... It is obtained by the ... effective use of resources through rational organization and full participation of the community....

Both writers, while recognizing the tendency for the specific task objectives to assume more importance than the general process goal, feel that the importance of "strengthening horizontal community ties" is not diminished.

Conversely, it is relevant to note Hogg's (1970) observation that in the process of local participation, longstanding local disputes may escalate to the point that horizontal ties are actually destroyed.

**Task-Oriented Approach**

It might be argued that the development of a process is not enough, that community development requires tangible results. It is certainly true that the process goal of community development must be tied to very specific task objectives in order to legitimize the effort of strengthening horizontal ties. Whether or not the attainment of a particular task objective constitutes community development depends on the definition of development employed.

There have been many attempts to define community development in terms of social welfare, but the difficulty of interpersonal comparisons of utility, and the lack of a clearly-defined social welfare function have stymied these efforts (Beattie, 1972). A more operationally meaningful economic definition relates community development to increases in some measurable economic variable or set of variables. Leven (1965) argues that different groups in society will define development in strikingly different ways. Bankers and businessmen might define it in terms of net product or gross cash flows, while workers may define development in terms of jobs or distribution of income. Such definitions may conflict, with one definition indicating that a particular project has furthered development, and another indicating no change or even a decrease in the degree of development.

To avoid the problems inherent in any single task-oriented indicator of development and to provide an operationally meaningful definition, several "possible development objectives" may be posited (Barrows, 1972). Increases in total community income and attainment of a more equal distribution of income are two possible task-oriented development objectives. Increasing employment opportunities in the community might be another specific objective of a community development program. Attainment of this objective could be measured by the increase in total employment in the area, or by the decrease in the number or percentage of local residents who are unemployed. Finally, decreasing the number of community households with incomes below the poverty line may be a community development objective. In addition to objectives related to economic change, other types of task-oriented definitions of community development may be constructed. For example, one goal might be to increase the percentage of registered voters, or to increase participation in local elections. For purposes of this discussion, however, task-oriented objectives will be considered to be economic changes such as those discussed above.

In conclusion, community development may be defined as a process of increasing community involvement in solving local problems, with the overall goal of strengthening the community's horizontal ties. Alternatively, it may be defined in terms of very specific, task-oriented objectives, such as increasing local income and employment, decreasing local unemployment and poverty, and producing a more equal distribution of income. Each of these notions of community development is important in assessing the implications of the changes in the nature of water resource projects. (The differences between the process approach and the task-oriented approach are discussed in more detail in Bromley, 1972.)

## THE CHANGING NATURE OF WATER RESOURCE INVESTMENTS

Before discussing the community development impacts of a change in the nature of water resource investments, it is necessary to outline ways in which future water resource projects are likely to differ from the "traditional" water project. First, the "purposes" for which projects are built, whether for flood control, irrigation, or municipal and industrial water, will differ significantly from more traditional purposes. Second, the "institutional setting" under which projects are constructed and financed will differ, not only in the ways they are planned and evaluated, but also in the extent to which those who benefit from the undertakings are held responsible for some of the financial costs. The first type of changes will be referred to as a "change in focus," while the latter will be termed "institutional changes."

**Changing Focus**

There are six probable changes in the focus of water resource investments: (1) a move away from hydroelectric generation, (2) more explicit recognition of recreation as a principle project purpose, (3) a greater reliance on nonstructural flood control measures, (4) more explicit recognition of municipal and industrial water supply as a principle project purpose, (5) increased emphasis on wastewater management, and (6) fewer irrigation developments.

*Energy Production*

One of the purposes of many water resource projects in the West has been the generation of electric energy. Because it is often a joint product of irrigation and flood control, hydroelectric generation is often thought of as a secondary purpose of most projects. But, secondary does not necessarily imply expendability. For instance, in a proposed Bureau of Reclamation Project in southern Idaho, "Power development was included as a function to supply the heavy irrigation pumping power demands involved in the plan *and to assist in project repayment"* (Bureau of Reclamation, 1966; emphasis added). In this project, power revenues were to be utilized to repay over 80 per cent of the reimbursable costs of irrigation. This repayment obligation, which became necessary once it was obvious that irrigators could not meet repayment obligations, has encumbered the Bonneville Power Administration to the extent that BPA recently raised its power rates for the first time in its history in order to meet its repayment obligations (Bonneville Power Administration, 1969).

In addition to the financial burden that small, inefficient generating facilities have placed on marketing agencies such as BPA, it is also evident that all but a few of the good hydroelectric sites have already been developed. Hence, the balance of facilities will probably be located on low-head sites suitable only for "run-of-the-river" generation.

The number of viable hydroelectric sites is now low enough, and the repayment burden great enough, that the future of hydroelectric generating facilities as part of the more traditional water resource development is not bright. In addition, recent estimates indicate that while 18 per cent of the national output of electricity in 1965 came from conventional and pumped-storage hydroelectric facilities, by the year 2020 the portion so supplied is expected to drop to approximately 5 per cent. This will be due primarily to greater efficiency of alternative sources of generation (Water Resources Council, 1968).

The main alternative source of energy will be nuclear generators. Creation of fast-breeder reactors promises to make power from such sources vastly cheaper than from present sources. However, this alternative has its drawbacks since nuclear fusion or fission demands great quantities of water for cooling. The Water Resources Council recently estimated that water withdrawals for cooling purposes at steam-electric plants constitute the largest nonagricultural diversion of water at present. It is anticipated that by 1980 these withdrawals will surpass those of agriculture (Water Resources Council, 1968).

*Recreation*

Traditionally, recreation has been a project output of convenience rather than of conscious design. The agency can count benefits from providing recreation as a project purpose, while the incremental costs of providing for recreation can often be held to a minimum. In addition, local repayment helps to defray a part of these costs. However, state conservation agencies have become less willing to agree to these traditional arrangements, arguing that paying a portion of the cost for afterthought recreation facilities may be less wise than paying the full cost of recreation facilities comprehensively planned by the state.

Recommendations of the National Water Commission (1973) are explicit with respect to recreation. The Commission recommended that recreation be "... elevated to a high priority program ... in coordinated planning, construction, operation, land acquisition, personnel, and funding." These recommendations suggest that future water resource investment policy is likely to place increasing emphasis on recreation-oriented projects.

*Nonstructural Flood Prevention*

As pointed out recently, "... floods may be 'acts of God,' but flood losses in human life, property, and social disruption often result from improper use of flood-prone lands" (Yanggen, et al., 1971). This obvious notion, so elusive to many responsible for building flood control structures, is finally gaining currency. The circularity concept of justifying flood-control structures on the basis of damages avoided (called "benefits"), while not restricting further development in newly-protected areas, has resulted in flood losses that continue to average over $1 billion annually (Yanggen, et al., 1971). Even though $7 billion has been spent on flood control since 1936, damages continue to exceed construction costs.

Yet, individual states and municipalities are exercising a broad array of police-power regulations to control land use in flood areas. As pointed out by Yanggen, et al. (1971), construction of dams and levees is controlled by some states or localities, as are bulkhead lines for rivers, streams, and harbors. However, principal local control of flood hazard area land is through adoption of broad zoning, subdivision regulation, building and housing codes, and sanitary codes with special flood hazard provisions.

The federal agencies have begun to respond imaginatively. For example, in Prairie du Chien, Wisconsin, the Corps of Engineers moved buildings out of the flood plain of the Wisconsin and Mississippi Rivers rather than employ traditional structural measures. There is every reason to believe that in the future, flood plain zoning and flood plain insurance will provide the means to reduce the economic and social losses from flooding without the necessity of resorting to elaborate structures. The National Water Commission (1973) recommended enactment of legislation authorizing the Water Resources Council to make federal grants to the states for "... mapping flood plains, determining flood hazards, making flood plain management plans, establishing state standards for flood plain regulation ..., and assisting local governmental entities in carrying out flood plain management programs."

In a more sweeping statement, the Commission urged that no federal funds should be made available for construction of engineering works to provide flood protection unless: (1) beneficiaries paid costs commensurate with their gains, and (2) the state or local government regulated use of flood plain lands to ensure against development that would make additional protective works necessary or would be subject to "... substantial damage in the event a flood exceeding the magnitude of the design flood" (Water Resources Council, 1972). It is quite certain that this trend toward nonstructural flood-loss prevention will continue, with increased emphasis placed on land use planning and zoning.

*Municipal and Industrial Water Supply*

Municipal and industrial water supply aspects of federal projects were traditionally subordinate to such purposes as irrigation, navigation, and flood control. However, Water Resources Council projections of withdrawal and consumptive uses of water for municipal, rural domestic, and manufacturing purposes through the year 2020 indicate a twofold to threefold increase. In the past decade, there has been a substantial increase in outlays by local governments for provision of water (Table I). The Department of Housing and Urban Development also increased its grant program for basic water and sewer facilities from $100 million to $500 million between 1965 and 1973. Over that same period, the Farmer's Home Administration also increased its program of grants for rural water and waste disposal from $20 million to $100 million.

Evidence indicates that adequate supplies of good quality domestic water will become a more important resource problem in the future, and it is expected that federal projects will increasingly reflect this concern. The National Water Commission recently recommended a number of specific guidelines for improving use of existing water supplies as a prerequisite to construction of water supply projects. Hence, it can be expected that water supply management will assume a more prominent position than in the past.

## Wastewater Management

The 1972 Amendments to the Federal Water Pollution Control Act provide for sweeping changes to prevent, reduce, and eventually eliminate water pollution by 1985. The federal government has the authority to spend up to $18 billion over the next three years to help local governments build needed sewage treatment plants, and authority to spend an additional $2.75 billion to reimburse local governments for facilities already built in anticipation of federal aid. Table II contains the estimated costs of treatment of all wastewater through the year 2000.

**Table I**

Expenditures by Counties, Municipalities, and Special Districts for Water Supply and Sewerage, 11 Western States, 1956-57 and 1966-67[a]

|  | Sewerage, in $ | | Water Supply, in $ | |
| --- | --- | --- | --- | --- |
|  | 1956–57 | 1966–67 | 1956–57 | 1966–67 |
| Arizona | 4,363 | 18,235 | 7,931 | 24,485 |
| California | 78,511 | 150,953 | 187,493 | 459,052 |
| Colorado | 9,317 | 16,153 | 36,301 | 69,539 |
| Idaho | 1,570 | 3,190 | 4,264 | 6,122 |
| Montana | 2,456 | 4,734 | 4,397 | 6,248 |
| Nevada | 3,859 | 7,108 | 2,407 | 7,002 |
| New Mexico | 3,890 | 6,531 | 10,367 | 13,808 |
| Oregon | 5,692 | 15,977 | 16,728 | 26,367 |
| Utah | 6,254 | 6,881 | 11,549 | 13,960 |
| Washington | 12,200 | 44,331 | 29,897 | 48,014 |
| Wyoming | 744 | 1,082 | 2,944 | 4,815 |
|  | 128,856 | 275,175 | 314,278 | 679,412 |

Source: U.S. Census of Governments, U.S. Department of Commerce, Bureau of Census.

[a]Thousands of dollars for relevant years.

The Corps of Engineers, quick to perceive the potential future in wastewater management, has recently sponsored five pilot studies (Boston, Cleveland, Chicago, Detroit, San Francisco) investigating the potential environmental impacts of massive schemes for wastewater management. The Corps, hopeful of a $4 million additional appropriation for further development work, has demonstrated good faith by shifting $2.7 million from other programs (Zwick and Benstock, 1972). Additionally, research is proceeding on perfecting systems for pumping municipal and industrial wastes into rural areas for sprinkling over farm or forest lands. The City of Muskegon, Michigan, has developed such a system for handling its liquid waste.

**Table II**

Estimated Annual Costs of Primary and Secondary Treatment of All Wastewater in the United States, By Source, 1973, 1980, and 2000.

| Source | 1973 | 1980 | 2000 |
|---|---|---|---|
| | Billions of 1971 Dollars | | |
| Municipalities | $ 7.0 | $ 9.5 | $12.0 |
| Livestock | 1.5 | 2.0 | 3.0 |
| Manufacturing | 10.0 | 16.0 | 40.0 |
| Paper and allied products | 1.3 | 2.0 | 4.5 |
| Chemicals and allied products | 3.4 | 5.2 | 18.9 |
| Petroleum and coal products | 0.6 | 0.6 | 1.1 |
| Primary metals | 3.4 | 6.2 | 11.2 |
| Other manufacturing | 1.3 | 2.0 | 4.3 |
| Total | $18.5 | $27.5 | $55.0 |

Source: Schultze, *et al.*, 1971.

*Future Irrigation Developments*

Speaking of present agricultural capabilities of the United States, former Secretary of Agriculture Hardin recently stated:

> Our agricultural production capacity is in excess of available outlets at home and abroad. In 1969, we harvested crops from 294 million acres, and paid for nonproduction on 58 million acres. Our analysts foresee no time in the early future when the gap between our capacity and our food requirement is likely to disappear unless farm prices drop sharply from present levels. Some kind of program is required if we are to avoid being inundated by a flood of crops and livestock (Hardin, 1970).

Studies indicate that if crop production were shifted to the most efficient regions, nearly 80 million acres would be idled by 1980 (Heady and Mayer, 1967). If all production were carried out with the level of efficiency now characteristic of the largest two classes of farms (census definition), output could be increased 24 per cent with no change in aggregate resource input (Tweeten, 1969). Fittingly, the National Water Commission recommended that subsidization of new irrigation projects should be discontinued (National Water Commission, 1973). The Commission argued that future irrigation of both new lands and existing croplands would only add to the problem of excess productive capacity in agriculture.

While the above evidence has existed for some time, indications now are that large-scale irrigation developments sponsored by the federal government are virtually a thing of the past. This conclusion is not affected by the increased price of food over the past two years. Rather than a food "shortage" in the U.S., we have witnessed the results of general inflation and some economic policies inappropriate to the food sector, coupled with a sudden *surge* in export demand. As a result, some shifts in resource allocation have occurred, but the capacity to produce even larger quantities of food remains undiminished.

**Institutional Changes**

While water resource programs are likely to change in focus and purpose, changes in the institutional setting for water-related investments can be expected to have significant impacts on the manner in which projects are initiated, planned, and financed. Three important institutional changes are: (1) the National Environmental Policy Act, (2) proposed changes in financial responsibility, and (3) a thrust for greater public participation in the planning and evaluation process.

*The National Environmental Policy Act*

The National Environmental Policy Act (known hereafter as NEPA) was passed without a great deal of Congressional debate or public awareness. Yet, in the words of Russell E. Train, chief environmental advisor to the President, it is "one of the most significant policy reforms in recent history" (Gillette, 1972). Basically, the heart of NEPA is Part C of Section 102 which directs federal agencies to:

> Include in every recommendation on proposals for legislation and other major federal actions significantly affecting the quality of the human environment, a detailed statement by the responsible official on—
> 1. the environmental impact of the proposed action
> 2. any adverse environmental effects which cannot be avoided should the proposal be implemented.
> 3. alternatives to the proposed action
> 4. the relationship between local short-term uses of man's environment and the maintenance and enhancement of long-term productivity
> 5. any irreversible and irretrievable commitments of resources which would be involved in the proposed action should it be implemented (Council on Environmental Quality, 1971).

The "102 statements" have become a major hurdle for federal agencies, with frequent lawsuits challenging the quality and thoroughness of the agencies' filed statement. It was NEPA that made it possible for environmentalists to delay the $3 billion trans-Alaska pipeline in 1970, and to stop the $400 million Tennessee-Tombigbee Waterway in 1971. Court rulings under the Act have delayed the operation of a half-dozen nuclear power plants and have "tied the Atomic Energy Commission up in such a tangle of paperwork that ... the AEC has been unable to complete a single licensing action since last summer" (Gillette, 1972). It was reported that district and appeals courts have handed down more than 160 decisions under NEPA, with new rulings coming at a rate of one per week. However, according to the Council on Environmental Quality, the rulings have curtailed less than 15 per cent of the projects of the federal government, most of which are mere delaying actions.

*Changes in Financial Responsibility*

Another recommendation of the National Water Commission is that Congress enact comprehensive legislation encompassing all aspects of federal cost-sharing in the water resource area. The Commission recommended that the users of project services bear an appropriate share of development and operating costs. It also urged that the trend toward self-financing municipal water supply utilities be encouraged. It was further recommended that the costs of all new irrigation facilities be recovered from irrigators directly or through contracting with irrigation districts, keeping interest rates consistent with current economic conditions.

Another suggestion was that those who benefit from navigation channel improvements should pay the costs through a system of toll charges and fuel taxes. Such a charge should cover all future operation and maintenance costs of existing facilities, plus all operation and maintenance costs and all construction costs (with interest) for new navigation facilities. In addition, all costs of operation and maintenance of future hydroelectric projects should be recovered through a realistic set of charges. Further, the Commission urged that consumers of electricity should not be expected to subsidize irrigators. The Commission argued that user charges should be assessed against all identifiable recreation users where revenues can be expected to exceed the cost of collection, with the objective of covering all operation and maintenance costs of federally-funded recreation facilities.

The Commission urged that charges for wastewater treatment be consistent with what charges would be if the service were operated as a utility. However, it was recognized that the large investment required to catch up with waste treatment needs precludes full user financing. Finally, it was recommended that existing cost-sharing arrangements for flood protection be revised so that beneficiary charges would provide for full repayment of the costs of protecting lands through flood control, drainage, and shoreline protection. Hence, the era of virtual cost-free water resource services for many citizens appears to be drawing to an end.

*Greater Public Participation*

The final category of institutional change arises from the National Water Commission's recommendation for a more vigorous pursuit of expanded public participation in the planning and evaluation process. The public participation program of the Corps of Engineers is a good example. It is a system that would: "(1) allow the public to establish its own goals and priorities early in the study, (2) let the public clarify and define its own problems, (3) permit public participation in the development and investigation of alternatives, (4) allow open public debate of conflicting views, (5) encourage two-way communication between the planner and the citizenry, (6) demonstrate that public comment had an effect on the proposed action, and (7) above all, keep the public involved from beginning to end (Sellevold, 1972)."

Additionally, the Corps' Institute of Water Resources has sponsored at least two studies dealing with public participation (Bishop, 1970; Borton, et al., 1970). The National Water Commission has urged that the Water Resources Council direct federal water resource planning agencies to adopt procedures and issue guidelines to create an opportunity for greater public participation. The Commission also recommended that each agency report on its program for such participation as a prerequisite for project authorization.

**Conclusions**

It is anticipated that the era of general purpose water resource projects is past. Instead, future projects will likely emphasize those outputs (recreation, municipal and industrial water supply) that have heretofore been considered secondary purposes, and will begin to include objectives not traditionally considered, such as water for cooling nuclear energy facilities, and wastewater treatment and management. Finally, two traditional project purposes, flood control and irrigation water, will become less justifiable outputs for public sector projects.

In addition to the inhibiting impact of NEPA, two forces of an institutional nature are at work that will change the basic nature of future water resource projects. The first is a change in the rules for cost sharing whereby those who benefit will likely be expected to pay project costs commensurate with benefits received. Second, the emphasis on greater public participation in the planning and evaluation process will remove project formulation from the restricted province of the agency and a few influential local individuals.

## IMPLICATIONS FOR COMMUNITY DEVELOPMENT

Changes in the nature of future water resource investments will likely bring about an increased emphasis on process activities, and less emphasis on task-oriented activities.

### Changing Focus

Some of the changes in the focus of water resource investments have implications for the task-oriented view of community development, some relate only to the process view, and some will affect community development according to both views.

The changes that have implications for the task-oriented view of community development are the de-emphasis of hydroelectric and irrigation projects, more emphasis on municipal and industrial water needs, and a shift toward greater use of nuclear energy. The de-emphasis of hydroelectric projects may result in less subsidized power available in specific communities. Since at least some areas have probably attempted to attract industry on the basis of surplus electrical energy, this change could have a negative impact on these task-oriented endeavors. In all likelihood, the impact will be relatively slight, and isolated in specific communities.

The shift to greater use of nuclear energy may imply a decreased demand for water for power generation in many areas, and a large increase in demand for cooling water in the few areas with nuclear power plants. Again, any predictions approach conjecture, but the impact may be less job creation, and thus less community development, in the task-oriented sense, than in the past.

On the other hand, the increased emphasis on municipal and industrial water needs may aid communities in attracting industry and creating jobs. Increasing the quantity or quality of a public service such as water supply may increase the attractiveness of many rural communities as places for industrial location. The results are not completely predictable for a particular community, although there is some evidence to indicate that investment in improved public services has attracted industry in at least some cases (Barrows, 1972). This would enhance community development according to the task-oriented definition.

Finally, the decreased emphasis on irrigation projects may result in fewer service jobs in rural towns and a less developed agricultural sector in some areas. This may be particularly evident in areas that would have qualified for large-scale irrigation projects, and in areas in which limited water for agriculture results in a sparse population and a low level of economic activity.

Other changes in the nature of water resource investments have implications for the process-oriented view of community development. The increased emphasis on nonstructural flood loss prevention may have important implications for the amount and intensity of local cooperation and interaction. The emphasis on inducing development outside flood plain areas, and the availability of funds for relocating existing flood plain development, may stimulate local land use planning and zoning.

Rural planning and zoning efforts typically involve significant local participation both in developing the zoning ordinance or the plan, and in the process of public hearings and community decision making. The process of planning and zoning may result in formulation of local interest groups that cut across occupational or other vertically-oriented ties, *e.g.*, formulation of a property owners' association in one part of a county. This strengthening of horizontal ties would constitute community development according to the process definition.

Finally, some changes in the focus of water resource investments might have community development implications according to both process and task-oriented definitions. Changes with respect to wastewater treatment and management provide two types of incentives for community organization and action in solving waste management problems. The first incentive concerns increasingly stringent regulations governing waste management and the increasing pressure on communities to upgrade their waste treatment systems. Second, the increase in available funds for wastewater management from federal agencies provides an incentive for many communities to plan and develop waste treatment facilities. Because of the large capital expenses and the existence of economies of scale in waste treatment facilities, there are incentives to organize waste treatment on a countywide or multicommunity basis. This may result in forging new ties between community leaders within a county and would qualify as community development under the process definition. At the same time, provision of a higher quality public service might qualify as community development under the task-oriented definition.

Emphasis on recreation as a major project purpose might also enhance community development according to both task-oriented and process definitions. Local communities would have an incentive to work together to plan recreation development in an area such as a small watershed. Recreation planning might involve members of several communities or occupational groups and might lead to a strengthening of horizontal ties and thus enhance community development by the process definition. In addition, the new recreation emphasis may stimulate employment and income in some rural regions by enabling some communities to obtain development projects that could not be justified other than on a recreational basis. This might constitute community development from the task-oriented point of view.

In summary, changes in the focus of water resource investments have important implications for community development by either definition. Hydroelectric and irrigation projects that would hinder community development, according to the task-oriented definition, by limiting the rate of growth of income and employment in some areas will be de-emphasized. On the other hand, new emphasis on municipal and industrial water supply may aid communities in attracting industry and stimulating employment and income. The stress on nonstructural flood loss prevention may result in increased local participation in land use planning and zoning, which would constitute community development according to the process definition. Increased emphasis on recreation development and wastewater management may lead to community development according to both process and task-oriented definitions.

**Institutional Changes**

*The National Environmental Policy Act*

It seems evident that the environmental impact statement required by NEPA will encourage more participation at the local level. Horizontal ties may be strengthened by bringing local individuals with diverse interests together to protect important aspects of their physical environment. However, increased local involvement may actually destroy horizontal ties by arousing conflict

# WATER RESOURCES AND REGIONAL DEVELOPMENT 101

that cuts across previously solid or tight social groups. Conflicts over environmental impacts did not often arise in the past, largely because such impacts were not specifically assessed in the decision process. NEPA requires that these impacts be made explicit, which may lead to conflicts that would not have occurred in the absence of such detailed information. Finally, NEPA may also have the effect of bringing nonlocal groups into conflict with local interests. This may either solidify local interest groups, or further sharpen the conflicts between local groups. In conclusion, NEPA will lead to much greater public participation, but may not necessarily enhance community development by the process definition.

*Cost-Sharing*

It is reasonable to expect that increases in the charges levied on residents in the project area will provide an incentive for greater local participation in the decision-making process. Local residents will want to know the exact benefits of the project since they will be paying more of the costs. As a result, there will be more incentive for residents to organize and work collectively to gather and evaluate information about project impact, and to act to encourage or discourage project approval by local and nonlocal officials. Additionally, the increased quantity and quality of information on project impacts may act to pull the community apart. The "gainers" and "losers" will be much more clearly identified and perhaps more sharply divided. The resulting conflict may destroy horizontal ties in the community. The increase in local participation might be called community development, although the result may well be a weakening of horizontal ties in the community, the antithesis of community development according to the process definition.

*Local Participation*

Increasing emphasis on community involvement in planning and evaluation of water resource investments should lead to community development by the process definition. Providing information on agency plans and interests, project plans, and impacts may stimulate encouragement or opposition by local organizations. Public hearings might provide opportunities for local groups to interact, and could lead to formulation of common goals and strengthening of horizontal ties in the community. At the same time, increased participation could serve to reinforce the divisions that existed in the community before the project. Once again, institutional changes

## 102  WATER AND COMMUNITY DEVELOPMENT

might provide enhancement of community development or lead to increasing division in the community.

### SUMMARY

It seems likely that the changes in water resource policy will de-emphasize some traditional task-oriented aspects of water projects. Less emphasis on hydroelectric and irrigation projects implies that certain communities may experience less growth in employment and income than would have occurred with a water resource investment. However, with municipal and industrial water supplies becoming increasingly important, with the emphasis on wastewater management, and with more explicit attention given to recreation, it may be possible for many communities to attract industry or other economic activity and increase the level of income and employment in the area. If community development is defined as the attainment of certain task objectives, such as increasing local employment and income, then it is not clear whether the likely changes in water resource policies would enhance or inhibit community development.

Changes in water resource policy will lead to increased public participation and involvement in planning and evaluating water projects. Emphasis on nonstructural flood loss prevention may stimulate local efforts at land use planning and zoning involving local cooperation. More funds for wastewater management, together with increasingly stringent controls over waste treatment and disposal, provide incentives for local planning and cooperation at the county or multicommunity level. Availability of funds for strictly recreational projects may stimulate local efforts to plan recreation development. Environmental impact statements required by NEPA may stimulate increased local involvement in project evaluation, but may sharpen conflicts between local groups. Cost-sharing changes provide incentives for local participation in project planning and may lead to formulation of common goals and interest groups. Thus, if community development is viewed as a process whereby residents use local resources in solving community problems, it seems safe to conclude that the water policy changes mean more community development. That is, if community development is seen as a process of strengthening the horizontal ties in a community, policy changes discussed earlier provide an opportunity for furthering community development. On the other hand, with the lessened interest in task-oriented activities, those who insist that community development implies specific measurable changes are likely to be disheartened.

The authors' views remain uncertain. It is their hope that these ideas will precipitate some thought about what constitutes "development," and how water resource projects are likely to affect that notion. But, until a single, generally accepted concept of development exists, it is impossible to derive unequivocal conclusions as to the effects of changes in the scope and purpose of water development projects on community development.

**ACKNOWLEDGMENT**

The work upon which portions of this paper is based was supported in part by funds provided by the U.S. Department of the Interior, Office of Water Resources Research.

**REFERENCES**

Barrows, R. L. *Regional Economic Development and the Public Sector: An Economic Analysis of the Economic Development Administration's Public Works Projects,* PhD dissertation, (Madison: University of Wisconsin, 1972) pp. 94-98.

Baskin, D. *American Pluralist Democracy.* (New York: Van Nostrand Reinhold, 1971) p. 94.

Beattie, B. R., T. H. Klindt, and G. L. Bradford. "Perfecting Methods for Predicting the Course of Rural Area Development," Part I, *Toward a Definition of Economic Development and a Framework for Evaluating Model Efficacy,* Research Report 11, (Lexington: University of Kentucky, College of Agriculture, Agricultural Experiment Station, Department of Agricultural Economics, 1972) pp. 4-13.

Bilinski, R. "A Description and Assessment of Community Development" in *Selected Perspectives for Community Resource Development,* L. T. Wallace, *et al.,* Eds. (Raleigh: Agricultural Policy Institute, North Carolina State University, 1969) pp. 143-180.

Bishop, B. "Public Participation in Water Resources Planning," U.S. Department of the Army, Institute for Water Resources, Alexandria, Virginia, IWR Report 70-7 (1970).

Bonneville Power Administration, "BPA Factbook," Portland, Oregon (1969) p. 16.

Borton, T. E., K. P. Warner, and J. W. Wenrich. "The Susquehanna Communication-Participation Study: Selected Approaches to Public Involvement in Water Resource Planning." U.S. Department of the Army, Institute for Water Resources, Alexandria, Virginia, IWR Report 70-6 (1970).

Bromley, D. W. "The Economist and Rural Development: Concepts and Conflicts," Staff Paper Series No. 46, (Madison: University of Wisconsin, Department of Agricultural Economics, 1972).

Bureau of Reclamation. "Southwest Idaho Water Development Project," Boise, Idaho (1966) pp. III-98.

Council on Environmental Quality. *Environmental Quality,* 2nd Annual Report, (Washington, D.C.: U.S. Government Printing Office, 1971) p. 269.

Gillette, R. "National Environmental Policy Act: Signs of Backlash are Evident." *Science* 176:30 (1972).

Hardin, M. Statement Before the Committee on Agriculture and Forestry, U.S. Senate, U.S. Department of Agriculture, Washington, D.C. (1970).

Heady, E. O., and L. V. Mayer. "Food Needs and U.S. Agriculture in 1980," National Advisory Commission on Food and Fiber, Technical Papers, Vol. 1, Washington, D.C. (1967).

Hogg, T. C., C. L. Smith, M. R. McComb, and R. A. Hart. "Impact of Water Development on a Community," in proceedings of the Oregon Water Resources Congress (1970).

Ingram, H. "Patterns of Politics in Water Resources Development," *Natural Resources Journal* 11:102 (1971).

Leven, C. L. "Theories of Regional Growth," in *Problems of Chronically Depressed Rural Areas,* Agricultural Policy Institute, North Carolina State University (1965).

Lord, W. B. and S. C. Smith. "Tools of the Trade in Policy Decision—PPBS, A Case in Point," *American Journal of Agricultural Economics* 51:1427 (1969).

National Water Commission. "New Directions in U.S. Water Policy—Summary, Conclusions and Recommendation from the Final Report, (Washington, D.C.: U.S. Government Printing Office, 1973) pp. 85-101.

Schultze, C. L., E. R. Fried, A. M. Rivlin, and N. H. Teeters. "Setting National Priorities: The 1972 Budget," Brookings Institution, Washington, D.C. (1971).

Sellevold, R. P. "Public Involvement Programs—The Corps of Engineers," in *The Grass Roots and Water Resource Management,* L. McKenzie, Ed., State of Washington Water Research Center, Pullman, Washington, Report #10 (1972).

Tweeten, L. G. "Theories Explaining the Persistence of Low Resource Returns in a Growing Farm Economy," *American Journal of Agricultural Economics* 51 (4):798 (1969).

Warren, R. *The Community in America,* (Chicago: Rand McNally and Co., 1963).

Water Resources Council. *The Nation's Water Resources,* (Washington, D.C.: U.S. Government Printing Office, 1968).

Wilkinson, K. P., and R. N. Singh. "Generalized Participation of Voluntary Leaders in Local Watershed Projects," Water Resources Institute, Mississippi State University (1969).

Yanggen, D. A., J. A. Kusler, *et al. Regulation of Flood Hazard Areas,* Vol. 1, Parts I-IV, Water Resources Council, Washington, D.C. (1971), pp. 3-16.

Zwick, D., and M. Benstock. *Water Wasteland,* (New York: Grossman Publishers, 1971) p. 389.

# 6. Institutional Reorganization for Water Resources Management

## STEPHEN C. SMITH

The basic purpose of this book is to explore the role of water resources in contributing to community development. The call to examine this subject is very timely because "community development" is being given new national programmatic thrusts and badly needs intelligent guidance.

Water resources policy may be characterized as being in a state of disarray as it moves into a new era carrying the "burden" of forty years of leadership in blazing the trail for public investment economics. For a century it has, in reality, been tied fundamentally to the neighborhood community and been caught in that "web of myth" that holds social structure together. An extreme position could be taken by stating that we are in a state of double trauma—the disintegration of the "traditional" community and the inability to define relevant water resources management systems. The term traditional community as used here means the social situation occurring when people living within a defined geographic area also have a concurrent community of interest covering major aspects of social and economic life, *e.g.*, religion, recreation, education, public service, and business relationships.

## WATER RESOURCES MANAGEMENT

Water resources management is certainly not a new subject. Yet like all of resource management it must be reassessed to meet the challenge of new conditions.

Historically water policy and management have been tied closely to community, regional, and national development. The Corps of

## 108 WATER AND COMMUNITY DEVELOPMENT

Engineers was assigned the task of improving harbors and keeping rivers navigable as the nation emerged from infancy. Canal building as an internal improvement of states was in vogue prior to the advent of the railroad. During the last half of the 1800's the legal and social basis for irrigation was laid in state and national legislation with community action firmly imbedded in the policy process. During this period also, local communities were draining the midcontinent and the South. Along the nation's rivers, communities built levees and dams to hold floods. As the technology of hydroelectric power developed, it became a component of water management, providing a community service and a means for repaying water development. Federal institutions were combined with those of the state to execute community action. As in flood control and irrigation, community externalities led to regional management organizations and regional financing, TVA, Missouri Basin Account, Central Valley Project, and Columbia Basin Project.

Today the West has been settled and resettled and continues to grow. Many old problems are still with us, but the chemical, biological, and viral content of water have new significance in view of expanded population and economic growth. What we might call the "native" values of water, for example, fish, stream biota, and scenic beauty, have taken on new meanings as their scarcity increases. Stream flow has new multiple uses. Ecological systems are being scientifically defined and elaborated in such a fashion that we can explicitly account to them. If we do not act on our knowledge, the costs will be assessed, irrespective of our desires and of our awareness. For example, the costs of salinity cannot now be ignored in many situations even though they were originally neglected or given low priority.

Water resources management is more complex than digging a well, diverting a stream through an irrigation ditch, storing surplus winter runoff for summer use, channeling flood flows, or eliminating an effluent. This complexity is not new, whether one lives in the great basin of the Columbia River, the Tennessee River Valley, the Delaware River Basin, the low flat land of Florida, or elsewhere. Yet the old theses keep coming to the fore as in the report of the National Water Commission (1973). The Report is a significant document dealing with issues in institutional reorganization for water resources management. In fact, the main issue may be found within the phrase "for water resources management." As a nation we are confronted with the question of how we are going to face the responsibility *for* water resources management.

The Commission's Report is eclectic in the sense that it compiles a list of significant water problems and addresses these questions through competent staff or contract studies, many of which will have lasting value. But no concept of *water resources management* emerges other than that which brings water explicitly into the market economy via recommendations such as developing a concept of demand rather than requirements (Smith, 1964), pricing for water service, and increasing the marketability of water rights. Clearly, adding the weight of the Commission to these concepts is important and could have a significant effect on water management and use. Likewise the intertying of water services with complementary or competing services has great merit. For example, considering water transportation as a component of a more general transportation policy, integrating land and water use policy around our cities, and dealing with irrigation as an explicit part of agricultural, food, and fiber policy. The general policy position that water cannot be considered in isolation from the economic activities with which it is associated has a validity that has been ignored too long. The Commission's Report helps to redress this balance.

The recommended tightening up of the system could lead to greater efficiencies in an economic sense. Hopefully water "quality" will be improved and the availability of water increased because of greater frugality of use due to a change in the system of incentives.

The tenor of the water rights recommendation is similar. Greater transferability of rights is encouraged plus granting rights to instream uses. The native values mentioned earlier should have proportional protection as legitimate, beneficial uses, even though no diversion takes place. The requisite of diversion to establish a right is a historical phenomenon with an understandable legal, social and economic origin (Hutchins, 1971). However, the value of instream uses cannot be denied in today's world and this value will undoubtedly increase.

My purpose in outlining a few salient points of the National Water Commission Report is to present neither a summary nor a critique. Rather, I hope to partially characterize the flavor of the overall report and to comment that the work will have valuable results as it deals with reorganizing many water resources institutions. Yet, a very central issue is not identified or handled by the eclectic approach or by what I call the "economist" approach of synthesizing marketability.

A prime need of the day is the development of a broad national concept and institutional structure for water resources management. Water management is the process by which the resource is defined and put to use in combination with other resources. It is a process for determining priority services and objectives without taking the services or the technology of management or the institutions of management as given. The Commission's Report deals with many of the related issues but the issue of institutionalizing management itself is not laid bare for full policy definition.

Institutions are used to interface people with resources and people with people. They define resources in terms of people's demands; thus, they encompass both social structure and value as well as physical and biological phenomena. This paper does not primarily probe methodology. Yet to approach the subject of institutional reorganization for water resources management an understanding must be developed of both the "resource" and the people. Thus, the basic point of view is important, namely, people define resources (Ciriacy—Wantrup, 1963). The effect of the concept of resource finiteness upon the human enterprise has not been fully probed. It has a "certain" validity, yet, it may be equally damaging to human survival as not heeding resource limitations.

At the outset, the Commission did not deal with the issue of institutionally defining water management problems. An over-all model, a characterization of the resource water in terms of the future was only partially developed. The important problem of water flow management was not really identified. Rather, attention was directed to important issues of water consumption in an economic sense. If this institutional problem is examined, a case can be made that concepts of property rights developed to bring land into the market economy were "applied" to water. But water *is not land.*

The flow characteristics of water have caused many institutional problems. Societies have had difficulties in dealing with flows, individuals have had problems with flows. The fixity of land space likewise is unique. But many of our institutions of market and property rights are deeply imbedded in the definability of land or other market goods for which property rights are exchanged. The application of landed property concepts to water has had social utility, but has it been wholly successful?

Useful concepts that have evolved from water rights law are the definitional elements of a water right. These elements vary among the states. Yet there is a broad spectrum of agreement. Namely, the volume of water, the time of diversion, the quality of water, and the place of diversion must be identified to provide the fixity of land. In other words, to bring water into our market economy, rights had to identify tangible traits of the resource in question. For over one hundred years litigation has established certain operational necessities, since the rights of A must be separable or identifiable from those of B. For example, the use of volume of water (acre feet) rather than a flow (cu. ft. per second) has proven more successful. Specification of quality has probably been performed most weakly, although the future may change the situation. On the other hand, time and place have generally been made clear.

What should be emphasized from this experience are (1) the legal necessity of dividing flows into distinct definable units and (2) that the rights to these units are owned and exchanged. When one of the elements—volume, time, quality, or location—is omitted, problems ensue. This lesson has not really been learned yet in dealing with other aspects of water management. There has been an attempt to separate quality from the body of water and treat it as independent from flow (or quantity), time, and place. In other words, one of the major roles of water institutions is to define water for the social structure, dealing with each of these elements simultaneously. Without this type of specification many of the other efforts are less effective or ineffective.

Another issue growing from the flow character of water is the fact that instream characteristics generally have not been subject to private appropriation. These have been held by the people of the State, with some Federal and Indian rights being dominant. I am not arguing that the instream water should be privately appropriated, but public ownership of the stream has meant that we have looked on the flowing stream through a different set of institutional eyes (no private ownership, ownership by the public, or any one) (Hutchins, 1971). The flowing stream has provided opportunities for diversion to private use, for dumping wastes, for pressuring for maintenance, for transportation, etc. These were institutional eyes generated from landed property concepts, eyes that attempted to define water so that it could be brought into our general property system—our general market economy.

But water is not land, and water has become so scarce that it must be managed far more conscientiously in the next quarter century than in the past. Past experience will give us tremendous insight, but it will not provide the blueprint for the future. The National Water Commission does not provide us with a blueprint nor did it intend to.

As we think about institutional reorganization in water resources, two points need greater conceptual clarity: (1) the flow characteristics of water should not be neglected and the historic institutional "public character" of the "natural flow" should not blind us from focusing explicitly upon placing management responsibility for surface flow, and (2) the overall concept of management. The elements of water, its uses and its combinations with other systems must be integrated into the broad management concept.

Ground water must be a part of the overall system. The integration of the management of ground and surface water is a much more clearly recognized concept than it was twenty years ago. This paper will generally bypass these critical issues. Their coverage on other occasions will have to suffice (Smith, 1962).

## THE COMMUNITY AND COMMUNITIES OF INTEREST

The present state of water resources management has been very dependent upon the local community. The multitude of community actions "created" the philosophy of checks and balances and a faith in plural structures that has been widely evident in water resources policy. Water resources management in the United States has evolved from what I term a "bottom up" philosophy (Lord and Smith, 1969). Even the present status of river basin management has emanated from this approach.

It was not until the economist approached the question from the point of view of allocating federal budget investments and national income that hierarchial concepts began to really take hold. (Engineers dealing with stream flows recognized hierarchial systems management before the 1930's.) This approach had its roots in national income accounting, the application of a theory of capital, and what might be termed Keynesian operationalism rather than water resources problems. In other words, it was not until the development of economic concepts, and the data they began to generate, and the studies from the Flood Control Act of 1936 that serious arguments began with local Chambers of Commerce, irrigation associations, etc. Today the "top down" view is often being reinforced by the hierarchial character of much systems analysis, increasing resource limitations, and the clearer definition of community externalities. These limitations force new difficult choices of priorities.

The "bottom up" policy has been clearly evident in dealing with water where the individual was able to capture his supply, dump his waste, etc. He did so without recourse to community action. But community action has a long history in dealing with water use because of technical and economic externalities (flows) to the individuals. Communities of interest have coalesced around water resource issues within a locality to provide a political basis for water management; where this community of interest was nonexistent, little management ensued since a public was not defined. Many of our water resources institutions have been created to test the extent of community commitment, the range of issues pertinent to a community of interest, and the relevant geographic locality to the water resources plan of action (Smith, 1962). The history of local district, municipal action, and the battles to enact the appropriate state legislation attest to water serving as a vehicle to define a local community and a community of interest.

The basic structure of federal water resources legislation can likewise be understood within this frame of reference. Namely, its content and purpose has been to provide local community service through federal organization and financing. The common characteristic is local community initiative. Benefit cost analysis later provided a presumed safe-minimum economic standard—a national income criteria. The prime allocation of investment funds created the ability for local initiatives to aggregate enough political power to achieve appropriations. The point of amassing political power has often been assessed on the basis of "pork-barrel," but there is another point. What is the required local community initiative necessary to bring a project to the point of congressional action? In terms of accomplishing an objective at the community level, what is the significance of the fact that such community initiative exists and is organized with the requisite political and economic power? Within a benefit cost analysis, there has yet to be a preproject costs tally. On the other hand, what national benefits accrue as a result of investing in those communities that achieve such initiatives? Is such community leadership transferable to solving other nonwater problems? There is an array of questions in this area that sociologists might address in their research programs dealing with community development.

The foregoing comments are made with the full recognition that through the process I have described large federal bureaucracies have been created. These creations have an independent momentum for survival and expansion. This characteristic of organizations may be necessary for viability; however, it may stimulate false community "labor pains" from goading local leadership. This aspect of water bureaucracies has been well-documented. For our purposes today, we need only acknowledge its significance and recognize that we are living in the 1970's and not the 1920's with respect to water development opportunities and the state of the economy.

The community viability test has not been analyzed as thoroughly. (The test is significant but too little explored. What are the criteria for identifying a community of interest that will be strong enough to carry out its job? The southeastern United States has a long history of community development programming and the question of why some communities "move" and others do not is still a puzzle in many respects.) From a national policy point of view what is the significance of having such a community test prior to allocating federal investments? Sound scientific research in this area is not wholly conclusive, but we can hypothesize that viability is an essential, although not a sufficient, factor for water project success. In analyzing such situations, falsely stimulated action due to bureaucratic prodding must be recognized.

Even though the foregoing points are interesting, the question of the relevance of this issue for the next 25 to 30 years, or even to decisions being made today, remains. From the point of view of the need for water management, one asks if the nation has moved to the point where the traditional community is inadequate for organizing the required water management program. On the other hand, one must also ask if the structure of the traditional community has so changed that it can no longer be organized to achieve water management. These are two quite different but critical questions.

One water management objective underlying much of the National Water Commission's work, as well as that of many others, is to increase the efficiency of water use and the quality of water in the stream. The Commission's general concept of demand and its suggestions that pricing be more analogous to other goods and services fits this view. However, the accomplishment of this water management objective cannot be achieved without a consensus of interests at the local community level. The attainment of this objective would cut deeply into the local structure of organizations and their procedures for achieving consent, for channeling anticipated and actual returns to resource users, for distributing the returns among the members of the community, and for assessing costs. If the "traditional communities" saw that it was within their interest to move in this direction, a very powerful force affecting the rate and distribution of aggregate water use would be released.

Due to the way in which returns from water use are currently generated and distributed, however, local community adjustment is difficult. (Note the significance of the organizational institutions in channeling returns and costs.) In effect, an old water organization procedure is often used, namely, adjust the boundaries of the community until a consensus is achieved rather than change the procedures for distributing returns or assessing costs. The traditional community is not organized to obtain a favorable response for increasing efficiency although the public basis for such a response is broadening with a growing feeling of environmental responsibility. A reason for the lack of favorable response is that much of the institutional structuring has been predicated on the principle that public water service be priced as an extension of the users operations, really more as a cooperative (Brewer, 1961). Water service should be provided at "cost" with returns accruing as increases of capital values. Institutional reorganization in this arena will be slow and difficult. Changes may well be achieved by developing new communities both in terms of interest and geographical extent. There is some evidence that these communities are beginning to take shape as noted due to an environmental consciousness.

From the point of view of water resources management, the management responsibility for water flowing in the stream remains critical. It is being neglected because no community exists to bring the interests together. The organizational structures that currently exist were put together to handle local developmental issues and welded into basic flood routing systems because the national view could identify the local externalities. Power production and irrigation contributed historically, particularly in the West. But McKinley's (1950) and Fesler's (1964) political analysis of twenty years ago concurs with Ingram's recent political science research (1971, 1973). The flow of the river is not of strong enough political-economic interest to establish a community. The traditional community has welded the present structure of the Corps and Bureau on the basis of community development as noted. This structure has been used to route flood flows; witness the Midwest in 1973. This fact is significant and should not be torn apart capriciously. Yet in a real sense, the integrating factor has been the porkbarrel. But what of the future?

The development and construction ethos within the bureaucracies and communities have been driving forces of water resources in the past. During this past period, the degree of complementarity between uses has been relatively high, but in the future quality management and other instream flow uses may be more directly competitive. The community is just now becoming seriously concerned with the quality of the water in the river, and with organizing the systems needed to bring the community's water quality up to some standard. How does the community participate in setting these standards? Communities have not been able to organize instream management.

The other question is equally important, namely, has the structure of the traditional community so changed in the last 50 years that it cannot function in the water management area? Water institutions have been subject to change, consolidation, and merger, with much difficulty at times. Yet irrigation districts have been converted to municipal water supply districts as subdivisions engulf agricultural land. The whole process of changing the economic power base of many communities places water management in a new situation. The problem is to identify the "right" community. Return flows from large scale agriculture pose new problems that transcend the historic community's wastewater treatment. A municipality may deeply involve the surrounding agricultural area in disposal processes. Frequently no readily available community structure exists.

In analyzing the second problem, the forces that pull the community apart must be handled. This is not a new problem, but our modern techniques of communication and the large scale merged businesses have changed our local communities as well as the communities of interest. Modern business has contributed: Arlans discount stores are now in national financial difficulty; when they close a store in the neighborhood shopping center, employees are transferred. The local grocery, home-owned for 80 years, is purchased by a tobacco company in Louisville, Kentucky, which in turn is owned by British-American Tobacco Company of London. A new 800 acre subdivision is going to be built, financed by ITT. An international paper company closes an old marginal mill because of the high cost of waste treatment. They open a new mill

# WATER RESOURCES AND REGIONAL DEVELOPMENT

in another region near water transportation. To mention another aspect of the community, we must not forget that water use is affected by community action through established building codes, union rules, and health standards. This aspect of the community and its water use has been neglected.

The centers of power have been shifted outside of the traditional community reducing the effectiveness of that locality as an integrating force for major aspects of today's mode of living. Does this limit the local community in its organizing to provide traditional water services? Does it provide an opportunity to create a new community within a much broader context?

At the "community" level the interaction of water and land has been well-documented. Those working in the water resources field have long used the phrase "water and related land resources." As we see increasing national attention being brought to land use planning and management, the phrase "land and related water resources" is becoming more prevalent. The point is interesting because it indicates a shift in priorities that will mean new problems demanding community attention, and it will cause new problems of organizing a community of interest for instream water management.

## COMMUNITIES FOR WATER MANAGEMENT

The state of double trauma still exists. The traditional community is losing its integrating ability and the management systems we are defining are not yet meeting the issues. (Please do not infer that I am arguing for the "so-called" internalization of all interests. Such an institutional reorganization would be neither a preferred solution nor possible.) We badly need new institutions for creating new communities of interest. Two sources make a very basic contribution: one, the drive of organizations to solve real problems and two, the creation of new knowledge and new systems.

From water management's point of view two issues have been given emphasis: (1) to specify more clearly a concept of water management and pin down the identification of quality for its integration with quantity, and (2) to place management responsibility for the water in the stream. As a part of dealing with these issues, the discovery of communities must be dealt with and new communities of interest must be created. If the forces of change are moving in the direction of creating new communities, there is a suggested way to develop our potentialities, a way that builds upon past research and experience. If systems analysis is carefully incremented so that the empirical content is real, it could serve to identify partially new communities and help create new institutions.

In a sense, the creation of ORSANCO (Ohio River Valley Water Sanitation Commission) was a step in this direction. Many other situations could be cited as illustrations. One of the big missing elements is a clear, well-established national system for collecting and analyzing water quality information. However, information and data collection for its own sake is the wrong way to go. The information should be generic, but it should fit into water management systems. Progress will be sporadic at best. However, without this quality information on a national basis, combined with flow, time, and place specification information, ecological systems may be placed on an irreversible path we may regret. A well-conceived national quality-quantity monitoring system would make it possible to raise questions seldom raised now. The massive investment in treatment systems cannot be judged without such a monitoring overlay. For example, the articulation of simulated water management systems as described by Butcher (see Chapter 4) could provide an added dimensional base for the necessary public arguments over community definition and assist in defining the boundary conditions.

The reader may be surprised at my suggestions. But I dare say, for better or for worse, the agricultural programs of the 1930's would not have come about if Henry Taylor and others had not organized a data collection system so that they could be used by the political process. The present state of national economic policy, for better or for worse, would not exist if it were not for long years of national income accounting research. We are at that state in water use that we can ill afford to be without the knowledge of quality, quantity, time, and place of water use. This information will help define the new water management communities.

**REFERENCES**

Brewer, M. F. *Economics of Public Water Pricing* (Berkeley, California: California Experiment Station, 1961) Giannini Research Report #244.

Ciriacy-Wantrup, S. V. *Resource Conservation, Economics, and Policies* (Berkeley, California: University of California. Division of Agricultural Sciences, Agricultural Experiment Station, 1963).

Fesler, J. W. "National Water Resources Administration," in *Economics and Public Policy in Water Resource Development,* S. C. Smith and E. N. Castle, Eds. (Ames, Iowa: Iowa State University Press, 1964).

Hutchins, W. A. *Water Rights Laws in the Nineteen Western States,* Vol. 1, Misc. Pub. No. 1206, Natural Resource Economics Division, Economic Research Service (Washington, D.C.: U.S.D.A., 1971) pp. 143-44.

Ingram, H. "Patterns of Politics in Water Resources Development," *Nat. Res. J.* 11: 102 (1971).

Ingram, H. "The Political Economy of Regional Water Institutions," *Amer. J. Agric. Econ.* 55 (1): 10 (1973).

Lord, W., and S. C. Smith. "Tools of the Trade in Policy Decision—PPBS, A Case in Point," *Amer. J. Agric. Econ.* 51 (5): 1427 (1969).

McKinley, C. "The Valley Authority and Its Alternatives," *Amer. Pol. Sci. Rev.* 44: 618 (1950).

National Water Commission. *Water Policies for the Future,* Final Report to the President and to the Congress of the United States, National Water Commission, Washington, D.C. (June, 1973).

Smith, S. C. *The Public District in Integrating Ground and Surface Water Management: A Case Study in Santa Clara County* (Berkeley, California: University of California, 1962) Giannini Foundation Report #252.

Smith, S. C. "Water in the Future Economy," in *Water, Ecology, and the Future,* A. Agnew, Ed. (Bloomington, Indiana: Indiana University Press, 1964).

# Part III
# Water Resource Development and Human Response

# About the Contributors

*Gordon L. Bultena,* Professor, Department of Sociology and Anthropology, Iowa State University, received his PhD from the University of Minnesota. His inquiries have dealt with human behavior in wilderness settings, with environmental orientations, and with agency-clientele relationships. Dr. Bultena's recent publications examine public attitudes toward environmental problems and patterns of public involvement in natural resource decision-making.

*Courtland L. Smith* is presently Associate Professor of Anthropology at Oregon State University, Corvallis. His investigations have concentrated on man-environment relations in complex cultures. He is author of the book, *The Salt River Project, A Case Study in Cultural Adaptation to an Urbanizing Community,* as well as articles dealing with human adaptation to riverine and marine environments. Professor Smith earned his PhD at the University of Arizona.

*Sue Johnson* is Program Assistant at the Center for Developmental Change at the University of Kentucky, Lexington. She is currently finishing her PhD program at the University of Texas at Austin. Her research includes the sociology of natural resources, ethical aspects of natural resource use, and the sociology of sex roles. Recent publications and planned research concentrate on forced migration due to eminent domain.

*Rabel J. Burdge,* Associate Professor of Sociology, University of Kentucky at Lexington, earned his PhD from Pennsylvania State University. His research focuses on the social aspects of land and water resource utilization. Professor Burdge is editor of the *Journal of Leisure Research* and co-author of the rural sociology textbook *Social Change in Rural Society.*

# Part III
# Water Resource Development and Human Response

Considerable emphasis in the environmental literature has focused upon the interrelationships of resources and species survival, especially when the resources upon which a given species depends are in some way altered. While most work has dealt with animal species other than man, most of us recognize that a similar examination is appropriate for man. He, too, is an animal, forming communities which are tied to natural resources. Social scientists have been concerned with the relationships between resources and human communities and the corresponding impact upon community structure when the natural resource base changes.

Natural resources as a factor in community development and/or change have been considered in two types of community investigations. First is an in-depth analysis of individual communities, characteristic of rural community research. Authors, more often than not, have focused entirely on institutional factors affecting communal life, without relating specific findings to events arising within the region or society at large. Their studies have traditionally been idiographic and descriptive. In each case when resources were linked to discussions of change in social structure or vice versa, explanations were generated in a limited way. The predominant treatment of resources and structure has been in the context of changing occupation-economic milieu, where service center communities depending upon a farm population were affected by changing land use patterns associated with agricultural production, forestry or mining.

In the second type of community study, emphasis has been

placed on explanations of community change in terms of the demographic factors associated with population growth or loss. A partial set of factors associated with change in communities has been placed in perspective by consideration of demographic variables.

Research emphasis on location, size, proximity to metropolitan centers, etc., however, has ignored institutional adaptation as a factor in population change and only implicitly acknowledges a changing relationship of resources and community as a factor in population growth or loss. Discussion of the joint effect between resources and community in both types of study has often been muted. This is not the case in the following papers.

The papers in this section have a common thread around which community-resource relationships are examined. In each case study the water resource has been, or is proposed to be, converted from a flow resource to a stock resource. Human response and impact upon community structure are emphasized in the ensuing analyses. Bultena focuses on how public interests in a small Iowa community are articulated and advanced through organized group action in the deliberation, decision-making and implementation of a water improvement project. Smith considers group action but, in addition, seeks understanding of the social processes for bringing about community adaptation to water development. His analysis is a comparison of public involvement from the Salt River Project of Arizona and the Willamette Project in Oregon. While Bultena and Smith examine community-public response and involvement in the decisions surrounding a resource alteration, Johnson and Burdge discuss the consequences for community stability and personal well-being after a water development project has been completed.

# 7. Dynamics of Agency-Public Relations in Water Resource Planning

### GORDON L. BULTENA

*Policy making is an inherently political rather than a deliberative process. (Rondinelli, 1973)*

Public concern with environmental quality has steadily increased over the past decade (McEvoy, 1972; Trop and Roos, 1971). Though there is a mounting consensus about the importance of a quality environment, there is also evidence of great popular disagreement as to what constitutes quality in specific instances, or what environmental programs should be pursued.

Fundamental to the realization of emergent public goals for the natural environment are the programs of federal, state, and local agencies charged with managing and developing natural resources. These agencies frequently operate under broad mandates from Congress or legislative bodies to formulate and carry out policies consistent with the "public interest" (Reich, 1962). How adequately these agencies reflect the public interest in their environmental programs, or what in fact constitutes the public interest, is much disputed (Henning, 1970; Wengert, 1961).

There is growing evidence of public dissatisfaction with the perceived insensitivity of some government agencies to citizens' aspirations for environmental use. Such agencies as the U.S. Forest Service, Bureau of Land Management, Bureau of Reclamation, National Park Service, and Army Corps of Engineers, among others, are drawing sharp criticism: (1) for maintaining elitist perspectives in which professional views are arbitrarily equated with the public interest, and (2) for failing to provide greater opportunity for citizen involvement in decision-making and program implementation. The intensity of public feeling about the need for more citizen involvement in resources management is dramatically revealed in the militant protests that have been erupting frequently against established environmental programs (Behan, 1969; Bolle, 1970; Friesma, 1971; Molotch, 1970).

Nevertheless, the extent to which citizens should be actively drawn into agency decision-making is controversial (Bolle, 1971; Wengert, 1971). A prevailing view among natural resource personnel is that environmental decisions must be entrusted to experts.

The "expertise model" of administrative decision-making is characterized by a complex division of labor around functional specialties and the recruitment of trained personnel capable of responding to narrow problems with speed, efficiency, and competence. A presumed advantage of this model is that it employs professional ethics and standards that are "value free" with respect to specific programs. It is argued by some that this arrangement helps agencies resist interest-group pressures and facilitates their serving the broader goals of the American public. Another perceived advantage of the expertise model is its use of rational decision-making processes in which goals are clearly defined, pertinent data are collected, the range of alternatives and their consequences are specified, and the most efficient program alternatives are rationally selected.

The expertise model of environmental decision-making, while appealing in principle, is open to serious challenge in practice. It needs to be recognized, first, that elected bodies often have transferred considerable authority to agencies not only to determine procedures for goal attainment, but also to establish these goals as well. Goal setting invariably involves value judgments about what are desirable, and undesirable, consequences of alternative management programs. Scientifically trained personnel are no more qualified than the general public to make these value-based decisions.

The prominent role played by political considerations in the decision-making of government agencies provides a second reason for rejecting the viability of the expertise model. Research reveals that environmental agencies frequently cater to special interest groups to expedite successful implementation of their programs and to secure public support of official policies (Foss, 1960; Henning, 1968; Ingram, 1971; Marshall, 1966; Selznic, 1949). Accommodation of agency objectives to interest group demands usually results in scientific judgments being compromised with "political realities." Many other questions can be raised about the expertise model as well. There is a growing body of literature, for example, that calls for reassessment of established institutional structures and decision-making procedures in federal agencies concerned with water resource development (Allee, 1971; Bromley, Schmid, and Lord, 1971; Smith and Hogg, 1971; White, 1971).

It is ironic that the expertise model of decision-making is both a product, and an object of attack, of conservation movements. The view that experts should be instrumental in the establishment of natural resource policies was promulgated in the 1900 conservation movement. The present environmental quality movement, on the other hand, seeks less reliance on expert judgment and more reliance on opportunities being made available for citizen participation in the planning and programming activities of resource agencies.

Government agencies are experimenting with citizen involvement from two perspectives. First, and foremost, this involvement is increasingly necessary if established programs are to remain viable and not engender destructive protest. A second reason for growing agency commitment to public involvement, and one not yet deeply instilled in the views of professional personnel, is that citizens have a proprietorial right to be involved in decision-making that encompasses goal setting and goal attainment considerations.

What is relatively unrecognized in the current debates over the need for greater public involvement is that some citizens have long enjoyed access to the policy-making processes of natural resource agencies. The resource management literature is replete with cases where special interest groups have successfully shaped public policy. The basic issue in the current demands for greater public access to agency procedures is not the challenging of the expertise model by a participatory model, but rather which citizen groups and concomitant public interests will prevail in the setting of environmental management goals.

Many state and federal resource agencies are experiencing a turbulent time in which their programs are under stiff challenge by public groups seeking greater agency commitment to what they perceive as emergent and priority values in the population for natural resources management. Agency programs long defended as consonant with the national interest are being subjected to close public scrutiny and, not infrequently, are found wanting. However, established programs, though occasionally under attack, are seldom readily altered to fit new public demands, for they typically are anchored in legal mandates, organizational philosophies, employee task commitments, and a myriad of agency ties with special interest groups.

The changing nature of public sentiment toward the environment and the effects of this change on agency efforts are illustrated in experiences of the Army Corps of Engineers with reservoir projects in Iowa. Although the Corps has long been active in building flood control and navigation facilities on the Missouri and Mississippi Rivers, it has been only in the past fifteen years that large reservoirs have been undertaken on inland rivers in the state. The initial reservoir project was built in 1958, followed by the completion of two projects in 1968. A fourth project will become operative in 1975.

Construction of reservoirs has met with growing public opposition in Iowa, as is true throughout the nation. A bill recently introduced in the Iowa State Legislature would declare a moratorium for several years on the construction of additional reservoirs. Another bill would restrict reservoirs to river basins where 75 per cent of the upstream land is managed under conservation practices. In addition, many environmental groups in the state have strongly opposed the reservoirs. Given this increasingly hostile public mood, the likelihood of additional reservoirs being approved is rapidly diminishing. In fact, several projects previously authorized by Congress have recently been shelved because of public opposition.

The politics of reservoir construction in Iowa, as in most states, has undergone significant changes. While the Corps has long faced bitter protests to its proposals, this opposition usually has been unorganized, ineffective, and easily ignored. Evidence from more recent reservoir controversies suggests that opponents of Corps' projects are becoming more aware of the agency's procedures and the deficiencies of benefit-cost analysis, are better apprised of political steps necessary for project approval or rejection, and are more often organized into effective interest groups. The formation of working ties and the exchange of information between protest groups has been especially important in opposition tactics.

Changes in the political climate for reservoir construction in Iowa have confronted the Corps with new dilemmas in obtaining necessary governmental approval of its proposals. Historically, many of the Corps' battles have been waged at the national level where it could resort to pork barrel politics (Douglas, 1969; Drew, 1970). It is with the emergence of militant and well-organized local interest groups that the Corps confronts a potent new adversary. The saliency of these local groups for the ultimate success or failure of reservoir proposals has been enhanced considerably by the Corps' need to include recreational benefits with flood control, water quality, and other benefits to economically justify its proposed projects. Where recreation benefits are involved, it is required that local or state matching monies be available for recreation development. Community interests opposed to reservoirs, while possibly impotent in the national political arena, may nevertheless enjoy sufficient influence in state and local politics to impede commitment of these required matching monies, and can thereby stymie proposed projects.

To better understand the dynamics of agency-community relationships in reservoir controversies, a study was undertaken in 1971 of activities related to a proposed reservoir on the Raccoon River near Jefferson, Iowa. The purpose of this investigation was to examine the public's attitudes toward the proposed project and to assess how various public interests were being articulated and advanced through organized group actions.

## THE JEFFERSON RESERVOIR PROJECT

The possibility of a reservoir being built on the Raccoon River near Jefferson, Iowa, has been of longstanding interest to some community residents. As described by proponents of the project, the idea of a reservoir was originally conceived about 50 years ago by civic-minded leaders who foresaw numerous ways that such a project could benefit the community. It was not until 1966, however, that the Army Corps of Engineers came to formally recommend construction of a reservoir. The Corps' justification of the project lay in the water quality, flood control, and recreation benefits it believed would be forthcoming.

While local proponents of a reservoir viewed each of these benefits as important, recreation held the widest appeal, especially since the flooding and water quality benefits would principally accrue to persons living downstream from the community. But an even more compelling reason for building the project in the minds of local supporters was the belief that a reservoir would bring economic prosperity to the area. [The belief that economic growth accompanies water resource development projects is a pervasive one in American society. Little objective information is available, however, on the actual economic impact of these reservoir projects (Haveman, 1972; Smith, Hogg, and Reagan, 1971). See the discussion by Butcher in Chapter 4 regarding the relationship between water projects and growth for a fuller explanation.] Project boosters could recite numerous instances where construction of reservoirs had precipitated community growth and economic revitalization. In the local case, economic expansion was seen as being sparked by a heavy influx of recreationists, by the attraction of industries to the area because of a stable water supply, and by residential development stimulated by the amenities of a nearby reservoir.

Because of their interest in securing government approval of the reservoir, several local business leaders organized a community group to promote the project. This group grew rapidly in size to about 300 members by 1972. Its existence was used as prima facie evidence by project boosters of widespread public commitment to a reservoir. The group's existence also provided a local base through which the Corps of Engineers could work in its promotion of the proposed project.

Although there was evidence of widening public support for a reservoir in the Jefferson community, opposition to the project was developing in rural communities upstream from the proposed dam. Residents in these places, rather than seeing a reservoir bring prosperity, felt it posed an economic threat. Specifically, they foresaw the displacement of numerous farm families, a drop in local business activity, and a substantial loss of tax revenues. They also felt, among other things, that recreational use associated with a reservoir would bring added pressure on local facilities without a compensatory economic return, and that the project would replace a scenic wooded valley with unsightly mudflats.

Several farmers who were particularly adamant in their opposition to the reservoir organized a group to fight the project. While their immediate personal concerns lay in saving local farms, they publicly pursued the reservoir issue in the broader context of irretrievable loss of prime agricultural land.

The opposition group, like the proponent group, was blessed with hardworking and committed leadership. The group's officers spent untold hours informing themselves about the project, investigating the political processes necessary for securing its approval, and exploring opposition tactics employed in earlier reservoir battles. To this end, they traveled to the Corps' offices in Chicago, Omaha, and Rock Island to consult with professional personnel; they sought out persons involved in similar controversies at other locales; and they contacted state and federal political leaders for advice. They also joined environmental groups, such as the Sierra Club, in hopes of winning wider public endorsement of their goals.

To sway public opinion, the protest group distributed circulars describing likely personal and community effects of a reservoir. They also organized several public informational meetings. One of the more effective protest actions was the establishment of a booth at the county fair at which maps of the proposed reservoir and materials describing probable social and economic costs of the project for the local area were displayed.

Both sides in the reservoir controversy were primed for battle at the time of the official public hearing in 1970, as evidenced in the three volumes of testimony, petitions, and letters that were produced. Despite the many arguments leveled against a reservoir, the Corps remained resolute in its endorsement of the proposed project. A major roadblock to the Corps' securing Congressional authorization of the project, however, lay in the importance of recreational benefits in the economic justification of the reservoir and in the requirement that state and/or local matching funds would have to be available for recreational development. It was around the issue of matching monies that the controversy moved out of the community to engulf the Iowa Conservation Commission, which held the key to financial support.

**The Reservoir Study**

Decision-making on the Jefferson Reservoir was stalemated at the time the author entered the field. Because of the prominence of proposed recreation values in the Corps' overall benefit-cost calculations, the fate of the project hinged on some state or local matching monies being obtained for recreation development. The Iowa Conservation Commission was the key agency involved in this financial commitment, for it was the only state agency with mandated responsibility for outdoor recreation development and with funds of the magnitude required.

For several reasons, the Conservation Commission had deferred making a financial commitment to the reservoir project. First, the agency found itself financially strapped by development needs at operative reservoirs. Second, it was experiencing public pressure to invest funds in other types of recreational facilities. Third, there was evidence of growing public resistance to the construction of more reservoirs in the state. This opposition was emanating from environmentalists concerned with destruction of natural river valleys, from agriculturalists dismayed over sizeable losses of productive land to reservoirs, and from citizens disturbed about siltation problems evident at established reservoirs. Perhaps the most telling pressure on the Commission was from organized interests in the Jefferson area. Leaders of the proponent group were working closely with the Corps in lobbying the Commission to commit funds to recreation development on the project. The opposition forces similarly were cultivating contacts in the Commission, in the state legislature, and in the Governor's office to ensure continued agency opposition to committing these needed recreation monies.

Several aspects of this controversy were of particular interest in this investigation. Leaders of both sides were claiming widespread citizen support for their respective positions, yet they lacked objective evidence to substantiate their claims. Despite this deficiency, neither side initially desired that preference data be obtained from local residents. Their resistance was severalfold: (1) they already had a good sense of local opinions on the reservoir issue, (2) a survey might get people "worked up" about the matter and create divisiveness in the community, and (3) a study of public opinion probably would not affect agency decision-making.

Both sides in the controversy were using public support as a major justification for their respective positions, yet neither group initially sought an objective solicitation of citizen views, nor did they feel this information would be useful in public decision-making. It appeared, in reality, that both sides were fearful that their claims of public support would be discounted by a study, and both were aware that an expression of citizen preferences might have greater bearing on any resolution of the issue than they cared to publicly concede. Of some importance here was the stance taken by the Conservation Commission that the controversy should be settled with regard to the "public interest," which this agency was defining as broader than the economic efficiency considerations reflected in the Corps' benefit-cost calculations.

A second purpose of this investigation was to explore the role that local citizens were playing in the reservoir controversy. Facets of citizen involvement that held particular interest were: (1) the extent of public awareness about the reservoir proposal, (2) public attitudes about the proprietorial rights of citizens to be involved in the decision-making of government agencies, (3) citizens' perceptions of the efficacy of individual and group-based action in affecting public decision-making, and (4) the behavioral involvement of citizens in the reservoir issue.

It was initially planned that data would be obtained from community leaders, from a representative sample of the local population, and from samples of the two community groups that had been actively supporting and opposing the reservoir. The sampling of group members was contingent on officers providing membership lists.

After several discussions with the study leaders, the group opposing construction of the reservoir conceded that a survey of their membership might hold value in improving public understanding of the controversy, and they came to fully endorse the research. However, leaders of the group supporting the reservoir were unrelenting in their opposition to a study. Their overtly expressed concerns were twofold: (1) that the names of their members might be made public, causing these individuals possible embarrassment or subjecting them to harrassment by members of the protest group, and (2) that the investigators were not impartial and might bring ridicule to the personal views of the members. This latter concern was tied to a belief by the group's officers that most University personnel were ecologists and, therefore, would not be sympathetic to a project that disturbed the natural environment.

The concern of reservoir boosters that a survey represented a potential threat to their position was undoubtedly heightened by an earlier University report that had raised serious question about the accuracy of the Corps' estimates of the amount of land to be acquired for the project. This report had become a major weapon in public attacks on the reservoir. An added, and more covert, concern by officers of the proponent group was that the research might indicate erosion in their members' commitment to a reservoir.

The data reported in this paper were obtained from interviews with several populations: (1) a representative sample of persons living in the area most directly affected by the proposed reservoir, (2) a representative sample of members of the group organized to fight the project, and (3) persons identified in the population interviews and through independent fieldwork as playing influential roles in the controversy.

The population sample was drawn from an area that included all townships and communities within 12 miles of the river from a point 15 miles above the proposed dam to 15 miles downstream. This area encompassed parts of the population in three counties. All persons 21 years of age or older living in the study area were considered eligible respondents. An area probability sample was used to identify household units. The sample was designed to ensure a representative inclusion of both rural and urban families. Individual respondents were selected through a screening interview that enumerated all adult residents of each household and provided a procedure for randomly selecting every third person for interviewing. Ninety per cent of the persons identified as eligible respondents were interviewed (N=268). The attrition of several potential respondents from the sample resulted due to their advanced age or their absence from the community while on winter vacations. Only three persons refused to be interviewed.

Members of the protest group were sampled by randomly selecting every fifth name from the group's membership list. All of these persons were interviewed (N=55). Depth interviews also were conducted with nine community residents who were identified in the population interviews as playing prominent roles in the reservoir controversy.

### Study Findings
*Public Awareness of the Reservoir Project*

The study revealed that the proponent group had been relatively inactive and enjoyed little visibility in the general population. It appeared that its officers were using the group's existence more to legitimize their claims of widespread public support than as a forum for securing participation and involvement of community residents in the reservoir issue.

The Army Corps of Engineers took a passive approach to public education on the Jefferson Reservoir. The agency did little to acquaint the public with possible pros and cons of the project. News releases prepared by the Corps stressed proposed benefits, particularly recreation, to the virtual exclusion of possible costs of the reservoir. Opponents of the project also bitterly complained that there was collusion among local newspaper editors who were favorable to the project to ignore or play down adverse information and news about the reservoir.

Leaders of the opposition group were particularly frustrated in their efforts to obtain detailed information from the Corps, especially with regard to the agency's procedures in calculating costs and benefits. These efforts largely proved futile despite assistance from the local Congressional representative. As the Corps indicated in a letter to the protest group:

> The problems and procedures involved in estimating the average annual costs and benefits of a proposed project, and of allocating them among the various functions of a multiple-purpose project, are highly technical and very controversial. Desirable as it would be to have some convenient, simple item of public information on this topic, we have not found it feasible to produce one that would not risk doing more harm, through conveying false impressions by over-simplification, than good. This is one of those rarified subjects that are pretty much reserved for trained economists who are also well-versed in federal law and policy in the field.

Despite the fact that construction of a reservoir had been a longstanding issue in the community, in the interviews a substantial number of persons in the population sample were found to be oblivious to the reservoir proposal, or were relatively uninformed about happenings on the project. Specifically, it was revealed that 20 per cent of the respondents previously had not heard about the possibility of a reservoir being built, and that an additional 20 per cent, while aware of the project, had given it little attention. Only a minority of persons (20 per cent) reported they had closely followed events on the project.

A lack of public awareness about what was being contemplated was further revealed in the fact that only about half of the respondents knew of the involvement of the Army Corps of Engineers in the reservoir proposal, and only one-third were aware that a public hearing had been recently held in the local area. Nearly all (90 per cent) felt they had not been kept adequately informed about the project by public agencies or local newspapers.

As expected, members of the opposition group, in contrast to the general population, were more adequately apprised of major developments on the reservoir issue. Seventy-five per cent said they had closely followed the proposal, and all were aware of the involvement of the Corps and of the fact that a public hearing had been held.

Because public support was claimed by both sides in the controversy, the attitudes of citizens about the desirability of building a reservoir were of interest. Nearly twice as many persons in the population sample were found to oppose the project (40 per cent) than supported it (22 per cent). Opponents, furthermore, were more adamant in their positions than were proponents. All members of the protest group were, as expected, unfavorable to the reservoir.

Three major benefits were set forth by the Corps as justifying the project: water quality, flood control, and recreation. The interviews explored the extent to which respondents viewed these as major problems and, if so, whether they concurred with the Corps that a reservoir represented an appropriate solution. Only 25 per cent of the population sample, and 10 per cent of the group sample, defined either water quality, flooding, or lack of recreational opportunities as a major problem. Furthermore, persons who saw one or more of these as problem areas typically rejected the reservoir as a solution, preferring instead such actions as restricting settlement in the flood plains, and clamping tighter restrictions on the disposal of municipal and industrial wastes in the river. Given the vested interests of the Corps in constructing the reservoir, and their role in the preparation of background studies, these and other solutions to the identified problems had not been given serious attention in the community.

*Perceived Propriety of Citizen Involvement*

The levels and nature of citizen involvement in government programs ultimately reflect public sentiment on the legitimacy of such involvement. Respondents were queried on their feelings about the propriety of citizens participating directly in public programs and about the role of expertise in agency decision-making. These questions were posed both in an abstract context and more specifically with regard to citizen involvement in the Jefferson Reservoir issue. As reported in Table I, a majority of the persons interviewed felt that citizens should be involved in public decision-making. Responses ranged from 52 per cent rejecting the notion that "a citizen's obligation to participate in decision-making by government agencies largely ends once he has voted," to 84 per cent rejecting the idea that "residents in this area should not expect to participate in the decision-making activities of federal agencies." The respondents, in even greater numbers, articulated a desire for public involvement in decision-making on the proposed reservoir. Virtually everyone (99 per cent) felt that "residents in the vicinity of the Jefferson Reservoir should make their views known on the project," and most (86 per cent) clearly rejected the idea that "it is not necessary for the government to consult the local population to make a correct decision about building the Jefferson Reservoir."

A further finding was that members of the protest group tended to be more committed than the general population to citizen involvement. Group members uniformly rejected the argument, for example, that "residents in this area should not expect to participate in the decision-making activities of federal agencies" (Table I).

Table I
Citizens' Attitudes on the Desirability of Public Involvement in Programs of Government Agencies and in the Proposed Jefferson Reservoir Project

| Attitude | Population Sample (Per cent) | Protest Group Sample (Per cent) |
|---|---|---|
| Programs of Government Agencies | (N=268) | (N=55) |
| 1. Responsibility for all public programs should ultimately rest with the public (agree)[a] | 69 | 80 |
| 2. Administrators in government agencies are better qualified to decide what projects are needed than is the general public (disagree) | 57 | 77[b] |
| 3. Residents in this area should not expect to participate in the decision-making activities of federal agencies (disagree) | 84 | 100[b] |
| 4. A citizen's obligation to participate in decision-making by government agencies largely ends once he has voted (disagree) | 52 | 69[b] |
| Proposed Jefferson Reservoir | (N=218)[c] | (N=55) |
| 1. Residents in the vicinity of the Jefferson Reservoir should make their views known on this project (agree) | 99 | 100 |
| 2. Residents in the Raccoon Valley are better qualified to decide the desirability of building the Jefferson Reservoir than is an agency in Washington (agree) | 82 | 91 |
| 3. It is not necessary for the government to consult the local population to make a correct decision about building the Jefferson Reservoir (disagree) | 86 | 89 |

[a] There were five responses to these items: strongly agree, agree, undecided, disagree, strongly disagree. The strongly agree-agree and strongly disagree-disagree categories were collapsed for this analysis. Percentages in the table are persons taking the response pattern noted by each item, which reflects an orientation toward maximizing public involvement in agency decision-making.
[b] Difference between population sample and group sample is statistically significant at the 0.05 level.
[c] Fifty respondents in the population sample did not respond to this section since they were unaware of the proposed Jefferson Reservoir.

This finding of high respondent commitment to citizens having a say in public decision-making is of particular interest when juxtaposed against the respondents' assessments of who is likely to wield power in the Jefferson Reservoir issue. They were asked to rate the likely influence of the Army Corps of Engineers, state-county-local officials, and local residents. The Corps came out a clear winner, with 55 per cent of the population sample attributing it "a great deal of influence," followed by 23 per cent who felt that state officials had such influence. Only 14 per cent of the population sample perceived community residents as having much say in this issue (Table II). This attribution of influence comes despite the respondents' feelings that citizen views are important, and despite their rather uniform belief that "residents in the Raccoon Valley are better qualified to decide the desirability of building the Jefferson Reservoir than is an agency in Washington" (Table I). An earlier study of citizen attitudes (Haas, Boggs, and Bonner, 1972) revealed a similar pattern of high citizen commitment to public involvement in official decision-making, as well as an accompanying belief that such involvement likely would have little effect on the outcome of the issue.

Members of the protest group differed in two important respects from the population sample in attributing influence on the Jefferson Reservoir issue. First, they more often than others saw the Corps as having a great deal of influence (84 and 55 per cent, respectively) and, second, they more often perceived community residents as being influential in the matter (45 and 14 per cent, respectively, Table II).

*Perception of Group Efficacy*

An important dimension in the efficacy of citizen action is the extent to which persons act individually or collectively. The effectiveness of grassroots efforts tends to be appreciably increased when citizens coordinate and advance their interests through group-based actions. Citizens' attitudes toward group processes would seem important to the nature and effectiveness of community actions that support or oppose government programs.

There was consensus in both the population sample and group sample on the likely efficacy of citizen groups in affecting public policy. A substantial majority of persons in both samples saw organized groups "having an effective voice in local affairs" and as "offering an effective way to tackle a local problem." A significantly larger proportion of group members felt, however, that

## Table II
## Perceived Influence of Several Groups
## on Jefferson Reservoir Decision

| Group | Perceived as Having a "Great Deal" of Influence[a] | |
|---|---|---|
| | Population Sample Per cent (N=218)[b] | Group Sample Per cent (N=55) |
| Army Corps of Engineers | 55 | 84[c] |
| State officials | 23 | 20 |
| County officials | 12 | 9 |
| Community officials | 6 | 18 |
| Community residents | 14 | 45[c] |

[a] Responses were: "great deal," "some," "very little," and "none." The latter three categories were collapsed in the analysis.
[b] This analysis does not include 50 respondents who were unaware of the proposed Jefferson Reservoir.
[c] Difference between population sample and group sample is statistically significant at the 0.05 level.

"setting up a group to fight a government program offers one of the best ways of influencing government decisions" (96 and 78 per cent, respectively, Table III).

A second dimension of the question of group efficacy involved respondents' notions about the democratic nature of community groups, particularly whether such groups were seen as responsive to membership views. As reported in Table III, members of the protest group were more solidly committed to the likelihood of democratic group processes obtaining desired results than were persons in the population sample.

*Behavioral Involvement*

A persistent problem in attitude research is the gap between what people say and what they actually do (Wicker, 1969). While citizens may verbalize commitments to action in support or opposition to a public program, the extent to which they actually become involved in various actions remains problematical. This study explored several facets of citizen involvement in the Jefferson Reservoir issue. Information was obtained on respondents' views of likely actions they would take if the government planned a program they opposed. Then, determination was made of actions they had actually taken in opposing the proposed reservoir.

As seen in Table IV (column A), most persons who opposed the

## Table III
### Respondents' Attitudes on Group Process and Group Efficacy in Public Action

| Attitude | Percentage Expressing Favorable Attitudes Toward Citizen Groups | |
| --- | --- | --- |
| | Population Sample (N=268) | Protest Group Sample (N=55) |
| **Group Efficacy** | | |
| 1. Members of groups can, through their leadership, have an effective voice in local affairs (agree)[a] | 94 | 95 |
| 2. Forming a group generally offers an effective way of tackling a local problem (agree) | 89 | 98 |
| 3. Organized groups usually have a great deal of influence in local affairs (agree) | 83 | 93 |
| 4. Setting up a group to fight a government program offers one of the best ways of influencing government decisions (agree) | 78 | 96[b] |
| **Group Processes** | | |
| 1. Most community groups are not very democratic in the way they are run (disagree) | 52 | 82[b] |
| 2. One problem with organized groups is that a few members usually have most of the say about what the organization does (disagree) | 26 | 60[b] |
| 3. Leaders of most organized groups have a way of using group members for their own selfish ends (disagree) | 57 | 84[b] |
| 4. For the most part, community groups truly reflect the views of their individual members (agree) | 76 | 89[b] |

[a] There were five responses to these items: strongly agree, agree, undecided, disagree, and strongly disagree. The strongly agree and agree categories, as well as the strongly disagree-disagree categories, were collapsed in the analysis. Percentages in the table are persons giving the response pattern indicated by each item, which reflects orientations supportive of citizen groups being influential in public affairs and of democratic processes characterizing community groups.
[b] Difference between the population sample and group sample is statistically significant at the 0.05 level.

Jefferson Reservoir were committed to taking some type of personal action against any government program they opposed; 85 per cent said they would join a group organized to fight the program; 77 per cent would write elected officials; 68 per cent would write agency officials; and 41 per cent said they would provide leadership in organizing a public meeting to discuss the program.

This abstract commitment to protest actions can be arrayed

against the actions these same persons actually took in opposing the Jefferson Reservoir. Only a small proportion had joined a protest group (7 per cent), had written letters in opposition to the reservoir (9 per cent), had talked with politicians or agency officials (11 per cent), had attended the public hearing (10 per cent), or had attended a community meeting organized on the reservoir issue (16 per cent). The most prevalent action was signing a petition, which was indicated by 23 per cent of the opponents (Table IV, column B).

This pattern of limited behavioral involvement of the general population stands in marked contrast to that of persons in the protest group. More than three-fourths of these members had attended the public hearing, had gone to a community meeting, or had signed a petition. One-half had written letters protesting the project, and over one-third had talked personally with a politician or agency official about the reservoir (Table IV, column C).

These data do not permit explanation of possible cause and effect relationships between group membership, attitudinal commitment to citizen action, and behavioral involvement in the Jefferson Reservoir issue. It may be that persons strongly committed to citizen action were disproportionately drawn to group membership, and that they would have acted in larger numbers than others regardless of this membership. Conversely, the availability of the group likely performed a facilitating function by raising the levels of personal action, by giving it coordination, and by ensuring that protests had a more potent impact on public decision-making than would otherwise have been obtained from individual efforts.

The data do indicate that persons were not drawn to the protest group out of their general environmental concerns; in fact, group members differed little from the general population in their attitudes on a variety of other environmental issues (Table V). However, group members were distinguished from the general population with regard to the impact they perceived the reservoir would have on their personal situations. Nearly all (93 per cent) of the group members, as compared to one-third of the population sample, felt they would suffer financial losses if the project were built. Similarly, a much larger proportion of group members, than the population sample (71 and 5 per cent, respectively), claimed they would lose land to the project. Thus, economic self-interest represented an important factor leading persons to group action in protest of the reservoir.

## Table IV
### Proportion of Persons Opposed to the Jefferson Reservoir Who Indicated They Would, or Did, Take Specified Protest Actions

| Abstract | | Issue-Specific | |
|---|---|---|---|
| Would Take Specified Action if a Government Agency Proposed a Program They Opposed | A<br>Proportion of All Reservoir Opponents (N=106) | Took Specified Action on Proposed Reservoir | B<br>Proportion of All Reservoir Opponents (N=106) | C<br>Proportion of Protest Group Members (N=55) |
| Write elected political officials | 77 | Wrote letter opposing reservoir | 9 | 51[a] |
| Write officials in agency proposing program | 68 | Talked with politician or agency official about reservoir | 11 | 38[a] |
| Try to meet personally with agency officials | 67 | Attended public hearing on reservoir | 10 | 75[a] |
| Take leadership in organizing a public meeting to discuss program | 41 | Attended community hearing on reservoir | 16 | 76[a] |
| Join a group organized to fight the proposed program | 85 | Signed petition opposing reservoir | 23 | 87[a] |
| | | Joined protest group | 7 | 100[a] |

[a] Difference between population sample and group sample is statistically significant at 0.05 level.

## Table V
## Proportion of Respondents Expressing a Conservationist Position on Selected Environmental Issues

| Issue | Percentage Expressing Conservationist Position | |
|---|---|---|
| | Population Sample ($N=268$) | Protest Group Sample ($N=55$) |
| State governments should be able to force individuals to adopt soil conservation practices (agree)[a] | 52 | 73[b] |
| Natural resources should be used wherever possible to increase the economic growth of local areas (disagree) | 21 | 36[b] |
| Present use of agricultural chemicals is seriously polluting our rivers and destroying wildlife (agree) | 69[b] | 44 |
| Greater regulation is needed on the use of chemicals in agriculture (agree) | 52 | 43 |
| Highway construction should be slowed to allow more attention to public transportation needs and the impact of roads on the environment (agree) | 50 | 66 |
| High air and water pollution standards should be maintained despite their possibly adverse impact on business (agree) | 79 | 86 |
| Economic progress that results in the destruction of places of natural beauty needs to be stopped (agree) | 83 | 88 |
| It is important that the government exercise greater control over the way individuals and companies use our natural resources (agree) | 79 | 69 |
| Protecting our remaining swamps and marshlands is of greater importance than draining them for the purpose of agricultural or commercial development (agree) | 56 | 71 |

[a] There were five responses to these items: strongly agree, agree, undecided, disagree, strongly disagree. The strongly agree and agree categories, as well as the strongly disagree and disagree categories, were collapsed in the analysis. Percentages in the table are persons taking a conservationist stand, as indicated by the response pattern following each item.

[b] Difference between population sample and group sample is statistically significant at the 0.05 level.

## Discussion

Citizen involvement in community issues obviously hinges on the level and quality of information available to the public. Previous research has demonstrated that persons often remain uninformed or poorly informed on issues that hold considerable importance for their lives.

There are several barriers that prevent citizens from being adequately apprised of public programs. One problem lies in the complexity of modern American society and the fact that the public is confronted with a broad spectrum of issues requiring resolution. It is difficult for any one person to be informed on all issues, or knowledgeable of even a few.

A second barrier to securing an informed citizenry lies in the present structure of public decision-making in American society. Primary responsibility for determining the desirability of natural resource projects, for example, is entrusted to government agencies holding vested interests in the outcomes of project evaluations. Because of these vested interests, agencies often are reticent to encourage public involvement for fear it may jeopardize realization of official plans. The fact that environmental agencies are restricted in the types of programs they can promote severely circumscribes public consideration of alternative resource management or development options. Often more potentially attractive resource programs go unexamined because of lack of an advocate agency.

The educational programs of natural resource agencies commonly are directed more at selling the merits of proposed projects and winning public endorsement than at providing a balanced assessment of their desirability. As a result of one-sided information campaigns, the average citizen may remain oblivious to possible social, economic, and ecological implications of proposed programs, and often must accept in good faith the recommendations of sponsoring agencies that such programs are meritorious.

The ways in which the nation's natural resources are utilized and developed reflects socio-political considerations as much as scientific-technical judgments. Socio-political aspects of resources management are not confined to the interchange between environmental agencies and legislative bodies in the review and funding of proposed projects, but permeate all facets of decision-making. Calculation of benefit-cost ratios to determine the economic desirability of water resource projects, for example, while offering a presumably "objective" approach to decision-making, actually harbors a set of value decisions (*e.g.*, the types of benefits and costs to be considered, the size of the discount rate to be applied, and the economic value of a recreation day). Hubert Marshall (1966) has proposed that a major use of benefit-cost analysis is to " . . . clothe politically desirable projects with the fig leaf of economic respectability."

Usually the same agencies that determine feasibility and desirability of projects become their staunchest advocates in the mobilization of political support. The considerable manpower and financial resources available to most environmental agenices, coupled with active clientele support, make them a potent political force in determining which of many possible programs will eventually come to fruition.

The fact that resource agencies usually serve as advocates of their own project proposals can pose a serious barrier to "rational" decision-making in that program opportunities lying outside an agency's mission typically are neglected. The public often is confronted with a choice, not between a set of alternative actions, but between having a specific project proposed by an agency or no project at all.

Typically, even the opportunity for the public to actively assess the merits of a proposed project is severely circumscribed. Given the advocacy role of resource agencies, it is difficult for citizens to obtain a balanced treatment of likely benefits and costs. Agencies control the types and amount of information about projects made available to citizens, they manipulate procedures for soliciting citizen input in ways to ensure a favorable public airing of their proposals, and they engage in interest-group and pork-barrel politics to ensure congressional approval of their proposals.

Whether or not the merits of resource programs are fully aired appears to be largely determined by the strength of any protest actions that emerge. While resource agencies have long encountered public opposition to their proposals, such opposition usually has been unorganized and relatively ineffective in stopping proposed programs. The environmental quality movement, however, has given rise to more sophisticated and effective pressure group tactics, as evidenced in recent adverse experiences of the Army Corps of Enginers in constructing reservoirs.

This study of a reservoir controversy in Iowa examined several facets of what proved to be a successful citizen protest action. Although the Army Corps of Engineers and prominent local supporters were actively promoting the Jefferson Reservoir as a desirable project and as being in the public interest, interviews revealed it received only minority support in the population. The amount of citizen opposition to the proposal could easily have been misjudged in the early stages of the controversy, however, because of the more vigorous and visible efforts of those promoting the project than of those opposing it.

Formation of effective citizen opposition to the Jefferson Reservoir was retarded by an inability of opponents to obtain detailed information from the Corps. The project was widely heralded by proponents as offering prosperity for the local community and as a source of expanded outdoor recreation opportunity, but the potential social and economic costs of the project remained obscure in materials prepared by the Corps for public consumption.

While many residents in the Jefferson area opposed a reservoir, relatively few had openly protested its construction (*e.g.*, by writing letters, signing petitions, attending hearings, and joining a protest group). This was despite the general commitment of these persons to taking such actions against government programs they opposed and their further conviction that citizens have the right to be heard in the decision-making of public agencies.

One probable source of behavioral paralysis among reservoir opponents was that many saw their actions as having little salience for the eventual resolution of this issue. They felt the Corps would eventually prove victorious in its efforts to win approval of the project. Persons who became actively involved in protest action, on the other hand, tended to be more convinced of the likely efficacy of their opposition.

It was not the appearance of adverse citizen reaction that stopped the Jefferson Reservoir, but rather that this opposition was mobilized into an effective interest group. Opponents of the project, through formation of a group, were able to effectively counter efforts by the Corps of Engineers and the local power structure to "sell" the project to citizens and state officials. Without this interest group, the Jefferson Reservoir project would likely have gone the course of many similar community controversies where hostile citizen reaction to proposals has been overcome by the skilled political tactics of proponents of these projects.

The present national concern with environmental quality has created a favorable climate for the emergence of protest actions similar to those evidenced in the Jefferson Reservoir controversy. It should be recognized that the group that formed in the Jefferson battle was not motivated out of a deep-felt citizen concern for obtaining a quality environment, or even of preserving a natural waterway. Rather, this action was precipitated because the project adversely affected the economic self-interests of some local residents. Once a citizen group had formed around these self-interests, however, it was able to capitalize on the environmental movement through the use of the proper rhetoric to draw wider citizen support to its cause. It was also able to expand its power base by drawing extra-local environmental groups into the political battle.

It appears that protest actions taken on the Jefferson Reservoir issue are a precursor for similar citizen actions in other Iowa locales confronted with reservoir proposals. Suddenly organized citizen action poses a new and potent force to counter what has long been an effective liaison between the Corps and local power structures in the politics of reservoir construction.

## ACKNOWLEDGMENTS

This project was partially funded by a grant from the U.S. Department of the Interior, Office of Water Resources Research, under Public Law 88-379, and made available through the Iowa State Water Resources Research Institute as Project B-020-IA. Funding also was provided by the Iowa Agricultural Experiment Station (Project 102-40-73-73-1858). I am indebted to the contributions of David Rogers, Sue Wright, Ken Barb, and Steffaney Lennard to the overall study from which this analysis is drawn.

## REFERENCES

Allee, D. J. "Management of Natural Resources for Optimum Development—Cutting the Costs of Decision-making," in "Issues in Natural Resource Use and Development," Report No. 1, D. Bromley and L. Fischer, Eds. North Central Regional Strategy Committee on Natural Resource Development (1971) pp. 32-47.

Behan, R. W. "The Lincoln Back Country Controversy: A Case Study in Natural Resource Policy Formation and Administration," Mimeographed. Missoula: University of Montana, School of Forestry (1969).

Bolle, A. "Public Participation and Environmental Quality," Nat. Resources J. 11, 497 (1971).

Bolle, A., R. Behan, W. Pengelly, R. Wambach, G. Browder, T. Payne, and R. Shannon. *"A University View of the Forest Service,"* Document No. 91-115, U.S. Senate. (Washington, D.C.: U.S. Government Printing Office, 1970.)

Bromley, D. W., A. A. Schmid, and W. Lord. "Public Water Resource Project Planning and Evaluation: Impacts, Incidence, and Institutions," Working Paper #1. Madison: University of Wisconsin, Center for Resource Policy Studies and Programs (Sept., 1971).
Douglas, W. "The Public Be Damned," Playboy (July), 182 (1969).
Drew, E. "Dam Outrage: The Story of the Army Engineers," Atlantic 225, 51 (1970).
Foss, P. *Politics and Grass*. (Seattle: University of Washington Press, 1960).
Friesma, H. P. "The Forest Service in Crisis in Northern New Mexico," Mimeographed. Evanston: Northwestern University, Department of Political Science (1971).
Haas, J. E., K. S. Boggs, and E. J. Bonner. "Science, Technology, and the Public: The Case of Planned Weather Modification," in *Social Behavior, Natural Resources, and the Environment*, W. Burch, N. Cheek, and L. Taylor, Eds. (New York: Harper and Row, 1972) p. 170.
Haveman, R. *The Economic Performance of Public Investments: An Ex Post Evaluation of Water Resources Investments*. (Baltimore: The Johns Hopkins Press, 1972.)
Henning, D. "The Politics of Natural Resources Administration," Ann. Regional Sci. 2, 239 (1968).
Henning, D. "Natural Resource Administration and the Public Interest," Public Admin. Rev. **XXX**, 134 (1970).
Ingram, H. "Patterns of Politics in Water Resources Development," Natl. Resources J. 11, 102 (1971).
Marshall, H. "Politics and Efficiency in Water Development," in *Water Research*. Allen Kneese and Stephen Smith, Eds. (Baltimore: The Johns Hopkins Press, 1966) pp. 291-310.
McEvoy, J., III. "The American Concern With Environment," in *Social Behavior, Natural Resources, and the Environment*. W. Burch, N. Cheek, and L. Taylor, Eds. (New York: Harper and Row, 1972) pp. 214-236.
Molotch, H. "Santa Barbara: Oil in the Velvet Playground," in *Ramparts* (Eds.), *Eco-Catastrophe*. (San Francisco: Canfield Press, 1970) pp. 84-105.
Reich, C. *Bureaucracy and the Forests*. (Santa Barbara: Center for the Study of Democratic Institutions, 1962.)
Rondinelli, D. A. "Urban Planning as Policy Analysis: Management of Urban Change," J. Amer. Inst. Planners 39 (1), 13 (1973).
Selznick, P. *TVA and the Grass Roots: A Study of Formal Organization*. (Berkeley: The University of California Press, 1949.)
Smith, C. L., and T. C. Hogg. "Benefits and Beneficiaries: Contrasting Economic and Cultural Distinctions," Water Resources Res. 7, 254 (1971).

Smith, C. L., T. C. Hogg and M. J. Reagan. "Economic Development: Panacea or Perplexity for Rural Areas?" Rural Sociol. **36**, 173 (1971).
Trop, C. and L. L. Roos, Jr. "Public Opinion and the Environment," in *The Politics of Ecosuicide*, L. L. Roos, Ed. (New York: Holt, Rinehart and Winston, Inc., 1971) pp. 52-63.
Wengert, N. "Resource Development and the Public Interest: A Challenge for Research," Natl. Resources J. **1**, 207 (1961).
Wengert, N. "Public Participation in Water Planning: A Critique of Theory, Doctrine, and Practice," Water Resources Bull. **7**, 26 (1971).
White, G. F. *Strategies of American Water Management*. (Ann Arbor: The University of Michigan Press, 1971).
Wicker, A. "Attitudes Versus Actions: The Relationship of Verbal and Overt Behavioral Responses to Attitude Objects," J. Social Issues **XXV**, 41 (1969).

# 8. Self-Interest Groups and Human Emotion as Adaptive Mechanisms

**COURTLAND L. SMITH**

Typically in the analysis of human adaptation, technological events are used as the horizon markers of change. The Stone Age, Bronze Age, Iron Age, agricultural revolution, irrigation revolution, and Industrial Revolution serve as examples of this pattern for the analysis of the history of human adaptation. Less attention is given to social, organizational and ideological changes as these may have influenced human adaptation. So predominant is the technological orientation to change that technology is very often viewed as the leading factor preceding social and ideological change.

Two case studies provide data indicating that ideological and social factors in the form of self-interest energized by emotional commitment were determinants of how technology of water development was employed. Reviewing the adaptation to water development in the Salt River Valley of Arizona and the Willamette Valley of Oregon suggests that the social and ideological factors of self-interest, energized by emotional commitment, brought to bear through action-oriented self-interest groups were important elements in the starting of water development in the case of the Salt River Valley, and in the slowing down of water development in the case of the Willamette Valley.

The Salt River Project of Arizona was one of the first five irrigation projects authorized under the National Irrigation Act of 1902 and the first to begin construction. The National Irrigation

Act and the choice of the Salt River Valley for a reclamation project would not have occurred had it not been for the self-interest energized by emotional commitment among many Valley residents and national leaders of the reclamation movement. On the other hand, self-interest energized similarly was instrumental in slowing water development in the Willamette Valley of Oregon. Earth Day, April 22, 1970, galvanized significant opposition to the continued damming of free flowing streams, and environmentalists blocked the construction of the Cascadia Dam on the South Santiam, a tributary to the Willamette.

The Salt River Valley and the Willamette Valley cases differ in terms of the actors, the technologies used, and the ideologies of the participants, but the two cases are remarkably similar in terms of the process for bringing about community adaptation to water development. Individuals, emotionally committed to what they believed to be right and acting for their self-interests, organized groups to bring their concerns before the public and a variety of decision-makers. Through voting behavior, testimony at public meetings, expressions of opinions, allocation of time, and allocation of personal resources, individuals and groups demonstrated their commitment to deciding the role of water development in the adaptation of their community.

## THE SALT RIVER VALLEY CASE

Utilization of the waters of the Salt River for irrigation dates back to 1868 when Jack Swilling initiated construction of the Swilling Ditch. (See Smith, 1972; Clark, 1936; Moore, 1961; Shadegg, 1958.) Water storage on the Salt River had been a topic for discussion at least since 1891 when the Maricopa County Surveyor prepared a map showing possible storage sites on the Salt River. At the turn of the century the Phoenix and Maricopa County Board of Trade, predecessor to the Chamber of Commerce, organized a committee of local business and agricultural leaders to consider alternatives for financing water storage. The alternatives identified were a direct appropriation from the federal government, ceding government lands to the state for sale to obtain revenues for dam construction, financing by private enterprise, and bonding Maricopa County. Bonding Maricopa County was the plan favored by a majority of Valley residents. Since Arizona was a territory, Congress had to be asked for authority to increase the county bonding limit.

Were it not for the interest of Theodore Roosevelt in reclamation, the National Irrigation Act of June 17, 1902, might not have been passed. In the spring of 1902 there were two courses that the citizens of Maricopa County could follow—bonding the county or securing federal aid. Those who favored federal aid were called "rainbow chasers." Most felt that the only feasible alternative was bonding the county.

When the National Irrigation Act passed, it was decided, much to everyone's surprise, that a storage project would be built on the Gila River at San Carlos for the benefit of the Pima Indians before any thought would be given to the storage dam on the Salt River. Yet there were a few eloquent and hopeful people who continued to support federal funding. Through the National Reclamation Association, George H. Maxwell had been working at the national level to promote the reclamation movement. On August 9, 1902, he addressed a meeting of Salt River Valley residents and exhorted the people of the Valley to get together to secure water storage under the National Irrigation Act. Leadership of Glendale farmer B. A. Fowler and Judge Joseph H. Kibbey resulted in the plan for a water users' organization, which became the Salt River Valley Water Users' Association, a publicly oriented private corporation that would manage the Valley's water resources.

The most difficult task lay ahead. This was convincing the landowners of the Valley that the association could and would act in their best interests, and that by committing their land to the association landowners had everything to gain and nothing to lose. Arthur P. Davis of the Geological Survey gave talks in the Valley in the late fall of 1902 about the benefits of water storage. Landowners did not stampede to sign their land. Commitment to the storage project meant agreeing to pay ten equal annual installments to return to the government the cost of the dam. It was estimated that a total commitment of $15 per acre would provide the two to three million dollars necessary to construct the dam. However, some of the older residents in the Valley had better water rights than the newcomers, and many oldtimers viewed the association as an attempt by newcomers to take their water. The resistance crystallized under the leadership of Dwight B. Heard. Heard was regarded as a progressive thinker and was a very large landowner. He felt that the rights of people along the Tempe Canal would be jeopardized by joining the association. Thus, the Salt River Valley Water Users' Association was having difficulty performing the task it was formed to undertake—uniting the land-

## 154 WATER AND COMMUNITY DEVELOPMENT

owners of the Valley behind a federally funded water storage plan.

In early June, 1903, the government was becoming impatient waiting for the people of the Valley to make up their minds. Water storage hung in the balance. Maxwell of the National Reclamation Association returned to the Valley in early June to rebut the arguments of Heard. Fowler worked tirelessly to get additional signatures. On June 19, 1903, one year after the passage of the National Irrigation Act, the following telegram was sent to Washington:

> Phoenix, Arizona, June 19, Walcott, Project Director, Geological Survey, Washington, D.C. Total acreage signed tonight one hundred fifty thousand. Will make it twenty thousand more next week without Tempe. The small landowners are all coming in.
>
> B. A. Fowler

So construction began in Tonto Basin on Roosevelt Dam, at the time the largest stone masonry dam in the world.

### THE WILLAMETTE VALLEY CASE

Instead of looking at the beginning of water development in the Willamette Valley, I will contrast the developmentally oriented Salt River Valley situation with factors that slowed water development in the Willamette Valley (Smith, 1973b). Between 1936, when the Flood Control Act was passed, and 1970, the Corps of Engineers had spent over half a billion dollars on flood control works and their operation and maintenance in the Willamette Valley of Oregon (U.S. Army Corps of Engineers, 1971). The result was 13 major flood control dams, revetments, channel improvements, and other developments. In 1970 the Corps, in conjunction with the Bureau of Reclamation, Soil Conservation Service, Federal Power Commission, Bonneville Power Administration, and 28 other local, state, and federal agencies presented an updated and comprehensive water plan that projected an expenditure of $3.9 billion more for water development projects through the year 2020. This plan, called the Willamette Basin Task Force Study (1969), was a coordinated water resource plan designed to meet the needs of Willamette Valley residents.

In the plan the Corps suggested 14 multiple purpose projects at a construction cost of $268 million, plus another $100 million for flood control and navigation. The Bureau had 11 projects at $495 million. The Soil Conservation Service suggested 69 projects at $116 million. A joint effort for $2 billion between the Corps, Bonneville Power

## WATER DEVELOPMENT AND HUMAN RESPONSE 155

Administration, and the Federal Power Commission proposed increasing the installed power generation capacity in the Valley by four times. An additional $400 million was projected for nonfederal power projects (Willamette Basin Task Force, 1969). The list of water and power development projected to optimize the well-being of Willamette Valley residents was substantial.

However, a shift had taken place in the variety of *public* interests to be served by water development. In the seven year period between the creation of the Willamette Basin Task Force in 1963 and the presentation of the plan to the public on May 20, 1970, considerable change had occurred in the interests of Valley residents and in the rules for evaluating water development.

When the task force was created, Senate Document 97 was the guide for evaluating water developments (U.S. Congress, 1962). It listed 10 primary benefit categories. The organization of the Willamette Basin Task Force report was to provide a separate appendix for each benefit category.

Federal legislation requiring environmental impact statements passed in 1969. The basis for water development evaluation was in the process of expansion to include regional economic development and environmental quality considerations. The Willamette Basin Task Force Plan was obviously prepared to meet the old requirements of Senate Document 97.

Emergence of several new environmental organizations was an indicator of change in the nature of public interest and support for water development projects. A Willamette Valley Project Committee, created by Governor Martin in 1935, had initially worked closely with the State Planning Board. When created, the committee did represent the public interest in the Valley and helped make Congress aware of the desire of Valley residents to benefit from the development of flood control works. In cooperation with the State Planning Board, the committee helped formulate a plan in 1937 for flood protection, known as House Document 544 (U.S. Congress, 1938). To implement the plan the State Legislature created the Willamette River Basin Commission, a state agency, to work with the Willamette Valley Project Committee in securing federal funds for major water development projects.

Yearly reports of the commission identified the success measure of securing federal appropriations for water development in the areas of flood control, bank protection, drainage, pollution abatement, navigation, irrigation, recreation, fish and wildlife maintenance, and power generation. When the commission was terminated in 1955 and the State Water Resources Board created in its place, the commission had won Congressional appropriations of $180,000,000 with a state expenditure of less than $90,000 (Oregon, 1956, p. 47).

During the entire period 1935 to 1970 the Willamette Valley Project Committee was the principle liaison between the water development agencies and the public. The same committee, called the Willamette Basin Project Committee, was the basis for public contact for the Willamette Basin Task Force study. However, the committee was no longer representative of the special interests in the basin. In 1963, when the Willamette Basin Task Force study was begun, the committee was composed of representatives from small communities who were interested in securing a water development project in their area. There was not a broad representation of labor, business, industry, and environmental interests.

The potential problem was identified by a spokesman for the League of Women Voters when she stated:

> We feel it is vital for local citizens groups and community organizations to be brought into planning at an early stage with continuing access to thinking as it develops and the right to comment. By this means, public acceptance and support of development projects is more readily achieved and decisions are made possible between alternative choices, not variations of a single plan (U.S. Army Engineers District, 1963, p. 282).

The recommendation was appropriate; however, no public hearings were held after 1963 except for a report in 1968 to the Willamette Basin Project Committee. At the time of the unveiling of the project report on May 20, 1970, there was increased concern with the environment. This was less than one month after Earth Week, a rite that intensified public concern for the environment. During this period urban and suburban-oriented concern for the environment manifested itself in environmental groups (surveys conducted by the Dept. of Anthropology and Harris, 1970).

New environmentally oriented organizations were being formed. Citizens for a Clean Environment, the Marys Peak Chapter of the Sierra Club, and the Oregon Environmental Council were three who worked through 1970, '71, and '72 to stop construction of Cascadia Dam on the South Santiam River, a tributary of the Willamette. The contention of the environmentalists was that the highest and best use of the South Santiam was as a free flowing stream. They contended that the flood control benefits were over enumerated, that flood plain zoning had already provided sufficient protection, and that there was strong public sentiment for no development on the South Santiam.

In May, 1970, it was clear that the basin developers were out of touch with the variety of self-interests they euphemistically labeled the *public interest*. The Willamette Basin Project Committee was no longer representative of the public interest. When confronted with the challenge of not involving the public, some of the developers asked, "How do we get input from others while the planning is going on? How do you get people to make an input into something like this?" The old pattern of using the Willamette Basin Project Committee as the link with the public no longer worked. This committee represented only those who wanted projects to serve their local self-interests.

All the blame did not rest with the basin developers. The public, too, bore some of the blame as the closing sentence of the League statement indicated: "As part of the 'public,' League will watch with interest the outcome of your study" (U.S. Army Engineers District, 1963, p. 282). The key words were the willingness to "watch" and accepting the fact that it was "your" study. Only when citizens' groups, acting in accordance with their self-interests, asked to be involved did the Corps, the Bureau, the Soil Conservation Service, and the other water developers begin to contemplate new planning procedures to make this public involvement possible.

## SELF-INTEREST GROUPS

Influencing action as reflected in the behaviors of George H. Maxwell, B. A. Fowler, Arthur P. Davis, and Judge Joseph H. Kibbey in the Salt River Valley and the personally dedicated environmentalists of Citizens for a Clean Environment, the Marys Peak Chapter of the Sierra Club, and the Oregon Environmental Council took more than just emotionally committed self-interest. Influencing action meant welding the force of commitment into self-interest groups who could influence action. Emotionally committed self-interest provided the impetus to act and to overcome the reasons for not acting. Yet the enthusiasm of the activists had to be directed to influencing action, and the self-interest group was a mechanism for accomplishing this end.

Self-interest groups are organized by people who first recognized a problem and second accepted the responsibility for dealing with that problem. The structure of a self-interest group consists of three major roles (Figure 1). First, there are a small group of activists. The activists are the people most strongly committed to the goals of the group and are the principle implementors of action. These are the B. A. Fowlers, George H. Maxwells, etc. The

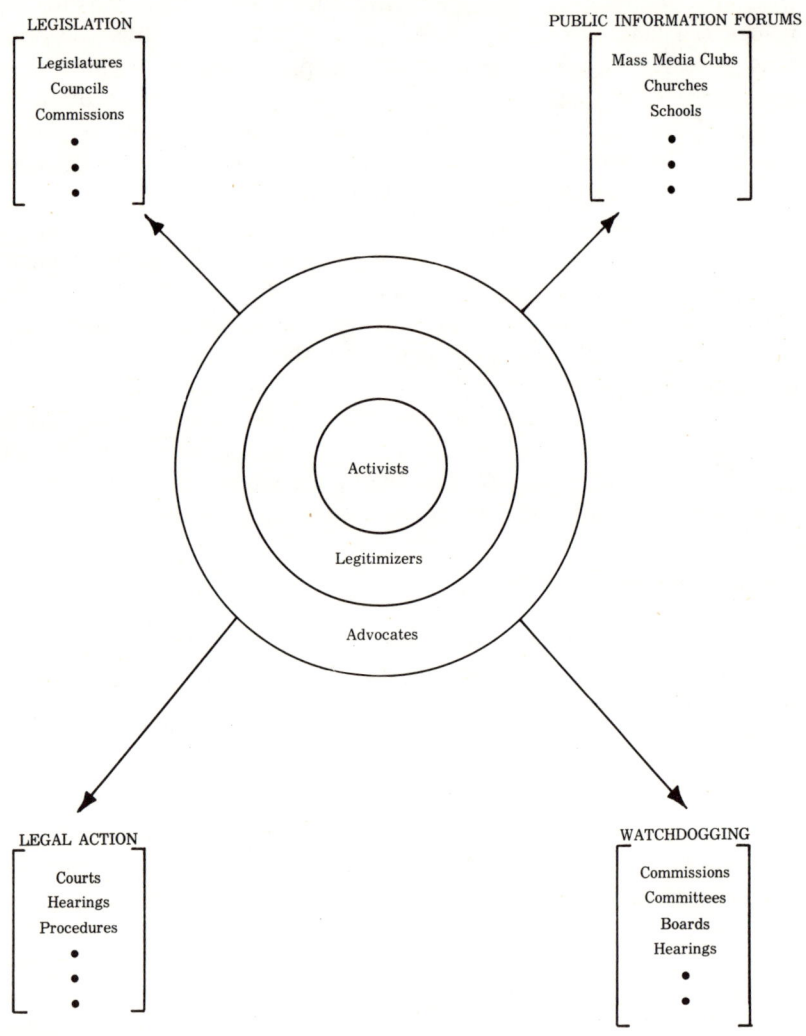

*Figure 1.* Self-interest group structure and action.

number of those committed to action to achieve a goal in spite of the personal costs is very small compared with the total membership of the self-interest group. For most newly formed groups the activists number 5-10 people. These are the ones who plan, organize, and carry out activities in the name of the group. These individuals accept the personal sacrifices of working for very little or no remuneration; they commit their time to organize and carry out the activities of the group; they provide the enthusiasm to keep the group going in spite of apathy, criticism, and obstacles. Without a core of activists no self-interest group could persist. They are highly motivated and committed people, giving freely of their time, energy, and resources for the success of the group's projects.

The next level of involvement is the legitimizers. This group is about three times larger than the group of activists and usually includes all the activisits. The legitimizers constituted a policy-making body.

In the Salt River Valley the legitimizers were representatives from each of the privately operated canals. They included local businessmen, bankers, developers, etc. who were respected citizens of the community. The legitimizers for the environmentalist groups were sought from a broad spectrum of the community to include logger and longshoreman as well as lawyer and landscape architect. Legitimizers are people whose roles are identifiable with the public at large and people whose roles add prestige to the positions advocated by the group.

If a single legitimizer loses interest in the activities of the organization, it is not as critical as when an activist drops out. The legitimizers made up a policy-making body. Because of this, their recognition in the community is often considered as a requisite for selection.

New members to the group of legitimizers are usually selected by the existing group on the theory that they do not want the organization to be infiltrated by members of groups with competing self-interests. In order for the legitimizers to be active, they are often divided into special committees which reflect the self-interests of each individual.

The third group is the largest—the advocates. This group usually numbers from a few to several hundred times larger than the group of legitimizers. The advocates are those who support the activities of the group enough to contribute, at the very least, dues and their name. The advocates, who are not activists or legitimizers, seldom became involved in the group's programs. Their primary support is financial and numerical (they lend the weight of numbers to the positions worked out by the activists and legitimizers). For example, the Oregon Environmental Council had a membership in 1972 of 1,800 advocates, a board of 30 legitimizers, and a core of 8 or 10 highly motivated activists. In the Salt River Valley the advocates identified themselves by signing their land to the Salt River Project, the legitimizers were farmers and businessmen who made up the Phoenix and Maricopa County Board of Trade, Water Storage Committee, and the activists were people like B. A. Fowler who followed through on the activities of the group.

If it is politically active, a group may develop procedures to get expressions of support from some of the advocates. When evidence of public support for a particular position was required advocates were solicited to telephone, telegram, or write the appropriate legislator, commissioner, or councilman. However, for the most part, the role of advocate was passive rather than active.

## COMPARISONS

Contrasting the two cases of the Salt River and the Willamette Valley water development shows different self-interest groups, both composed of activists, legitimizers, and advocates. In both cases public information, information to legislators and congressmen, and stirring up the community were the actions the activists promulgated. These actions were sanctioned by the legitimizers and supported in name and by contributions of name or money by the advocates.

Naturally where there are advocates, there are also derogates; people also acting on the basis of emotionally committed self-interest for the goals they believe to be right. Only the retrospect of history casts B. A. Fowler in the role of advocate and Dwight B. Heard in the role of derogate. The Salt River Project has been judged by many to be successful. The Tempe farmers later joined the association and thus, from the position of an observer examining the development of the Salt River Valley, Heard's actions were those of a derogate. B. A. Fowler, testifying before a Senate committee, summed up the opposition of the derogates:

> ... reasons for not wishing to join the association were ... fear that the association would usurp local control of the water; and such personality

constraints as ignorance, selfishness, and resistance to change (Fowler, 1904, pp. 141-142).

In the Willamette Valley the Western Environmental Trade Association and the State Water Resources Board derogated the environmentalists who were attempting to scuttle the massive water development plan proposed by the Willamette Basin Task Force.

> For some unexplainable reason the advocates of the free enterprise system, business and labor have not been able to convince these radicals, these pessimists, their friends in government and their cheerleaders within the national media, that the only real progress made toward any ideal environment has been made by this country; and only by that segment which is being punished for making a profit—the free enterprise system (Western Environmental Trade Assoc., 1971).
>
> A matter of even more immediate concern, to the State of Oregon, is what appears to be blind opposition to construction of Federal projects . . . (Oregon, 1972).

The environmentalists were advocating that slowing down of the water development movement would be better community adaptation. In the Salt River Valley 70 years before, growth was the emphasis for community adaptation. In the Willamette Valley growth was being called into question. The environmentalists did not agree with the spokesmen from business and labor that man was the best manager of nature, that population and economic growth were desirable, that multiple purpose management was always better than letting nature take its course, and that development always increased the quantity of resources available to man. Surveys made in the Willamette Valley between 1968 and 1972 showed a strong and growing antidevelopment sentiment among Valley residents.

For two of these surveys in a small community and a suburban area I analyzed the attributes of the antidevelopmentalist group. On the variables age, sex, occupation, and length of residence there were no significant differences between those favoring and those disfavoring population growth. With higher levels of education there was a tendency, although not significant, for people to oppose population growth. The only variable for which there was significant difference between those favoring and those disfavoring growth was on whether they had thought about solutions to the environmental problems. Those who had thought about solutions were more likely to disfavor population growth (Table I).

There were other indicators of public sentiment. Voting behavior

## Table I
### Attitudes Toward Solutions and Growth

| Attitude Toward Growth | Considered Solutions (%) | Did Not Consider Solutions (%) |
|---|---|---|
| Strongly favor population growth in community n = 22 | 19 | 81 |
| Neutral about population growth in community n = 40 | 36 | 64 |
| Strongly disfavor population growth in community n = 42 | 57 | 43 |
| ($p < 0.05$) | | |

was one. In the Salt River Valley the electorate voted to bond the assets of Maricopa County in order to get water storage. The Willamette Valley electorate strongly supported water pollution control bonds and a scenic waterways proposal in the 1970 primary and general elections, respectively. This voting behavior was an indicator to decision-makers of public sentiment regarding water development.

In both cases the derogates pointed to the outsiders among the advocates. Arthur P. Davis was with the Geological Survey and George H. Maxwell was from the National Reclamation Association. Neither were residents of the Salt River Valley. At a public hearing to consider scenic waterways status for the South Santiam River the mayor of Sweet Home, the town closest to the river said:

> The group which is advocating the designation is made up almost entirely of persons who live outside Linn County and it gets impetus from a national organization which has reached a decision without understanding the facts of the situation (Oregon, 1971, p. 10).

A local resident was more colorful in his characterization:

> ... we are being victimized by a bunch of professional protesters that I would easily describe by—kind of like my dog, "Bennybone." He is not a college man or anything like that but he's pretty slippery and he's pretty smart. Now when I turn him out for his dirty work, he don't go next door; he don't go across the street; he don't even go in the neighborhood; he goes out of the neighborhood; and he is pretty well thought about around home (Oregon, 1971).

# WATER DEVELOPMENT AND HUMAN RESPONSE 163

Ridicule, personal criticism, and appeals for a rational and unemotional approach were some of the social sanctions used to mitigate the actions of those advocating new forms of community adaptation to water. Yet the outsider, someone with different perspectives, was a key element in the change process.

Being a derogate does not mean that the emotionally committed self-interest was any less, or that the self-interest group was not well organized. In the opinion of the observer, the advocate-derogate distinction merely indicates whose actions are regarded as promoting community adaptation and whose actions are regarded as inhibiting it. Implied in the way I have presented these data is that it was better for community adaptation to advocate the Salt River Project at the turn of the twentieth century, and it was better for community adaptation some 70 years later to advocate slowing of water development in the Willamette Valley. I could have assigned the advocate role to those opposed to the Salt River Project on the grounds that their water rights would be adversely affected and to those who proposed that more water resource development was what was needed in the Willamette Valley. This serves to emphasize the nature of emotionally committed self-interest. To some it will be viewed as a good and useful force. To others it will be viewed as a bad and misguided force (Smith, 1973a and 1974).

In discussing advocates and derogates, however, the terms are assigned, I have tended to overemphasize action and activism. In both the Salt River Valley and the Willamette Valley citizen apathy was a problem activists and self-interest groups had to confront. The National Reclamation Service almost abandoned the Salt River Project because of lack of support. After nine months of discussing the project and attempting to convince the people of the Salt River Valley of the need to commit their land, there was still insufficient public participation. The federal government was considering withdrawing authorization of the project, or at least it took this kind of a threat, more speeches by backers of the project, and considerable personal effort on the part of B. A. Fowler to get 60 per cent of the land eligible for the project signed. In the Willamette Valley, the Oregon Environmental Council's membership was less than 1 per cent of the state's population. Citizens for a Clean Environment was a local community organization, as was the Marys Peak Chapter of Sierra Club. In each of the councils discussion of public apathy was not uncommon.

These examples illustrate that small numbers of emotionally

committed individuals, organized into self-interest groups, can have an impact on decision-making. In this endeavor they not only have to contend with advocates of other positions but with the absence of public participation as well. (In certain situations the absence of public participation can work to the advantage of self-interest groups.)

## ADAPTATION

Of what value is self-interest and emotional commitment for human adaptation? All animals adjust to their environment by organic means of adaptation. This may be genetic change or by the plasticity of the animal. Social organization, too, is a common adaptive mechanism used by many populations of animals. I am emphasizing that self-interest, energized by emotional commitment, is another important adaptive mechanism (Darwin, 1897; Hamburg, 1963; Lund, 1930; Plutchik, 1970).

The primary value of self-interest is in the rate at which changes can be made. Clearly man is an animal who can manipulate his environment. The water development programs of the Salt River and Willamette Valley demonstrate this. Self-interest, energized by emotional commitment, both stimulated and retarded these environmental management programs.

Self-interest has the potential, then, for stimulating change in man's relation with his environment more rapidly than genetic change, which is a process occurring over generations, and more rapidly than changes in social organization, which from experience are known very often to be slow. Self-interest, energized by emotional commitment, has the potential for rapid change *vis a vis* the relations people have with their environment. It, too, can be a retardant to change, thus mitigating the quickness of response, and possibly preventing detrimental changes.

I am not suggesting self-interest as a panacea. I am merely identifying it as an important mechanism in human adaptation. It, along with genetic change and social organization, is one of the many adaptive mechanisms available to man.

Self-interest, like genetic change, can lead to the detrimental mutants of greed, lust, exploitation of others, narrow vision, uncooperativeness, irrational action, and many of the other commonly identified frailties of man. Self-interest is one feature of human adaptation; it is not necessarily good or bad, but it manifests itself as both. As with emotionalism, what is good and what is bad are relative to the ideology of the observer.

This diversifying feature of self-interest is one of its important adaptive attributes. Self-interest maintains populations accepting a variety of different ideologies. Environmental decision-makers were faced with the problems of charting a course between a variety of competing extremes regarding human and natural resource ideologies. My research findings are that those individuals and groups acting in accordance with their own self-interests were critical to this process. These people organized themselves to change decisions when they perceived the course to be wrongly charted. In doing this they were energized by emotional commitment to support a set of ideas they accepted as true.

How does mankind chart the course for choosing between the conflicting ideologies? These case studies of environmental decision-making suggest that separate groups of individuals, each charting a somewhat different course and each with access to the system for influencing action, helped in deciding the way the community evaluated and worked out its adaptation with the environment.

**IMPLICATIONS**

Nothing can be proved from two case studies. However, perhaps ideas about the nature of human adaptation can be modified and supplanted with new hypotheses for testing, new hypotheses which emphasize inclusion of new variables. I am suggesting that emotionally committed self-interest is a force in community adaptation. Indicators of emotionally committed self-interest are unique levels of commitment of personal resources and actions which seem difficult in the face of public sentiment or apathy. Through the creation of self-interest groups the force of emotional commitment is directed to influencing decision-making and action.

Several questions should be given further attention. Can there be too much or too little emotionally committed self-interest? This was the hypothesis advanced by the Western Environmental Trade Association when they questioned the "irrational, irresponsible, fanatic environmentalist." Too little emotional commitment would be illustrated by public apathy. Why were the Salt River Valley landowners so slow to commit their land? Why were only 1 per cent of Oregon's population members of environmentalist groups when majorities were passing local bond issues for water cleanup, passing bonding authority for pollution control, and passing a scenic waterways act?

Are there forces in the society that can dull or stimulate the expressions of emotionally committed self-interest? I would expect that situations of abundance and severe deprivation might have these affects. Should emotionally committed self-interest and the groups that result from this self-interest be limited or controlled? Environmentalists were criticized by many for being emotional in their statements before decision-making bodies. Many decision-makers argued for pursuit of an unemotional and rational approach to decisions. Emotionalism did get people's attention. It did energize a force for change in the water development policies in both the Salt River Valley and in the Willamette Valley. Assuming a well-informed electorate, is this sufficient control?

In my mind these are important questions about the process of human adaptation. New technologies may be scientifically justified and validated, but new technologies must also stand the tests of human experience and the verification of social and ideological processes as yet incompletely known. I am suggesting that emotionally committed self-interest, organized into self-interest groups, is an important force that stimulates people to act to change the direction of policies when such a position is not popular, and it is part of a process that modifies the utilization of technology. Only retrospect can assign the advocates and the derogates, and even this depends on the ideology of the observer. Self-interest, energized by emotional commitment, brought to bear on policy decisions through action oriented self-interest groups, is a process basic to human adaptation and is a process in need of more careful scientific scrutiny.

## ACKNOWLEDGMENT

The research upon which this paper is based was supported, in part, by the Office of Water Resources Research, U.S. Department of the Interior as authorized by the Water Resources Research Act of 1964. In preparing this paper, I have benefited from the comments of William H. Buckley, John A. Dunn, Thomas C. Hogg, and R. Bruce Shepard.

## REFERENCES

Clark, V. "History of the Salt River Valley Water Users' Association," typewritten manuscript (Phoenix: 1936).

Darwin, C. *The Expression of Emotions in Man and Animals* (New York: D. Appleton and Co., 1897).

Fowler, B. "Salt River Valley Water Users' Association," U.S. Geograhpical Survey Water Supply and Irrigation Paper No. 93, F. Newell, Compiler (Washington: G.P.O., 1904).

Hamburg, D. "Emotions in Perspective of Human Evaluation," P. Knapp, Ed. *Expressions of The Emotions in Man*, (New York: International Universities Press, Inc., 1963).

Harris, L. and Associates, Inc. "The Public's View of Environmental Problems in The State of Oregon," Study No. 1990 for Pacific Northwest Bell Telephone Co. (Portland, 1970).

Lund, F. *Emotions of Man* (New York: Whittlesey House, 1930).

Moore, H. "The Salt River Project, an Illustrious Chapter in U.S. Reclamation," *Arizona Highways*, 37:2-15 (1961).

Oregon. State Highways Division, "Scenic Waterways," Hearing at Sweet Home, Salem (Nov. 17, 1971).

Oregon. Water Resources Board, *Newsletter* 3:1 (1972).

Oregon. Willamette River Basin Commission, *Biennial Report No. 6*, Salem (1956).

Plutchik, R. "Emotions, Evaluation, and Adaptive Processes," M. Arnold, Ed., *Feelings and Emotions* (New York: Academic Press, 1970).

Shadegg, S. "The Phoenix Story, An Adventure in Reclamation," Phoenix, Salt River Project (1958).

Smith, C. "Transfer of Cultural Values: Problems for Arid Areas," C. Hodge and C. Hodges, Eds. *Urbanization in The Arid Lands* (Lublock: Texas Technological College, 1974).

Smith, C. "Differential Participation as a Criterion for Evaluating Development Decisions," *Human Organization,* 32(2): 177-183 (1973a).

Smith, C. "Public Participation in Willamette Valley Environmental Decisions," Water Resources Research Institute, Publication No. 15 (Corvallis: Oregon State University, 1973b).

Smith, C. *The Salt River Project: A Case Study in Cultural Adaptation to an Urbanizing Community* (Tucson: University of Arizona Press, 1972).

U.S. Army Corps of Engineers. "Water Resources Development by U.S. Army Corps of Engineers in Oregon," Portland, North Pacific Division (1971).

U.S. Army Engineers District, Portland. "Willamette Basin Review," Transcript of Public Hearing: Eugene, McMinnville, Albany and Oregon City (1963).

U.S. Congress. House. "Willamette River and Tributaries, Oregon," House Document 544, 75th Congress, 3rd Session (Washington: G.P.O., 1938).

U.S. Congress. House. "Columbia River and Tributaries, Northwestern United States, Appendix J.," Willamette River Basin (Washington: G.P.O., 1950).

U.S. Congress. Senate. "Policies, Standards, and Procedures in the Formulation, Evaluation, and Review of Plans for Use and Development of Water and Related Land Resources," Senate Document No. 97, 87th Congress, 2nd Session (Washington: G.P.O., 1962).

Western Environmental Trade Association. "Remarks of Edward J. Whelan," McMinnville (1971).

Willamette Basin Task Force. "The Willamette Basin Comprehensive Study of Water and Related Land Resources and Appendices." Vancouver, Pacific Northwest River Basins Commission (1969).

# 9. An Analysis of Community and Individual Reactions to Forced Migration Due To Reservoir Construction

### SUE JOHNSON AND RABEL J. BURDGE

—to reveal the human meaning of public issues
by relating them to personal troubles (Mills, 1973)

"There ought to be a law to make some men wear a black fur coat with a white stripe down the back." So said Miss Babe Williams, 75, of Paducah, Kentucky, about the Army Corps of Engineers who bulldozed her 135-year-old home for Barkley Dam over 15 years ago (*Courier-Journal*, 1972). She still refuses to cash their check for $6400 because "They didn't have any right to take my home, and by accepting the money I would be agreeing that they did have." When she was evicted from her home and 60 acres in 1958 she had ten thousand dollars in the bank. "I don't have anything now, except this old house, some second-hand furniture, and a few clothes." Social Security pays her about sixty dollars a month. The old house she now occupies in Paducah was condemned by a city building inspection in January, 1968, yet no serious effort has been made to move her. Neighbors bring her fresh water for drinking, cooking and bathing. When she feels "homesick," she lives in an even more decrepit house near her old home, in full view of Barkley Dam. She wants the government to buy this old house for her and fix it up so she can spend the rest of her life near her childhood home. This is one woman's adjustment to forced change in the form of reservoir development.

## THEORETICAL BACKGROUND

Utilizing data from four reservoir studies, the authors of this paper attempt to follow Mills' imperative of revealing the human meaning behind public policy. This revelation of human meaning, as described here, opens a veritable Pandora's box of personal difficulties. In some cases, the policy of eminent domain has uprooted the central cognitive and social foundations of affected individuals. Some families have been spread over several counties when they used to live in one "holler." The paper shows the suffering some people endure for the "greater good of the community" or the region, while gaining little or nothing for themselves.

We have let these people speak for themselves where possible, and have purposely focused on the negative aspects of forced migration. These personal and community changes are seldom included in cost-benefit analyses; for that matter, the plight of these migrants is seldom the topic of systematic research for social scientists. This investigation reports one of the first such studies, describing longitudinally the process of relocation from the first warning of impending migration to settlement in new homes, although the data is taken from four separate studies at four points in the migration process. In addition to personal interviews, secondary data from Kentucky newspapers supplements the discussion.

Before migration, the interaction during migration and the adjustment to the new location are the topics around which this paper is organized. Although the paper is not intended to be theoretical, the underlying assumption is that we have described the clash of agents representing two alien social processes; those seeking to impose change and those passively or actively seeking to resist such change. It is a clash between the bureaucratic, efficiency-minded, goal-oriented behavior of the Army Corps of Engineers and the traditional, isolated mountain culture of Appalachia. From the affected migrant's point of view, it is almost as if the Corps used a literal interpretation of Al Capp's portrayal of Lil' Abner as their guide to interacting with the mountain culture.

## PEOPLE WHO HAVE TO MOVE: BEFORE RELOCATION

### The Location

The major group of people who pay when reservoirs are constructed, and pay most heavily if the subjective costs are added to the objective ones, are those who have to move. Since reservoirs are usually constructed in fairly isolated rural areas, those who must vacate their land and homes are not a representative cross section of the country's population. They are often mountain people, or plain rural people who are older than the population at large, and who form a distinct subculture. They fall in the lower socio-economic status brackets; some are subsistence farmers. It is almost as if they stepped out of the past. Their values are person-centered, traditional, fatalistic and familistic (Becker and Burdge, 1971). Sociologists often call them "laggards" and see them as stumbling blocks to reservoir construction and watershed programs. "Laggards" tend to have small farms, low incomes, relatively little formal education, and are tradition-directed (Rogers and Shoemaker, 1971). Findings concerning negative attitudes toward water resource construction are usually reported as the converse to positive correlations. Other than standard structural variables, no extensive research has been reported regarding the reasons for negative attitudes toward water resource construction.

**Knowledge of the Project**

Lack of knowledge is also thought to be a factor in negative attitudes toward water resource development. An interesting case concerning a reservoir is currently causing a furor in Paintsville, Kentucky. Many of those most vocal in opposing the project, technically in the construction phase, have the characteristics just described. What is fascinating is that knowledge about the project seems to be engendering negative attitudes rather than positive ones. Burdge and Ludtke (1970) found in their study of the Taylorsville reservoir, that although previous studies on watershed development predicted that knowledge of the project had a positive effect on attitudes, when persons are totally affected by being displaced, knowledge is not an important consideration. In fact, they suggest that under the conditions of involuntary and unwanted migration knowledge does little or nothing to ameliorate people's attitudes or to facilitate ease in moving. It is particularly important in light of the Corps' supposition that their public information policy of telling people why, when, and how they are to move will yield positive attitudes toward the move. Possibly, the more people know, and the more they interact with the Corps, the more negative their attitudes become.

## Awareness of the Project

A random cluster sample of respondents was interviewed in Paintsville and surrounding Johnson county during the summer of 1970. Very little awareness of the impending project was found. Even among urban Paintsville residents recognition of the impending project was poor. However, over three-quarters of the county residents were in favor of the proposed reservoir (Korsching, 1972; Becker, 1971). However, this past spring 1200 residents in the Paint Creek Valley signed a petition opposing the dam. This represents almost 95 per cent of the valley's inhabitants of whom 250 must move if the reservoir is built.

## Attitude Toward Reservoir Development

The questionnaire included information on attitudes towards reservoirs. Table I shows the distribution of responses, largely positive. Only items five, six and eight show negative majorities. However, if one looks closely, the scale items, though valid, are subject to bias in the responses. Items five, six and eight were the only ones scored backwards, yet the majority responses fall in the same "disagree" point on all the items. In spite of the apparent lack of reliability in terms of responses, the Spearman-Brown coefficient of reliability is 0.75 for all eight items, and 0.83 for items 1, 4, 5, 7, and 8. It is possible, of course, that the population is "schizoid" in its responses, but another explanation seems more plausible.

From a phenomenological point of view, it can be argued that this is a highly acquiescent population; it is interesting to speculate as to why. It is our guess, based on knowledge of the community, that because the people were not aware of the reservoir, their responses were disinterested. They said what they thought the interviewer wanted to hear. Moreover, there were 20 people in this random sample whose land was directly affected. When we compared their scores on the reservoir scale with the means of the rest, there was no significant difference, indicating that they too had little awareness of the proposed reservoir. Whether the community was ambivalent in 1970 or just unaware, the situation has definitely changed.

Informal evidence was found in a recent newspaper article regarding the attitude of the affected population towards the dam (*Courier-Journal*, 1973).

## Table I
Responses to Reservoir Development Scale Responses
(Paintsville Reservoir, Johnson County, Kentucky N=400)

| Statement | Strongly Agree Per Cent** | Agree Per Cent | Undecided Per Cent | Disagree* Per Cent | Strongly Disagree Per Cent |
|---|---|---|---|---|---|
| (1) More dams are being built than are necessary for flood control. | 2 | 10 | 15 | 69 | 4 |
| (2) Money spent on building reservoirs exceeds the benefits we get from them. | 2 | 20 | 23 | 53 | 2 |
| (3) Reservoir construction often floods land that is worth more than the land it protects. | 2 | 24 | 25 | 46 | 3 |
| (4) Reservoirs should only be constructed when they won't take people's homes or good farm land. | 4 | 37 | 11 | 46 | 2 |
| (5) Flood control projects always help more people than they hurt. | 1 | 11 | 13 | 71 | 4 |
| (6) Fish and wildlife development alone provide reasons for reservoir construction. | 0 | 19 | 17 | 61 | 3 |
| (7) Since floods only occur once in a while, it is foolish to give up good land for reservoir construction. | 0 | 17 | 11 | 66 | 6 |
| (8) Reservoir construction is a good investment for reducing flood losses in the long run. | 0 | 3 | 9 | 83 | 5 |

*Response-set items.
**All per cents rounded to the nearest whole number for purposes of clarity.

Local people have two major complaints about the dam. The first is that the Corps tends to buy land on a hilltop-to-hilltop basis in the valley to create a "buffer zone," taking much more land than will be actually affected by dam construction and resultant lake and recreation sites. The second complaint (perhaps more interesting) is that the public feels that until last April it was inadequately informed about specific details of the proposed Paintsville reservoir.

The first public hearings about the desirability of the proposed dam were held the day President Kennedy was assassinated, and were abruptly adjourned when that event became known. However, a former Morgan County sheriff who attended this meeting says, "There never were any dams mentioned—period." The Corps called another meeting in December, 1963, when the overall plan was discussed. The Corps forgot to notify the major newspaper in Morgan County of the second meeting, and Morgan County too is affected by the Paintsville Dam. Consequently the residents say the first time they were aware of the project was April of 1973. The Corps plans no further meetings with landowners, which means the next time they see the Corps, it will be taking their land. A land acquisition office has been established in Paintsville and the initial acquisition proceedings have begun.

Reading the newspaper article, one is struck by the characteristics of the affected Paintsville residents. Their ages are from 60 to 80. Many farmlands are in the hands of direct descendants of the original settlers, and unusual in this area, many are self-sustaining. The people speak of "being friends and neighbors for over 34 years," of "farming this valley all my life," and one lady who runs the general store in Relief, Kentucky, says "I haven't the faintest idea where I'd go." "I was a Hamilton and this land was originally homesteaded by Hamiltons," says another woman of her farm that would be flooded. An old man, 69, says "Of course, I'm not able to work much, but I hate to be run over and run off."

Perhaps the whole hypothesis that knowledge of a water project tends to engender positive attitudes should be amended with the qualification that *if* knowledge of the project leads to a realization of potential personal benefits, then forced migrants tend to have positive attitudes toward water resource construction. A suggested corollary hypothesis would be: if knowledge of the project does not lead to the realization of potential benefit, then knowledge will engender negative attitudes. Burdge and Ludtke (1970) found that those who felt they would benefit from the Taylorsville dam were not so apprehensive about moving and were willing to undergo major life changes. Those who most feared having to move, to whom knowledge of the project made no difference, were those who strongly identified with their present homes and land.

**Premigration Stress**

In an anthropological study of the Taylorsville reservoir site, Smith (1970) found that those waiting to move were subject to considerable stress and anxiety. For all practical purposes, it was as if they were already mourning the loss of their homes, their familiar lives, and their friends even before they moved. In addition, they are victims of bureaucratic foot-dragging because they still have not moved.

Mr. and Mrs. Harper (data-based hypothetical constructs) have lived all their lives in Van Burean, Kentucky, which is in the take line for the Taylorsville reservoir. The house and land has been in the Harper family for over a hundred years. They are in their early sixties, and have a nice garden that keeps them busy since Mr. Harper retired as a truck-driver several years ago. They live on about $200 a month, and they make ends meet by canning and freezing vegetables and fruit from their garden and splitting a beef with their next-door neighbor every fall.

When the news was released in 1961 about the proposed reservoir, Van Burean was a town of 70 people with a school, two churches, four stores, one bank and a few other services. To date (May 1973) the Army Corps has not even started land acquisition procedures, so Mr. and Mrs. Harper are still waiting to be told when they have to move.

The news that they would have to leave their beloved home struck the Harpers quite hard. They quit planting new fruit trees since their land would eventually be flooded, and every spring they worried whether they'd get to harvest their garden or not. Their house deteriorated because, after all, what's the use of fixing up a hundred-year-old house that's going to be destroyed? The front porch has practically fallen off, and Mr. Harper sprained his ankle badly one day when the edge crumbled and he fell to the ground. All the stores have closed, except for a tiny grocery; Van Burean looks like a ghost town, except the people are still in it. Gasoline is available in the nearest town, seven miles away down a deteriorating road, as are groceries and other goods. Mr. Harper refuses to buy a new car until he sees how much the move is going to cost him. Their 1955 Chevy which still runs fitfully, takes them to town when they need to go. If it quits their neighbors will have to take care of them.

The "causers of change" are unaware or unsympathetic to the plight of people like the Harpers. These older people wait like criminals who are to be banished, not knowing when. Mr. Harper says "Ida's headaches are worse every year, and I know it's because she don't want to move." He also wishes the Corps would just go away and leave them in peace, let him fix up his house and orchard, and live out the rest of their lives there. Many old people like the Harpers fear change—they don't want to move, and they don't want to change their lives. The older people get, the less flexible they usually are, and the harder it is for them to adjust to change, especially forced change. It would have been more merciful to move them immediately than to leave them lingering under the stress of uncertainty.

**Attachment to Place**

The mean age of those having to move from the Cave Run reservoir site in Eastern Kentucky was 58, modal education was eighth grade and mean total income was $4031 per year. Those having to move in the Carr Fork reservoir area had a mean age of 56 for males and 53 for females with modal education of eighth grade, and mean income of almost $5000 per year.

Freeway construction, which tends to run through slums, and urban renewal, which forces poor residents to move, have similar consequences. A recent study done of urban slum dwellers slated for relocation due to urban renewal shows basic residential stability among them, and that they see their slums as "home" (Fried and Gleicher, 1972). It is more the "neighborhood" and its attendant lifestyle they perceive as "home," since only 13 per cent say their attachment is an irreplaceable tie to specific people and places. This is even more true for rural dwellers forced to relocate. Burdge and Ludkte (1970) found over half so strongly attached to their place of residence that it was the "only place I can call home." But we cannot understand the true costs of having to move unless we understand the strength of attachments not only to places but to neighbors, ways of life and pace of doing things. All this is disrupted when forced migration occurs. The mountaineer lives a life based on personal, individualistic, familistic relationships to the environment around him. The loss of this personal identification can have catastrophic results. The magnitude of the problem can be better understood when we think of our own lives. Moving causes disruptions even when we want to move. How much greater must the disruption be when giving up a precious old house in which one has lived many years, tilling its gardens and reaping the harvests of its fields.

## PEOPLE WHO HAVE TO MOVE: THE PROCESS OF RELOCATION

### Land Negotiations

Given the law of eminent domain, people are sometimes forced to move even if they do not want to. In view of Miss Williams' and others tenacious and negative responses, it would be reasonable to expect public agencies to do their best to help forced migrants find new homes. Data from the Carr Fork reservoir about the Army Corps of Engineers' behavior concerning land acquisition and help in moving, however, suggest that this is not always the case.

After sending notification that one must move, the Corps then appraises the value of the land. An offer is then tendered to the landowner. Table II shows that eighty per cent of the first offers to heads of household by the Corps were *lower than the appraised value of the properties*. These data suggest that the Corps may be minimizing acquisition costs by offering landowners less than the appraised price.

### Table II
Comparison of Initial Settlement Offered by the Corps Relative to the Appraised Value (Carr Fork Reservoir, N=200)*

|  | *Offer Lower* | *Offer Same* | *Offer Higher* | *Total* |
|---|---|---|---|---|
| Number | 100 | 6 | 18 | 124** |
| Per cent | 80.6 | 4.8 | 14.5 | 100.0 |

*This table was constructed from two sources. The value of each of the properties was copied from the Corps of Engineers files. During personal interviews, respondents indicated the initial offer tendered to them for their property by the Corps.
**No Response (21) and Not Applicable (55) excluded from the analysis.

Respondents were then asked if they accepted the first offer, and twelve (8%) did. These twelve cases were older, long-term residents of Knott County. Perhaps they were unwilling to undergo the complexities of bargaining with the Corps, or did not know they *could* bargain with the government. The mean age of those taking the first offer of the Corps is two years older than the mean age of the population for males, females, and heads of household. However, the mean is misleading in this case since half the respondents were over 60, and three taking the first offer were in their early forties, thereby lowering the mean.

Table III shows the final amount accepted for the property by the remaining landowners in relation to the appraised value. Those who took the first offer were paid less than its worth for their land. Among those who bargained with the Corps, a majority won higher prices for their land. Or as one respondent volunteered, "The smarter people got the best deal."

**Table III**
Final Amount Received for Property in Relation to Appraised Value (Carr Ford Reservoir, N=200)

|  | Lower | Same | Higher | Litigated | No Response | Not Applicable | Total |
|---|---|---|---|---|---|---|---|
| Number | 11 | 4 | 108 | 7 | 3 | 67 | 200 |
| Per cent | 5.5 | 2.0 | 54.0 | 3.5 | 1.5 | 33.5 | 100.0 |

When the staff at the University of Kentucky Law Journal studied the Cave Run Reservoir project (located near Morehead in Eastern Kentucky), they found there was a "horsetrading" mentality on the part of the Corps toward condemned property. These researchers charge that the bargaining process was an "unfair attempt to circumvent the constitutional requirement of just compensation" (Goebel, 1969-70).

Several Carr Fork respondents complained that some got fair deals and others did not: "There was no rhyme or rhythm to it," notes one, "Some got twice what it (the house and land) was worth, others got half of what their property was worth." Table IV shows how the Carr Fork sample felt about how they did compared to their neighbors. Forty-nine per cent felt they had done worse than their neighbors, and only 7 per cent felt they had done better, raising the question: who was used as a comparison point? Presumably it was the 39 per cent who felt they had done just as well as their neighbors. Also, those who did do better than their neighbors may have become a source of local gossip with attendant exaggeration.

### Table IV
Response to the Question for How Respondent Thought He/She Did in Relation to What Neighbors Received for Their Homes and Property (Carr Ford Reservoir, N=200)

|          | Not Applicable | Worse | Just as Good | Better | In Litigation | Total |
|----------|---------------|-------|--------------|--------|---------------|-------|
| Number   | 55            | 71    | 57           | 10     | 7             | 200   |
| Per cent | *             | 49    | 39           | 7      | 5             | 100   |

*Not applicable were excluded from the percentage calculation.

Of more general concern is the effect of the Corps' attitude towards condemned property and its owners on the spending of governmental funds. The Cave Run researchers point out that trying to minimize the cost to the government by offering to buy the land for less than its worth is actually quite costly to the government due to litigious delay. Only 6 per cent of the 96 surveyed in Cave Run accepted the government's initial offer, and fully 22 per cent preferred to endure a trial and gamble on a jury verdict. Their gamble was profitable: jury awards exceeded government appraisals by as much as 78 per cent in the Cave Run area. Almost 5 per cent of the Carr Fork cases were in litigation at the time of the study.

It appears from Carr Fork and corroborative data from Cave Run studies that the Corps' willingness to negotiate land prices is basically an attempt to minimize costs to government. Also, if one is unwitting enough to accept the government's initial offer, one is in all probability going to be paid less than the land is worth, less even than the Corps' own appraisal. Data from the Cave Run project suggest that persons who go to court will probably receive more money for their land.

**Moving Expense**

The Muskie Bill of 1971 states that the Army Corps of Engineers must assume all reasonable costs of moving residents from condemned locations. Although this policy was not operative at the time of the Carr Fork and Cave Run land acquisitions, Table V shows the likelihood of the Corps' paying the full costs of moving. Forty per cent of those moving were paid less than full expenses, two per cent made a small profit from the move, while a majority, 58 per cent, were adequately reimbursed. It is to the Corps'

## 180   WATER AND COMMUNITY DEVELOPMENT

credit that in most cases they adequately reimbursed the migrants for the move. However, under the new law more moving expenses will be paid.

**Table V**
Resettlement (Moving) Payments Made to Carr Ford Residents by the Army Corps of Engineers*

|          | Payment Less Than Cost | Payment More Than Cost | Payment Same As Cost | Total |
|---|---|---|---|---|
| Number   | 80 | 4 | 116 | 200 |
| Per cent | 40 | 2 | 48  | 100 |

*These data were obtained by recording the price paid to the migrants for moving from the Corps Records. The respondents were then asked how much it cost them to move. A comparison provides the data for Table V.
TABLE VI

As a check on our data we asked the respondents if the payment was adequate to cover moving expenses. As shown in Table VI, 35 per cent said it was not. This figure is surprisingly close to the 40 per cent figure shown in Table V. We have no way of knowing whether the underpayment by the Corps was a little or a lot. Nevertheless, over one-third were dissatisfied with the amount they were required to pay for a move that they did not want.

**Table VI**
Response to the Question: "Was the Corps Payment to You Adequate to Cover Your Moving Expenses?" (Carr Fork Reservoir, N=200)

|          | Yes | No | No Response | Total |
|---|---|---|---|---|
|          | 65.0 | 45.5 | 0.5 | 100.0 |
| Per cent | 65.0 | 34.5 | 0.5 | 100.0 |
| Number   | 130 | 69 | 1 | 200 |

### The Search for a New Home

When asked if the Corps actually offered to help or advise them, 51 per cent said "no" and 47 per cent "yes." The response of the 47 per cent to the open-ended question of what type of help the Corps volunteered is shown in Table VII. The respondents were most likely to receive the moving expenses as the major contributions by the Corps. Other responses included assistance with moving vans and advise on reimbursements and procedures.

**Table VII**
Kinds of Help or Advice Offered by the Corps to
Carr Fork Forced Migrants (N=98)

|  | Number | Per cent |
|---|---|---|
| Moving expenses | 78 | 80 |
| Assistance with moving vans | 5 | 5 |
| Advice on reimbursement procedures | 8 | 8 |
| Other | 3 | 3 |
| No response | 4 | 4 |
| Total | 98 | 100 |

## PEOPLE WHO HAVE TO MOVE: AFTER RELOCATION

Moving changes almost every aspect of our lives, from such mundane concerns as relocating family possessions to the more important concerns of interrupting smooth relationships with friends, relatives and immediate family. The Carr Fork migrants were asked a number of questions about how their lives changed since moving. They were asked about their plumbing as well as how their children adjusted. The categories are too numerous to discuss in depth in this paper. However, summary data gives an overall impression of how well people fared after moving.

When asked how they fared financially after relocation one-third of the respondents noted their financial situation had changed for the worse (the majority said it was due to relocation) and 22 per cent said theirs had improved. The remainder experienced no change in financial situation. For the persons whose financial condition worsened, such reasons were cited as the lack of a garden, the increase in rent or cost of homes, and the distance from their work.

When asked which social activities had changed the most upon relocation, the major answer was visiting friends who were now further away; some respondents found themselves more isolated from major roads in their new homes. Sixty per cent said they visited less with friends and 46 per cent said this was true of visits with relatives as well. Five families were split by the relocation. Many of the hollows had been filled with members of the same family, and now several respondents complained that their families were scattered all over the place, some in four different counties.

Thirty-eight per cent noted a change for the worse in family activities like picnics, drives, and shopping trips. Twenty-eight per cent noted that the family was at home less frequently. Fully *fifty-five* per cent said the relocation change was for the "worse" overall, compared to twenty per cent who said it was for the better. Nineteen per cent said they had not adjusted well at all to the move. When asked what had changed the most one woman replied, "My home life. We began having trouble when we had to find a place to go." The couple is now getting a divorce. Others complained about the debts they took on when they were forced to move and find a new place.

Of the 77 families that had children, 27 per cent said their children had fewer recreational opportunities than before, and 25 per cent said their children were not as happy as before.

Of those having to change employment (N = 30), 80 per cent said they were not paid enough to look for a new job. Two respondents were offered help by the Corps in job retraining, and 32 said they would have found that kind of aid useful. Twelve found themselves unemployed after relocation.

Of the 110 families or single people who had a garden before relocation, 40 per cent (44) no longer had one. The role of the garden in mountain culture is a very important one, generally unknown to outsiders. Respondents often volunteered information about the loss of their gardens, even before the interview began. Knott County has a scarcity of tillable bottom land like most of the mountainous areas of Kentucky, and it appears the Corps took the most fertile land. More than half the people who bought acreage after relocation had less land, of inferior quality, and less tillable than what they previously owned. A number of respondents commented on the high cost of buying land elsewhere even if they thought they were paid fairly for their original land. A sizeable number also mentioned that their food costs had skyrocketed because they had no garden. Among these people with sparse incomes, this kind of change has a great impact.

The major consolation to most migrants was that their new homes were physically superior to their old homes. Only 18 per cent had inferior housing after moving, while 39.4 per cent had superior housing. Sixty-three per cent were satisfied with their new homes: they had better plumbing, gas as opposed to coal heating, and newer dwellings.

**CONCLUSIONS**

The major theme of this book concerns water as it relates to the community. Sometimes water and its proper use will contribute to the enhancement of community life. Our studies show that in many cases reservoirs lead to the destruction of community life. This destructiveness appears to be directly related to the number of persons who must be moved, the number of neighborhoods, towns and even cemeteries that must be relocated, and the degree to which the transportation and communication facilities are disrupted. Rural neighborhoods and communities are built around an interlocking set of social relations based on kinship and occupational similarity. These strong social relationships are rooted in ancestral lands and cemeteries. Obviously, flooding a valley branch severs the natural social linkages. The population must now go around the reservoir to be with friends and relatives. The traditional location for small communities (at least in mountainous Kentucky) has been where two valleys meet. Most of these are moved or destroyed when reservoirs are constructed. Hence, that community, like Van Burean or Relief, has vanished from the map.

These are neither the first nor the last episodes of persons being forcibly moved to make way for highways, reservoirs, airports, urban renewal and the like. Whether people have the right to refuse to be "developed" is a question full of sticky ethical issues, and it is far from being answered.

Just what have these people lost? They have newer houses than before, a little land, their same jobs, by and large, and most live in the same community. The intangibles, the immeasurables, that is, the fragile webs of community, social, and self-identity have been disrupted, and for older persons this disruption can be fatal.

The mobile mass of middle class America can in no way empathize with small community life that depends upon a strong identification with place, with stable, long-enduring patterns of social relations with friends and relatives, and with 'hollers' populated with familiar names and places. "Moving to town" is not necessarily what these people want to do; many of them just resettled into other "hollers," even if they were further from the main roads because that's where they wanted to live. They wanted to resume the same traditional patterns and daily routine guiding their former lives. However badly they wanted to keep their lives much the same as possible, our data have shown that many found adjusting to a new location very difficult.

Since the interaction with the Corps was alienating too many of these people, it is likely that whatever negative attitudes were held toward the government or reservoir construction were deepened by this contact. Many of the respondents, even those who didn't suffer unduly from moving, still thought the money ill-spent, and that it could have been used on something else, like helping poor people. This is interesting, in that part of the rationale for reservoir construction is that the economy of the area will prosper, and even the poor will benefit by better services. Several respondents were quite cynical about who would benefit—"the big guys" and tourists were frequently mentioned.

If the events we have described here concerning forced migration were an isolated instance, there would be little cause for alarm. The Army Corps has been "disciplined" lately by budget cuts and the Muskie Bill concerning relocation; however, there probably has not been a basic change in the values of the Corps or their attitudes toward those to be relocated. Moreover, a recent editorial called Kentucky, "The Corps' Happy Hunting Ground," because there are so many projects pending in the state (*Courier-Journal*, 1973). It is understandable in a sense. Kentucky has more miles of running streams than most states and is a logical place to build lots of reservoirs. Also, the political structure of the state is personalized, and being reelected depends upon cosmetic improvements rather than structural change.

The aforementioned Paintsville dam is an interesting case in point because the Corps' cost-benefit rationale for the project is heavily weighted in terms of recreational benefits, and the flood control aspect is not only minimal (six inches off peak floods at Paintsville), but the reservoir's flood-control effectiveness is dependent on the existence of ten other dams, most of which are not yet built, that empty into the Ohio River. It appears that the Corps is behaving in an opportunistic fashion to defend itself with larger and larger machinations to expand its territory and thereby its viability. What it means in human terms is that more and more people will have to be moved, with the attendant problems and pains of readjustment. There is a clear need for a more humane means of relocating people so affected.

A tragedy of cost-benefit analysis as a rationale for the construction of reservoirs is the paucity of studies that have investigated whether or not the projected benefits have ever accrued after the reservoir has been in operation. Community life is undoubtedly enhanced in some cases; for example, Lexington, Kentucky, with a safe and plentiful supply of water from the nearby Cave Run Reservoir (and proposed Red River Gorge Reservoir) can now expand its suburban development. However, it does seem to be true that the "economic development" benefit usually found in cost-benefit studies requires total resource development, and not just water (Hargrove, 1971). We think that the trend in recent years for the Corps to overestimate the value of recreational benefits may be misleading for two reasons. While the demand for recreation is growing, the economic activities of such enterprises do not often help the local population. More recreation does enhance the quality of life, but only for those who use the facility, most of whom are from the middle class. Secondly, the construction of new reservoirs will draw recreationists from existing reservoirs. Thereby, the pie of "water-based recreationists" will be cut in smaller pieces.

Perhaps decision-makers and planners are asking the wrong questions, questions of a basically technical nature, when they ought to be asking the public what it wants and what priorities it sets on public problems. For instance, the current trend toward more public participation in water resources still puts the emphasis on what the public thinks about a certain plan, and whether they want it or not. In reality, once a plan has been approved by governmental agencies the plan goes into effect unless the public outcry is extreme. The public has definite opinions about where their tax money ought to go. Building more reservoirs may not be high on the priority list. That is why a valid assessment of public priorities is needed. Simple attitude surveys will not do; it is what the public is willing to pay for (with taxes) that needs to be known.

A secondary purpose of this paper is to resist the tide of optimism that pervades much of our functionally-specific research in water resources which serves to grease the wheels of bureaucracies who foster massive social change, oblivious to the real human and social costs. Much sociological research has made it easier for planners and decision-makers to make public water projects palatable to those affected, and to keep the public calm and malleable while the planning, and the implementation of projects operates smoothly. Most public projects have negative consequences that do not find their way into cost-benefit analysis, (though the economists with their externalities of pollution are trying), and we should try too, by making clear the costs that public projects extract in people's private lives. We should even go further and show the public the best means of fighting projects it does not want—what agencies and congressmen to contact, and what in project plans is being done carelessly, erroneously, or ignored, and would have definite negative impact. Social scientists might work on an "anti-adoption" strategy that would result in successful nonadoption of bureaucratic decisions.

This paper can be seen as a first step toward operationalizing human and social costs for a nonmonetary calculus of costs and benefits, or it may be the first step toward alerting decision-makers to more humane ways of dealing with the human problems of relocation. A problem with this investigation, and for that matter with most work done by sociologists, is that no solutions are offered. The concerned members of government agencies, and in particular the Army Corps, have a right to ask for the alternatives. Short of the most desirable state of turning everyone into a humanist, we have no immediate solutions. Perhaps one way of alleviating the relocation trauma is to ask people what kind of future they want, and to help them obtain it. Do they need and want a house by the road? Do they want their favorite apple tree dug up and moved? Do they want to live in the town or the country? Do they want their relatives nearby? Do they need job-retraining? The intangible costs of being forcibly relocated are great enough that it seems that merely covering the monetary cost perpetuates injustice. The real need is to preserve and enhance the sense of personal, social and community integrity that gives the migrant's lives meaning, and money alone cannot buy that. Time and care from federal agencies is necessary to lessen the social costs of projects built for the public good.

Beyond this kind of alternative future suggestion, we are working on an alternative methodology that will place the concerns of the affected persons before the "general good" philosophy guiding Corps decisions today. A massive restructuring of the values and operating procedures that the Corps utilizes is necessary. Economic utilitarianism has been the *modus operandi*; an alternative philosophy must now be employed. So must post-construction studies become an integral part of the study of reservoir construction in order to see the real benefits and costs of projects in other than monetary terms.

If people are allowed truly to participate in decisions affecting their immediate lives, and allowed to move, if they must, at their own speed to locations they desire, with due consideration given their social and psychic needs, and if sufficient data were available so that the actual magnitude of the true costs and benefits of public projects were known, then perhaps those involved would not feel as if they had to say "The Corps' meaner than a barrel of fishhooks."

## ACKNOWLEDGMENT

Funds for this investigation were supplied in part by Project A-043-KY, Office of Water Resources Research.

## REFERENCES

Becker, C. J. "Factors Associated with Attitude Toward Reservoir Construction" unpublished M.A. Thesis, Lexington, University of Kentucky (1971).

Becker, C. J., and R. J. Burdge. "The Effects of Familism, Traditionalism, and Socio-Economic Status on Attitudes Toward Reservoir Construction in an Eastern Kentucky County," Paper presented at the 1971 Annual Meeting of the Rural Sociological Society, Denver, Colorado (August, 1971).

Bernard, J. "My Four Revolutions: An Autobiographical History of the ASA," *Amer. J. Soc.* 78(4): 773 (1973).

Burdge, J., and R. Ludtke. *Factors Affecting Relocation in Response to Reservoir Development*, Research Report #29 (Lexington, Kentucky: Kentucky Water Resources Institute, 1970).

Burdge, J., and R. Ludtke. "Forced Migration: Social Separation Among Displaced Rural Families," Paper presented at the 1970 Meeting of the Rural Sociological Society, Washington, D.C. (August, 1970).

Donnermeyer, J. F., P. F. Korshing, and R. J. Burdge. "An Interpretative Analysis of the Economic and Material Costs of Reservoir Construction," Paper presented at the Association of Southern Agriculture Workers, Atlanta, Georgia (February 1973).

Fried, M. and P. Gleicher. "Some Sources of Residential Satisfaction in an Urban Slum" in *Environment and the Social Sciences: Perspectives and Applications*, J. F. Wohlwill and D. H. Carson, Eds. (Washington, D.C.: American Psychological Association, 1972), pp. 137-53.

Goebel, E. R., et. al., "Government Acquisition of Private Property in Rural Areas: The U.S. Army Corps of Engineers and the Cave Run Reservoir Project," *Ken. Law J.* 58(4): 731 (1969-70).

Hargrove, M. B. *Economic Development of Areas Contiguous to Multi-Purpose Reservoirs: The Kentucky-Tennessee Experience*, Research Report #21, (Lexington, Kentucky: Kentucky Water Resources Institute, 1971).

Korsching, P. F. "The Effects of the Mass Media of Communication on Attitudes Toward Change in an Eastern Kentucky County," Unpublished M.A. Thesis, Lexington, University of Kentucky (1972).

Korsching, P. F., and R. J. Burdge. "The Effects of Mass Media Exposure on Attitudes Toward Reservoir Development in a Low-Income Eastern Kentucky County," in *Rural Sociology in the South*, Maurice E. Voland, Ed., Proceedings of the Rural Sociology Section, Association of Southern Agricultural Workers, (Lexington, Kentucky, Kentucky Agricultural Experiment Station, 1972).

Louisville *Courier-Journal* and *Times*

Mills, C. W. *The Sociological Imagination* (New York: Oxford University Press, 1959).

Rogers, E. and F. F. Shoemaker, *Communication of Innovations* (New York: The Free Press, 1971).

Smith, C. R. *Anticipation of Change, A Socioeconomic Description of a Kentucky County Before Reservoir Construction*, Research Report #28, (Lexington, Kentucky: Kentucky Water Resources Institute, 1970).

# Part IV
# Community and Leisure

# About the Contributors

*Joseph T. O'Leary,* a PhD candidate in the College of Forest Resources. University of Washington, Seattle, received his MFS degree from Yale University. His research interests include social behavior in the utilization of natural resources and community relationships to natural resources. Current publications involve methodological considerations for leisure participation. Mr. O'Leary is now working on his dissertation examining rural community-natural resource agency relationships.

*Gerard F. Schreuder* has received degrees in forest resources, statistics and economics. He served four years with the United Nations in Latin America in the area of forest resources. After his doctorate he joined the faculty of Yale University and recently moved to the University of Washington as Associate Professor, College of Forest Resources. His main interests have been in the areas of quantitative resource economics, mathematical modeling and operations research.

*Dean R. Yoesting* is Associate Professor in the Department of Sociology and the Department of Forestry, Iowa State University, Ames. His interests include human behavior and its relationship to leisure with recent emphasis related to the impact of childhood recreation experiences on adult recreation behavior. Dr. Yoesting's most recent publications concern social factors influencing leisure behavior and methodological issues in the study of leisure. He earned his PhD at the University of Wisconsin, Madison.

*Herbert H. Stoevener* is Professor of Agricultural Economics at Oregon State University. He received his PhD from the University of Illinois. His principal interests are in research and teaching in the economics of natural resource use, especially in the economics of environmental quality and outdoor recreation, and his publications are concerned with research areas. Dr. Stoevener serves as consultant to the U.S. Environmental Protection Agency.

*R. Bruce Rettig* is Associate Professor of Agricultural Economics, Oregon State University. His PhD was received at the University of Washington. Federal, state and local public policies governing natural resource use are the center of his research interests. Professor Rettig's current publications concern local conflicts over land use and international conflicts over use of marine resources.

*Stephen D. Reiling* is a doctoral candidate in the Department of Agricultural Economics at Oregon State University where he also earned his MS degree. His research interests are in the area of natural resource economics, with an emphasis on environmental economics, community development and the economics of outdoor recreation.

# Part IV
# Community and Leisure

Sociologists have emphasized the inherent social meaning and/or definition of resources in terms of the social structure man creates to deal with varying environmental conditions. Whether we further exploit natural resources as a basis for increased productivity or set aside lands for nonconsumptive appreciation, the decision to change present man-resource relationships will have consequences for the existing institutional structure of communities. The impact upon small rural communities may be most pronounced, as indicated by other chapters in this volume.

Thus far, emphasis has been placed on natural resource modification for community development without considering the institutional adaptation required when such a change alters the leisure or recreation patterns of a region. A change in recreation patterns brought about by a modification of the resource base does have an impact upon communities located in proximity to the recreation development; it may be positive or negative. Research investigations of community-water resource development for recreation portray economic benefits for the community when, in many cases, few economic benefits are derived by local residents. Papers in this section consider recreation opportunities created by development of a water resource. Consequences for a community are illustrated in terms of the impacts upon traditional recreation patterns and impacts upon the local economy.

O'Leary, *et al.* expand upon the growing body of literature documenting the importance of the social group as a determining factor in leisure participation. The authors suggest that social groups respond to a water-based recreation area by selecting among a set of recreation activities those which accomplish the objectives established for a given outing.

Yoesting measures the impact of an Iowa water impoundment project upon leisure patterns of the residents in the vicinity of the project and his conclusions parallel those of O'Leary. By developing activity clusters, Yoesting develops a scheme whereby planners can accommodate both local and tourist recreational demands. The authors of both papers point out that the development of a water recreation complex may provide greater recreation opportunities but, in so doing, development may alter the character of the area and the composition of people who utilize the area. Efforts made to attract tourists often deter local use, or in some cases entirely displace local use.

While O'Leary and Yoesting measure sociological impacts of water development upon local leisure patterns, Stoevener and his colleagues point out the economic impacts borne individually and collectively by residents within commuting distance of a recreation resource. They succinctly identify the benefits and costs of recreation development which should be examined by community decision-makers, prior to embracing recreation development as a stimulus to the local community. In many cases the costs exceed the benefits.

# 10. Social Groups and Water Activity Clusters: An Exploration of Interchangeability and Substitution

### JOSEPH T. O'LEARY, DONALD R. FIELD AND GERARD SCHREUDER

Rural and urban communities alike are assessing recreational development as an income producer as well as an alternative employment opportunity for local residents. Such a consideration is logical when commissioned reports dealing with regional development suggest entry into this untapped market as a basis for economic growth (State of Washington, Community Development Services, 1972). For growing and prospering communities a recreational industry is viewed as another step toward obtaining a diversified employment structure. For declining and stable communities the turn toward recreational development may be viewed as a panacea for a dwindling employment base.

Community leaders should examine closely the nature of the recreation industry as a solution to local or regional employment problems prior to expending scarce resources to implement recreational development schemes. Recreation as a solution may be more myth than hard fact, linked to rather extravagant claims attributed to the development process. One such statement by a prominent congressman during the public hearings on the formation of the North Cascades National Park is an example of purported economic gains for communities who cater to recreationists:

> The fastest growing industry in America is tourism/recreation. These people come to your community. They help make it green. They just leave dollars behind. You do not have to build schools. There are not any smokestacks, none of things that cause problems for a community. They just come and leave their money and depart, and have a good time while they are there.[1]

A few communities within a region will be successful in attracting and supporting enterprises that in turn may contribute to the regional or community economic base; however, the majority of communities seeking recreational enterprises will be unsuccessful. Alone, communities rarely will be able to provide the comprehensive recreational facilities attractive to diverse visitor publics. The seasonal nature of recreational business diminishes its attractiveness (Fuguitt, 1965) as a solution to what may be an already sagging employment base. The tendency for recreational developers to import key personnel further accentuates an imbalance in the local labor force.

Nevertheless a consideration of recreation as "revenue generating" and as an employment alternative will continue. The basis on which these intended outcomes are derived will be fundamental to their ultimate realization. Recent examination of recreational demand models, whether prepared by state agencies or consulting firms, suggests that many use incomplete and/or invalid indicators of the amount of participation that will occur in a given place, by whom, and the extent to which it will vary. Therefore, the purpose of the present paper is to propose additional criteria for assessing leisure participation so that communities contemplating recreation development can more accurately assess their potential.

The paper is developed in the following manner: First, a discussion of recreation demand studies is presented, outlining from a sociological perspective the most pertinent deficiencies hindering accurate assessment of leisure participation. Second, the methods

---

1. Hearings before the Subcommittee on National Parks and Recreation of the Committee of Interior and Insular Affairs, House of Representatives, on H.R. 8970 and related bills. 90th Congress, 2nd session, part 1:115, 1968.

of data collection and statistical procedures employed in the investigation are identified. Third, the basis on which most people participate in leisure (*i.e.*, within a social group) is introduced. Fourth, the utilization of the social group in conjunction with two other variables permitting a composite description of activity clusters is developed. In this section the concepts of interchangeability and substitution are defined and their importance for understanding the relationship between human behavior and activity selection noted. Finally, the implications for community development are discussed.

## RECREATION DEMAND STUDIES: AN INCOMPLETE MODEL[2]

State agencies involved in outdoor recreation are charged with the responsibility of providing information about current use as well as preparing predictions for future demand at state recreation facilities. The information is gathered to facilitate acquisition and development of new recreation areas and the improvement of existing facilities to meet anticipated user demands. The development of a data base is also designed (perhaps primarily) to satisfy regulations dealing with the receipt of federal funds for state recreation projects.

The majority of these recreation demand studies rely on a limited set of factors for predicting participation. In many of these cases it has been suggested that those factors employed have been used incorrectly (Knetsch, 1968 and 1969; Burdge and Hendee, 1972). Similarly, few of the studies include behavioral factors. Many behavioral aspects of group dynamics cannot be independently considered. If the intention of the demand study is to measure how human beings participate in outdoor recreation, then a representation of these factors in terms of selected sociological variables has merit. A brief sketch of demand formats as utilized by many state agencies will illustrate these deficiencies. Such an examination becomes more appropriate in light of the fact that many private consulting firms have adopted similar procedures in the development of demand studies for communities.

---

2. This section of the paper was prepared independently and without prior knowledge of another, somewhat parallel treatment of the problem. See Rabel Burdge and John Hendee, The Demand Survey Dilemma: Assessing the Credibility of State Outdoor Recreation Plans, *Guideline,* 2 (1) (1972).

## The Demand Study Examined

Justification for expansion of existing facilities and/or acquisition of new areas is often based on recreation demand studies prepared for or by the agencies involved. These are not demand studies in the traditional economic sense, *i.e.*, a schedule of volume or quantity in relation to price. Instead, they are often expressed as a total number of visitors (visitor-days, user-days, etc.) in relation to a site or facility, or in terms of participation rates (activity-days) for specific activities. Using different guidelines or standards (usually expressed on a users/acre basis) a determination is made regarding the adequacy of recreation facilities.

A perceived demand for specific recreation sites as commonly emphasized in these studies may represent a desire on the part of recreational publics to have additional recreational sites regardless of the type provided. Unfortunately, this point is seldom addressed in traditional demand studies. The result leads to a proliferation of the same kinds of facilities with little innovation, and to a perpetuation of old problems. Most studies rely on measures of participation in the form of rates of participation for specific recreational activities. Such an approach (1) is normally based on population aggregates and (2) assumes that the activity in which people participate, like swimming, boating, fishing or walking along a beach, represents the only attraction or reason for being at a given site.

The prevailing strategy focusing on population aggregates should be carefully reviewed. A major goal of these studies is to develop a data base about social characteristics or participants, users and visitors. In general, these social aggregate variables are examined alone and the variables considered in 1973 do not vary from those originally assumed to be appropriate for explaining participation in the ORRRC study reports on demand and participation that appeared in the early 1960's (ORRRC). While appropriate for some purposes these models do not fully reflect participation or the nature of human behavior in leisure settings. Burdge and Field (1972) have emphasized this point by suggesting that demand analysis has been incomplete since aggregate variables represent a statistical group, but do not include interpersonal interaction. They state:

> Because participation in outdoor recreation is culturally influenced, the cultural environment of participants must be considered an explanatory variable. Accurate measures of demand are presently, and will

continue to be, inadequate unless the analysis goes beyond the commonly employed social indicators. (p. 64)

Either through pictures, or explicitly in the text of the report, almost every demand study makes reference to the presence of the family and friendship group in recreational participation. For example, see the State of California Public Outdoor Recreation Plan (1960) and the State of Washington Statewide Outdoor Recreation and Open Space Plan (1967) for a variety of references. However, this observation has not been incorporated into the subsequent analysis. What role does the social group play in defining demand and participation in recreation? This question is not answered through an exclusive examination of aggregate variables. To the extent that the shortcomings of aggregate variables have not been confronted, there appear to be serious flaws in interpretation of traditional recreation demand.

If the social variables appropriate for assessing participation are inadequate, then difficulties are also presented in interpreting related information gathered about activities. Demand studies tend to treat each activity as if it were unique. If a "visitor" goes to an area and engages in two or more activities in the same day or part of a day, the activities are treated separately. When a calculation of "activity days" is prepared a count is made that suggests a participant did one activity for one whole day, another activity for another whole day, etc. Little effort is made to examine the interrelationships among activities with respect to participants. Similarly, allocating one full day to each activity in the analysis seems to continuously overestimate the duration of participation.

Although there have been efforts to seek out activities that conflict[3] (*e.g.*, swimming and ice skating) or would not naturally be found together, the results have not been pursued to develop inferences about activity-participant or activity-activity relationships. The emphasis on searching for activities that conflict has muted efforts to search for a network of activities that are *complementary* and perhaps mutually exclusive in terms of the way in which people play in outdoor recreation.

A growing body of literature is emerging suggesting that studies based on the above assumptions may be misleading due to the incompleteness of the criteria considered. The goal of present de-

---

3. An interesting treatment of this can be found in the State of Missouri Outdoor Recreation Plan, Vol. 1, 1970 (Plate 11, opposite p. 45). Unfortunately it has not been exploited further to assess participation.

mand studies may be to satisfy the "letter of the law" to obtain federal funding, and not to understand the mechanics of leisure participation. An activity may be only a means to, not the basis for, participation. In terms of human behavior, too much emphasis has been placed on what individuals do. Activities may be interchangeable depending on who participates with whom. The basis for participation in any recreational activity may well be linked to the social bonds generated by a particular set of people. That is, for particular people who have gathered together to enjoy the outdoors, several activities and a variety of leisure settings may provide equal opportunity to achieve the participation desired by the group.

## DATA AND METHOD

The data for this investigation were gathered as part of a joint effort by the National Park Service in conjunction with the University of Washington. The universe for the larger study includes the adult population 18 years of age and older who reside in western Washington, western Oregon and northern California. Geographically, the study area is bounded by the Cascade Mountains and Sierra Nevadas on the east, the Pacific Ocean on the west, the U.S.-Canadian border on the north and the greater San Francisco metropolitan area on the south.

A probability sample of 1,504 residents was selected from within this universe for examination. All interviews were completed by telephone during the months of August and September, 1971. Sampling criteria ensured that an equal number of interviews were completed by male and female heads of household. The average length of time per interview was 20 minutes. A complete description of the sampling procedures including respondent selection and interview items are reported elsewhere (Field, 1973).

Data were obtained from respondents within leisure information sets. A leisure set is nothing more than a self-contained set of items focused on a specific resource base, in this case, water. The dependent variable is the frequency with which participation occurs in an activity. The major independent variables are: (1) the social group within which participation takes place, (2) 11 water-based activities for which participation was recorded, and (3) selected sociodemographic characteristics of male and female household heads.

## Statistical Procedures

Often violated in multiple variable regression analysis is the assumption of mutual independence of the independent variables, which is often the case for income and education. This is the problem of multicolinearity. While it undoubtedly accounts in part for the lack of success in assessing participation in outdoor recreation, variations in statistical technique can accommodate the problem. Recently, statistical techniques have been developed that offer promise to the social scientists by allowing correlated variables. These go collectively under the name of multivariate techniques, and it was decided in this study to employ one of these in order to obtain some understanding of the patterns of participation and variation among social groups. A principal component analysis was selected.

The main objective of principal component analysis is the parsimonious summarization of a mass of observations. In other words, it is useful to summarize a sample of correlated variates. These correlated variates are transformed linearly into a set of orthogonal (uncorrelated) variates that are called principal components or factors. Since these principal components are mutually independent, they can be considered separately. Finally, the principal components are determined in such a way that a decreasing order of variance is associated with each following component, *i.e.*, the first component accounts for the largest variance, the second component for the second largest variance, etc. The idea is that possibly only one, or only two, or very few of the components are needed to summarize the whole of the variability and covariability of the original variates. Thus, each principal component is a composite of one or more of the original variates, containing a maximum variance.

Considered in the broadest context, principal components can be viewed in two different ways. In one sense they are artificial variables containing aspects of the original variates. More importantly, such combination into a new variable contributes to a composite assessment of those factors associated with participation, which heretofore has had to be treated individually. For example, when attempting to describe a human being one can measure length, width and height. A principal component constructed from these three variables might be thought of as representing the non-measurable variable called "shape." In our case we combine several activities and group types into a composite called "leisure activity cluster" representing overall frequency of participation.

In another way principal component analysis might be compared to regression analysis. Regression analysis attempts to summarize a wealth of data into a single equation consisting of independent variables that explain the one dependent variable (we ignore here the subject of simultaneous equations, where more than one dependent variable exists). Principal component analysis likewise summarizes the wealth of data by reducing one, or at most three, new and mutually independent variables. If this can be done by statistical procedures, then researchers may concentrate their data acquisition in the future into more meaningful units such as these new variables representing "leisure clusters."

Ideally, principal component analysis should not be based on variates measured on different scales. Since all variates were expressed in number of times participated, this requirement was fulfilled in the first application reported here.

## SOCIAL GROUPS AND LEISURE PARTICIPATION REVISITED

Although the primary group has been accorded an important priority for consideration in social research, seldom do we find a measure in which the social group is used to examine leisure participation as one aspect of the human social drama. Much of the recreation and leisure literature has focused on the social person (often called the "visitor"), thereby overlooking the observation that leisure appears to be associated with the social organization phenomenon of the primary group.

Taking part in leisure activities does not occur randomly. It is a product of the cultural milieu and boundaries within which members of a society reside. (In leisure participation, the roles assumed by members, the statuses assigned and the composition of the social group in which the social person is found contribute to establishing group norms for leisure behavior.) Taken together these factors are a few of the criteria that orient the social group to effect how participation may occur. As indicated elsewhere, while what people do is important, it may be more important to consider how they organize themselves to do it.

Meyersohn (1969), Burch (1969), and Cheek (1971) are but a few of the authors who have noted the absence of research attempting to assess the role of the social group in leisure behavior. Both

Meyersohn and Cheek reviewed a number of leisure studies, separating them according to what specific aspect was studied. They failed to find an analysis examining group behavior. Burch noted that one of the failures of leisure research was to treat statistical aggregates as if they were social groups, when no such relationship could be said to exist (Burch, 1969). His concern for the inadequacies of some contemporary hypotheses purporting to explain leisure behavior led to his expression of a "personal community" hypothesis. It suggested that one's leisure style would, to a large extent, be a reflection of relationships with, and socialization by, work mates, friends, parents, and one's spouse. He noted:

> Interaction in specific occupational, familial and friendship settings seem likely locations to search for determinants of leisure behavior. . . . It seems likely that post-industrial man, just as his tribal and peasant counterparts, finds the shape of his free time formed within small circles of work mates, family and friends. (p. 143)

However, the intricacies of these relationships and the effect on activity selection were not explored further.

Cheek (1971) suggests that characteristics of social organization might be used to ascertain differences between "work" and "not-work"; the latter is the area within which leisure would be found. In his data, "work" was engaged in by the *social person*, while "not-work" was characterized by the presence of the *social group*. He explored the activity of park going, and found a significant difference between male participation "alone" versus "with others."

Yancey and Snell (1971), investigating leisure activities among lower, working and middle class blacks and whites living in Nashville, reinforced Cheek's results when they showed that "leisure activities are social activities." In almost every activity that was studied, family and/or friendship groups were involved, not individuals participating alone.

Field and O'Leary (1973), investigating water activities in the western United States, found that by adding the social group as a variable to the commonly employed social aggregate variables, statistical explanation was enhanced providing greater accountability for variation in the frequency with which participation in selected water activities occurs.

To suggest that the *social group* is an important variable in studying leisure behavior is not sufficient, however. If the group emerges as an important dimension for explaining leisure behavior, how will the organizational characteristics affect the specific activities in which people participate? As Field and O'Leary (1973) have noted:

> If the relationship with various "others" influences leisure style, does the transmittal of style into action mean that sets of activities become linked to the group in which the social person finds himself a member? (p. 3)

## SOCIAL GROUPS AND WATER ACTIVITY CLUSTERS

One objective of all sociological research into leisure may be identified as an attempt to describe the nature of leisure participation in societies and to differentiate among participating groups, utilizing as few variables as possible. If successful, this quest for a parsimonious set of sociological factors indicative of human behavior in leisure offers a new dimension to planning recreation facilities for people. We suggest that the social group is one variable and that age and sex may be two others whereby leisure participation can be described meaningfully.

Such descriptions could include differences reflected within the life cycle, generational variation in terms of orientation toward recreation, and variation due to male-female socialization. Each contributes to the formation of activity clusters appropriate to a specific grouping of people. It is to activity clusters that we now turn our attention.

Field (1971) was able to demonstrate with data collected in the western United States that leisure settings are not necessarily unique in terms of the types of activities being performed within those settings. In fact, they were interchangeable. In addition to sharing similar social groups, a set of activities accounting for most participation in the outdoors emerged as common to all leisure places. When the analysis was extended to consider leisure setting, leisure activity and social group simultaneously, a clustering of activities by group type became evident. It was found that regardless of setting, specific groups selected similar activities. As the construct of the group changed (*e.g.*, from friends to family), certain activities dropped out and were replaced by others. This new activity set then remained constant for each leisure setting.

These findings imply that the social group responds to a leisure setting by establishing, or engaging in, activities that are used to deal with the current social and environmental conditions. Activities are not all-encompassing, but vary in outcome according to the composition of the group, previous leisure experience, cultural background, and specific purposes for which a given setting was visited. Consequently, the parameters for establishing sets of activities in terms of the social group and of individual participation are often predetermined. Indeed, there is the possibility that the social meaning established between a group and specific water activities facilitates movement, as an actor alters his group type (*e.g.*, from family to friends).

Two variables, age and sex, are introduced along with a social group variable as a basis for describing leisure clusters and variation among such clusters.[4] When this is done, explanation for leisure choice becomes more apparent.

**Age**

The first factor in a principal component analysis accounts for the greatest amount of variance for participation frequency as explained by group type and activity. For Factor I in Table I, a relationship between group type and activities for the various age categories is noted. Within the age categories 18–29, 30–39 the most frequent participation occurs among friends, while for those older adults frequency shifts to family groups or a combination of family and friendship as in the case for those respondents in the 50–59 age category. The one exception is salt water fishing, where those 60 and over take part more often in the company of friends.

At this juncture two changes in activity choice are worth mentioning across age groups. Powerboating, which can be separate or supportive for other water-based activities, accounts for higher participation frequency in four of the five age categories (Factor 1, Table I). Notice, however, that the group type changes with increasing age. Similarly, in contrast to swimming at a beach and clamming with friends for younger adults, those in the age categories 50 and older swim and clam at a beach most often with family members present.

The association of activities by group type within age categories

---

4. While other social characteristics might have been employed, several writers have suggested that these two variables combined with a social group variable reflect social system properties operating to differentiate human behavior in "non-work" environment. See, for example, Lionell Tiger, *Men in Groups* (New York: Vintage Books, 1970) and Neil H. Cheek, Jr. and William R. Burch, Jr., *Myth, Taste and Leisure in Society* (New York: Harper and Row) in press.

## Table I
### Ranking of Variables Comprising Three Main Factors of a Principal Component Analysis for Age by Social Group and Activity

| Factor | 18-29 | | 30-39 | | 40-49 | | 50-59 | | 60 and over | |
|---|---|---|---|---|---|---|---|---|---|---|
| Per cent of variance explained | 56.2 | | 56.0 | | 57.4 | | 65.2 | | 55.6 | |
| 1. | Water ski, fr | 0.913 | Powerboat, fr | 0.833 | Powerboat, fa | 0.841 | Powerboat, ff | 0.815 | Powerboat, fa | 0.939 |
|  | Swim beach, fr | 0.670 | Clam, fr | 0.561 | Ob nature, fa | 0.803 | Fish, salt, ff | 0.755 | Swim beach, fa | 0.925 |
|  | Powerboat, fr | 0.664 | | | Fish, fresh, fa | 0.688 | Clam, ff | 0.554 | Clam, fa | 0.918 |
|  | Clam, fr | 0.600 | | | Visit beach, fa | 0.595 | | | Ob nature, fa | 0.836 |
|  | | | | | | | | | Fish, salt, fr | 0.706 |
| 2. | Water ski, ff | 0.623 | Powerboat, ff | 0.641 | Water ski, fr | 0.858 | Fish, fresh, fr | 0.611 | Ob nature, fr | 0.745 |
|  | Powerboat, ff | 0.592 | Fish, salt, ff | 0.595 | Powerboat, fr | 0.794 | Powerboat, fr | 0.540 | Fish, fresh, fr | 0.744 |
|  | Powerboat, fa | 0.550 | Swim beach, ff | 0.565 | Swim beach, fr | 0.731 | Swim pool, fr | 0.513 | Swim beach, fr | 0.638 |
|  | | | | | Visit beach, fr | 0.608 | | | Powerboat, fr | 0.580 |
| 3. | Water ski, fa | 0.552 | Swim beach, fr | 0.570 | Powerboat, ff | 0.736 | Hunt, fa | 0.664 | Clam, ff | 0.661 |
|  | | | | | Swim beach, ff | 0.603 | Swim pool, fa | 0.648 | Swim beach, ff | 0.628 |
|  | | | | | Water ski, ff | 0.555 | | | Powerboat, ff | 0.552 |
|  | | | | | Fish, salt, ff | 0.531 | | | | |

fr = friends   fa = family   ff = friends and family   ob nature = observe nature offers another perspective for understanding the role of a social group in activity selection and clustering as an initial basis on which interchangeability may be projected. For adults 18–29, four activities account for the bulk of participation. Powerboating and water skiing, along with clamming and swimming at a beach are more often done with friends. These activities form a leisure cluster describing recreational choice by a particular kind of social group. When the type changes from friends to family, a new leisure cluster emerges. Those activities that reappear (powerboating and water skiing) become *interchangeable* among groups. If an activity is added to a group where it did not appear before, a *substitution* has taken place. If an activity reappears in more than one factor in the same way, it is the dominant activity associated with participation by a given group for a specific sociodemographic category. If more than one activity appears they are co-dominant. For this age group a substitution did not occur. It appears that the activity functions as a vehicle by which particular intragroup interaction is facilitated. The objectives and nature of association among friends appear different from those that emerge from family groups while powerboating. As Berger (1961) suggests, the normative structure operating may be different depending on the situation in which play takes place.

The ability to denote clusters of activities where interchangeability and substitution take place is enhanced by the nature of the statistical test employed. If a set emerges within one factor the strength of relationship between group type and activity set is intensified, because those activities appearing in a factor *together* account for differential frequency of participation as indicated by the amount of variance explained for a given factor.

As was the case in the first age category, four activities together account for the greatest frequency of participation for those 40–49. They are: powerboating, observing nature on water-based sites, fresh water fishing and visiting a beach. When the social group changes from a family unit to a friendship group the set associated with a higher participation frequency changes. Two activities, swimming at a beach and water skiing, are substituted for family activities, fresh water fishing and observing nature. Visiting a beach and powerboating become interchangeable. A third set of activities is associated with a higher frequency of participation in a combination family-friendship group. As was true above, two activities replace two others to form a new set. It should be carefully noted though, that activities facilitate participation, and therefore shared activities among social groups would not be inconsistent with the possibility that activities might be treated differently.

Two of four activities connected with a higher frequency of participation in a family-friendship group for those 40–49 likewise are associated with a higher frequency for the next age group. The difference, of course, is that for those 50–59 participation is more often undertaken with a family-friendship group. When friends gather, freshwater fishing (a substitution) and powerboating (an interchangeable activity) are important activities comprising a new set. Swimming in a pool with friends is very seldom done. Comparing other activities there is a disproportionate amount of waterfowl hunting and swimming in a pool when the social group participating is a family. In this latter case only substitution has taken place.

The greater the number of activities comprising each set, the wider distribution of participation among activities. Those adults who are 60 and over, like those 40–49, have three and four activities with a high frequency of participation per set. In this last age category clamming, observing nature, swimming at a beach and powerboating are more often done with family than other groups. With friends, three activities are interchangeable with family, while two are substituted. For a family-friendship group swimming at a beach and powerboating are shared while clamming is not. Greater congruity among leisure sets might be expected with increasing age. Yoesting (1973), for example, notes that the number of activities in childhood is related to the number engaged in as adults. While we do not have comparable data, it may be that as one gets older a limited set of activities is shared among a wider variety of social groups.

**Sex**

Differential socialization patterns that operate to establish appropriate social roles for males and females appear to be reflected in leisure participation. The substitution of activities as group type shifts from all male groups to mixed sex groups, like family, may illustrate the socialization process and role playing. Burch (1965 and 1969) observed that leisure participation is characterized by sets of recreational alternatives that are appropriate to the social roles and life styles of participants in a group. Burch (1965) defined a number of play action types within which different activities are located. These types when considered together composed a play system. He noted:

> Within the social drama, numerous subplots are simultaneously and constantly unfolding. However, these subplots are not randomly distributed but are assigned attributes of given performing groups. Each of these subplots adds up to the total configuration of the unfolding play system. (p. 605)

A play action type represented "... the predominant form of action in a given social situation" (Burch, 1965). He considered a number of different natural settings where he believed different types would become apparent. Perhaps most important was his observation that as the social group varied, the activities pursued also varied. For certain of these types he noted:

> ... the dominant model is apparently companionate marriage and family togetherness. (p. 608)

He identified rock collection, driving, swimming and hiking as examples. However, even though these activities may occur in a fishing camp situation, when people fish a different group orientation occurs:

> ... the male fisherman steals away in the dark of morning with his male conspirators, not returning until afternoon or evening when he resumes his family role obligations ... contexts of action vary as does the extent of the division of play. (p. 608)

Although these observations are made to distinguish sexual differentiation and identity in activity engagement, they demonstrate specific group orientation to certain activities as well.

As with age factors, a relationship appears between differential participation in water-based activities and group type by sex (Table II). Males engage most often with friends in water-based activities. Females take part more often within a family group. Powerboating is an important choice for both sexes. For males greater frequency is in association with friends, while for females greater participation happens with families. The same is true for swimming at a beach.

An unexpected finding emerges in Factor 1 for females. We have noted previously that female participation in fishing and waterfowl hunting is substantially less than for males, but when females do participate in waterfowl hunting they are more often found in a family group. The same feature was noted concerning fresh water

## Table II
### Ranking of Variables Comprising Three Main Factors of a Principal Component Analysis for Sex by Social Group and Activity

| Factor | Male | | Female | |
|---|---|---|---|---|
| Per cent of variable explained | 52.3 | | 52.4 | |
| 1. | Water ski, fr | 0.776 | Fish, salt, fr | 0.632 |
| | Swim beach, fr | 0.713 | Powerboat, fa | 0.577 |
| | Powerboat, fr | 0.674 | Swim beach, fa | 0.543 |
| | Visit beach, fr | 0.667 | | |
| 2. | Powerboat, fa | 0.752 | Clam, crab, fr | 0.707 |
| | Water ski, fa | 0.692 | Sail, fr | 0.696 |
| | Swim beach, fa | 0.646 | | |
| 3. | Powerboat, fr & fa | 0.605 | Powerboat, fr & fa | 0.778 |
| | Fish, salt, fr & fa | 0.516 | Water ski, fr & fa | 0.771 |

fr = friends    fa = family

fishing. We find here that females participate in salt water fishing more often with friends.

Clustering of activities for males associated with participation frequency suggests again the interchangeability of activities for social groups. Four activities account for differential frequency for males. With friends, water skiing, swimming at a beach, powerboating and visiting a beach typify greater leisure involvement in water-oriented activities. The leisure set remains almost identical for family groups. Only visiting a beach drops out. Two activities account for more participation in a family-friendship group: powerboating and salt water fishing. Because of the appearance of powerboating in each of the three factors, it becomes an important activity explaining male participation. It is also an interchangeable activity.

More often than not females swim at a beach and powerboat with family, whereas the three activities comprising the leisure set for friends are distinct. When family and friends gather, a higher frequency of participation takes place in water skiing and powerboating.

## DISCUSSION

It is apparent from previous research and findings reported here that predictability of leisure participation is enhanced by considering sociological variables in conjunction with specific recreation activities. The meaning is clear: several activities equally can satisfy objectives established by a group when they arrive at a leisure setting.

We often forget that recreation sites, whether water-oriented or not, are leisure settings, settings in which human groups define what a recreation experience is to be within the boundaries of their culture and community of orientation. Adaptation to a recreational site occurs within the above context. Activities facilitate but are not the basis for participation. For example, if a group (like a family) arrives at a given site intending to swim, but the nature of the area and other people present preclude such participation, there is a high probability that another activity will be substituted so that the family interaction desired can be achieved. If there are activities that are interchangeable for different social groups, the greater the allowance for adaptation provided within the leisure environment, the greater the probability an area will be used and reused by many different groups. Sets of activities can be associated with groups, and activities do become interchangeable depending on the configuration of the group and the purpose for taking part in water activities.

Therefore, clues for recreational development can be identified among participating groups themselves. Recreational sites with a great deal of development and single purpose facilities may constrict the ability of social groups to adapt to the site. Thus, the opportunity for various types of social groups to partake is greatly reduced. There appears to be a direct relationship between flexibility of a site and diversity of social groups present. Flexible leisure settings allow social groups to organize their own human activities with a minimum of site constraints. Finally, single activity facilities oriented to a particular clientele are usually more expensive, and subject to the ebb and flow of leisure choice from year to year.

## IMPLICATIONS FOR COMMUNITY DEVELOPMENT

Emerging theoretical insights and growing methodological sophistication in the social sciences have led to a greater understanding of the nature of leisure participation which should facilitate planning, implementation and operation of recreational projects. However, the proliferation of these projects provided by public agencies or private entrepreneurs, resulting from increased knowledge in and around communities, should not necessarily be considered synonymous with community development. New projects may represent real development if they contribute to the overall well-being achieved within the community. This will depend on how community goals and institutional arrangements are considered in relation to the project. Resolution of the question: Is recreational development an aspect of community development? requires examination of both "the recreation business" and the range of impacts created which affect non-economic sectors of the community.

Recreation projects are often presented as development which provides an array of benefits for the local population. These may be in the form of more jobs for the local populace, the sale of more goods and services by local business, the enhancement of property values and improvements in the tax base for the local community. While each of these examples implies positive gains for the community, there is also potential for negative consequences. The remaining discussion will identify a few consequences of recreation development upon local population.

The thrust of a development project attempts to capitalize on local resources as economic ventures to attract tourist populations and/or generate additional revenue. Local populations often view this capitalization as an erosion of the original "character" of an area that once made it attractive. Efforts made to attract and facilitate the tourist often infringe upon traditional activities participated in by local residents. For example, activities that are developed tend to be only those that are revenue generating or that represent the most common denominator attractive to the widest segment of the recreation public. Traditional leisure places where local residents would gather are oftentimes altered, due to a changing composition of people who use such places. This creates an antipathy between locals, tourists and the agency or entrepreneur responsible for the project. Rarely do the intended projects attempt in some way to complement or supplement local community recreation resources, so that recreational alternatives are expanded for residents as well. The tendency is for local leisure patterns to be displaced.

Private projects are often initiated by nonlocal entrepreneurs because of an absence of adequate local capital. While new jobs may be introduced, outsiders are usually employed in key managerial positions and remain only during the recreation season. The resulting contribution to the local employment base becomes marginal. The rapid improvement of a local market picture for goods and services may lead to the introduction of national or regionally controlled chain stores to exploit this demand. Local businessmen, put in the position of being unable to compete, find themselves having to stay open longer hours, perhaps while earning less.

Property values may increase, but to the point where local residents are no longer able to meet tax responsibilities, possibly resulting in forced movement away from the community. Expanded community services required to maintain recreation development often generate a similar effect upon those with the least ability to pay.

Finally, population composition of a recipient community catering to recreation often changes. Local traditions and culture may be eroded, while community leadership and decision-making may shift to outside interests.

## ACKNOWLEDGMENT

This project was funded in part by a grant from the U.S. Department of Interior, Office of Water Resources Research as authorized under the Water Resources Research Act of 1964, and made available through the State of Washington Water Research Center as Project A-047 WASH. Funding also was provided by the National Park Service, U.S. Department of Interior, through the Office of Natural Sciences, Projects SO-S-201 and SO-S-500.

## REFERENCES

Berger, B. M. "The Sociology of Leisure: Some Suggestions," *Ind. Relat.* **1**, 31 (1961).

Burch, W. R., Jr. "The Play World of Camping: Research into the Social Meaning of Outdoor Recreation," *Amer. J. Soc.* **70**, 604 (1965).

Burch, W. R., Jr. "The Social Circles of Leisure: Competing Explanation," *J. Leisure Res.* **1**, 125 (1969)

Burdge, R. J. and D. R. Field. "Methodological Perspectives for the Study of Outdoor Recreation," *J. Leisure Res.* **1**, 63 (1972).

Burdge, R. J. and J. Hendee. "The Demand Survey Dilemma, Assessing the Credibility of State Outdoor Recreation Plans," *Guideline* **2**, 65 (1972).

Cheek, N. H., Jr. "Toward a Sociology of Not-Work," *Pac. Soc. Rev.* **14**, 245 (1971).

Cheek, N. H. Jr. and W. R. Burch, Jr. *Myth, Taste and Leisure in Society* (New York: Harper and Row) forthcoming.

Clawson, M. and J. L. Knetsch. *Economics of Outdoor Recreation,* for: Resources for the Future, Inc. (Baltimore: The Johns Hopkins Press, 1966).

Davis, J. A., J. L. Spaeth and C. Huson. "A Technique for Analyzing the Effects of Group Composition," *Amer. Soc. Rev.* 26, 215 (1961).

Field, D. R. "Interchangeability of Parks and Other Leisure Settings." Paper presented at the AAAS Symposium, Philadelphia, Pa. Dec. 26-31, 1971.

Field, D. R. "Telephone Interviewing in Leisure Research," *J. Leisure Res.* 5, 51 (1973).

Field, D. R. and J. T. O'Leary. "Social Groups as a Basis for Assessing Participation in Selected Water Activities," *J. Leisure Res.* (1973).

Fuguitt, G. V. "The Small Town in Rural America," *J. Cooperative Extension,* 3, 19 (1965).

Knetsch, J. L. "Outdoor Recreation Demand and Benefits," *Land Economics* 39, 387 (1963).

Knetsch, J. L., "Assessing the Demand for Outdoor Recreation," *J. Lesiure Res.* 1, 85 (1969).

Meyersohn, R. "The Sociology of Leisure in the United States: Introduction and Bibliography, 1945-1965," *J. Leisure Res.* 1, 43 (1969).

Mueller, E. and G. Gurin. *Participation in Outdoor Recreation: Factors Affecting Demand Among American Adults.* ORRRC Study Report 20. Report to the Outdoor Recreation Resources Review Commission. Washington, D.C. (1962).

Richardson, R. C. and J. S. Peery. "Recreation in Utah: A Profile of the Demand for Outdoor Recreation by Utah Residents," Bureau of Economic and Business Research, College of Business, Economic and Population Studies, University of Utah (Jan., 1966).

State of California. *California Public Outdoor Recreation Plan* (March, 1960).

State of Missouri. *State of Missouri Outdoor Recreation Plan, Vol. 1.* Prepared for State Inter-Agency Council for Outdoor Recreation (Saint Louis: R. W. Booker and Associates, Inc., 1970).

State of Tennessee, Department of Conservation. *Tennessee Statewide Comprehensive Outdoor Recreation Plan,* Division of Planning and Development, Nashville, Tenn. (1969).

State of Washington. *The North Cascades Highway: Its Impact on Community Economies.* Prepared by Community Development Services, Inc. for State Parks and Recreation Commission (November, 1972).

State of Washington, Department of Commerce and Economic Development. *Statewide Outdoor Recreation and Open Space Plan* (January, 1967).

Tiger, L. *Men in Groups* (New York: Vintage Books, 1970).

U.S. Congress. House. Committee on Interior and Insular Affairs. *The North Cascades, Hearings before the Subcommittee on National Parks and Recreation on H.R. 8970 and related bills.* Part 1. 90th Congress, 2nd Session (1968).

Warringer, C. K. "Groups are Real: A Reaffirmation," *Amer. Soc. Rev.* 21, 549 (1956).

Yoesting, D. "Impact of New Water-Based Recreation Facilities: Behavior and Management Implications." Paper presented at the Water and the Community Conference Lake Wilderness Center. University of Washington (May 23-25, 1973).

# 11. Impact of New Water-Based Recreation Facilities: Behavior and Management Implications

## DEAN R. YOESTING

Speculation continues concerning the impact of new recreation facilities on the surrounding communities or regions. Local chambers of commerce and certain government public works agencies are usually optimistic of the impact, although some sociologists, economists, and environmentalists have been more cautious about the relationship of social and economic costs to benefits obtained with recreation development.

The planning process that precedes construction of new recreation facilities involves substantial uncertainties. It usually involves study of public preferences, cost estimates, relationships to the activities provided by other existing or planned facilities, and related considerations. In view of scarce funds, an attempt is made to provide for as many users of a given kind and quality of facility as possible, at a given cost level. This means that estimates of probable use are extremely important. These estimates are commonly developed by surveying current use patterns using representative sampling techniques and then projecting these patterns, based on expected changes in the composition of the population, income levels, and related socioeconomic factors.

These are useful estimates, but they do have shortcomings. One of the most serious relates to the effects of new kinds of recreation facilities. It is simply not possible to estimate probable use of new kinds of facilities by working directly from current use patterns of the area residents. If there are no facilities for a particular activity in a given region, there is little or no current participation in that activity, and direct projections will indicate that there never will be. Obviously, data are needed to enable resource managers to provide facilities affording the greatest satisfaction from the recreation experience.

Merely providing facilities is not enough, however. These facilities must be managed to enable expansion of choices and opportunities for the residents as they seek to satisfy their personal goals. Managers must be provided information to help them in their decision-making related to facility development. Although many residents may not use the new facilities, they are likely to be affected by the existence of the facilities in the area.

This paper explores an alternative method of estimating the impact of a new reservoir on the leisure patterns of residents of the area. The factor analysis technique is used to examine substitution among several recreation activities to determine if patterns exist that could be used in estimating response to new kinds of facilities. It also directly examines a new and relatively large facility in Iowa in order to gain a limited, but useful, perspective of the magnitude of changes in use patterns brought about by new kinds of facilities. This approach may be of value to social scientists concerned with leisure behavior and to natural resource specialists concerned with the planning and implementing of recreation programs.

## MANAGING FOR MULTIPUBLICS

Resource managers are feeling increasing pressure from a multitude of publics who make diverse and conflicting demands on the environment (Lime, 1972). These publics consist of various government agencies, special interest groups, and the general public, who desire an array of services that may include local, state, regional, and national interests. When a particular recreation area is to be developed, a number of diverse pressures are brought to bear as the plan is being implemented. It is the resource manager's responsibility to consider the various alternatives available, make decisions, and justify these decisions to "the publics." The dilemma lies in deciding which public to consider because there are so many (Lime and Stankey, 1971), and in determining the proper balance among the interests of various publics.

Recreation planning agencies continue to use various social, economic, and personal characteristics of recreationists to justify development of recreation areas, but their ability to accurately predict future use from these variables has been inadequate. A better understanding of the recreation experience, of the importance of that experience to the recreationists, and of the projections that are made must be achieved. As Lime (1972) stated:

> If managers are to know how to manage their lands in order to maximize user satisfaction, they must, in part, know who their clientele are ... and know something about what these people like and dislike. Learning about their clientele implies the need to listen, not only to people who visit the area but also to those who do not come but still have an interest in it.

If user satisfaction is the goal of natural resource managers, then they must know what recreation activities are desired and what environments and circumstances produce a satisfying experience (Clark, et al., 1971).

To provide every kind of activity at every facility is not feasible. Lucas (1963) stated: "No recreation supplier need feel obligated to meet all demands. Each public agency could aim clearly at a part of the demand, and refer people who want something more, less, or different to a more appropriate area." But some selection criteria must be implemented enabling the resource manager to select the kinds of activities that will provide the greatest public satisfaction. One such technique may be the classification of recreation types or activity-aggregates that are definite and consistent.

If recreation types can be isolated, it is hypothesized that the recreationist may substitute one recreation activity for another activity within that same type. Ferriss (1970) stated:

> The positive and negative reinforcements provided by both the natural environment and the sociocultural system condition the individual's preferences for the out-of-doors. Thus, his recreation preferences arise out of experiences. Since outdoor-recreation preferences are learned, they may, through appropriate schedules of reinforcement, be unlearned, and other responses and patterns of behavior substituted.

Moss and Lamphear (1970) conducted research on the relationship between personality and the ability to substitute recreation activities to meet the needs and drives of people. They stressed that:

> ... it seems reasonable to suppose that unlike personalities are more apt to choose different forms of recreation, and like personalities would tend to choose similar activities ... a particular activity may be related to several needs, but is more likely to serve similar needs for similar people ... several activities may be related to the same or similar needs.

Their findings indicated that activities could be clustered into meaningful groups and that the groups were related to certain measureable human needs. In addition, other needs within the cluster seemed to have meaningful relationships to each other. Their findings have been supported by other researchers, even though the same recreation activities have not been used (Proctor, 1962; Burton, 1971a, 1971b; Holme and Massie, 1970).

Development of recreation types seems to provide a reasonable mechanism for aiding the recreation planner in satisfying the needs of recreationists. If stable types can be isolated, planners may be able to select at least one activity from each cluster (type) and avoid excessive duplication of one type with no activities in another type. Selection will depend upon the feasibility of an activity at a particular recreation site and compatability of all activities at that facility. Physical features also may influence the selection.

## METHODS

### Sample

Data were obtained by personal interviews using a stratified area random sample in seven Iowa counties. Counties were selected to include a major central Iowa water-basin recreation facility (Red Rock Reservoir) and the six contiguous counties. The area contains both urban and rural counties with a range from 92.9 to 39.8 per cent urban population.

The universe consisted of all individuals 12 years of age and older residing in the seven counties during the fall of 1970. A total of 298 respondents were interviewed, with the sample consisting of 46.9 per cent (140) males and 53.1 per cent (158) females. The mean age of the respondents was 38.0 years, and the mean education was 11.6 years of schooling. Both recreators and nonrecreators were included in the sample but there were no control groups. Therefore, establishment of a causal relationship was not possible, because reported behavior, not observed behavior, was used.

## RESULTS

### Reservoir Impact on Leisure Behavior

The reservoir under consideration in this study was first put into operation in the spring of 1969, although none of the recreation facilities around the lake were opened until early 1970. Therefore, the data on impact provide a benchmark for future study. Of the 298 respondents, 199 or 66.8 per cent had visited the reservoir by the time of the interview. Of the 199 who had visited the area, 82 or 41.2 per cent (27.5 per cent of the total sample) of the respondents had participated in at least one recreation activity at the reservoir. A number of the respondents had participated in more than one activity, with a mean of 1.5 activities per participant. In total, 124 occasions were mentioned by the 82 respondents (see Table I). Only 22 of these activities had not been participated in by the respondents before the reservoir development.

### Table I
#### Present Participation in Recreation Activities by Participation Prior to Reservoir Development

| | Prior Participation | | | | | |
|---|---|---|---|---|---|---|
| | Yes | | No | | Total | |
| Activity | N | % | N | % | N | % |
| Swimming | 7 | 6.9 | 1 | 4.5 | 8 | 6.5 |
| Water skiing | 7 | 6.9 | 2 | 9.1 | 9 | 7.3 |
| Fishing | 29 | 28.3 | 1 | 4.5 | 30 | 24.3 |
| Boating | 19 | 18.6 | 6 | 27.4 | 25 | 20.3 |
| Camping | 4 | 3.9 | 1 | 4.5 | 5 | 4.0 |
| Hiking | 13 | 12.7 | 3 | 13.7 | 16 | 12.9 |
| Picnic | 16 | 15.7 | 2 | 9.1 | 19 | 15.3 |
| Sailing | 2 | 2.0 | 1 | 4.5 | 3 | 2.4 |
| Horseback riding | 1 | 1.0 | 0 | 0.0 | 1 | 0.8 |
| Watching boat races | 0 | 0.0 | 1 | 4.5 | 1 | 0.8 |
| Duck hunting | 1 | 1.0 | 2 | 9.1 | 3 | 2.4 |
| Bird watching | 2 | 2.0 | 0 | 0.0 | 2 | 1.6 |
| Motorcycling | 1 | 1.0 | 0 | 0.0 | 1 | 0.8 |
| Sightseeing | 0 | 0.0 | 2 | 9.1 | 2 | 1.6 |
| TOTAL | 102 | 100.0 | 22 | 100.0 | 124 | 100.0 |

Because most activities had been participated in by the respondents before the development of the reservoir, the intensity of present involvement as compared with involvement before development was determined. The intensity of participation was indicated for 99 of the 102 activity occasions participated in previously (see Table II). Of these 99 activities, 53.5 per cent were participated in

### Table II
Rate of Participation Change in Activities at Red Rock Reservoir

|  | Total | |
|---|---|---|
|  | N | % of 99 |
| Much less | 5 | 5.1 |
| Slightly less | 4 | 4.0 |
| Same | 53 | 53.5 |
| Slightly more | 17 | 17.2 |
| Much more | 20 | 20.2 |
|  | 102 | 100.0 |

at the same intensity, 9.1 per cent at less intensity and 37.4 per cent with more intensity than before the reservoir was built. Activities showing the greatest increase in involvement were fishing, boating, hiking, and picnicking.

In analyzing the activities in which respondents began participation after development of the reservoir, no one activity stands out (see Table I). The greatest impact was in boating and hiking, but the basic finding is that few people changed their behavior. The reasons respondents began participation in recreation activities at the reservoir are listed in Table III.

### Table III
Reasons Why Respondents Began Participation in Recreation Activities at Red Rock Reservoir

| Reasons | N | % |
|---|---|---|
| No response | 2 | 9.1 |
| Better fishing | 2 | 9.1 |
| Closeness | 7 | 31.8 |
| Entertainment-relaxing | 5 | 22.7 |
| Friend or relative influence | 6 | 27.3 |
| Total | 22 | 100.0 |

Respondents were asked to comment on anticipated changes in their recreation patterns resulting from the reservoir. Only 31.9 per cent (95) of all the respondents anticipated a change. The reasons for anticipating changes can be categorized into three broad categories: (1) want outdoor experience (27.4 per cent of 95); (2) want water-related experience, but not boating (48.4 per cent of 95); and (3) want boating and water-skiing experience (24.2 per cent of 95). The remaining 68.1 per cent of the sample did not anticipate any change in their recreation patterns.

At the time of this study little impact had been made by the new facility, due mainly to its recent development. The question arises as to whether the concept of recreation types will aid the planners in the decision-making process, considering anticipated change and the need and desire to develop the area.

**Classification of Outdoor Recreation Activities**

*Development of Recreation Types*

Respondents were asked to indicate which of 45 recreation activities they had participated in from Labor Day 1969 to Labor Day 1970. The "yes" and "no" responses were then subjected to the principal components, factor analytical techniques with the varimax rotation (Harmon, 1967; Nunnally, 1967). This technique was used to determine if respondents could be grouped into recreation types according to the activities in which they had participated. Results of the analysis indicate if individuals are more likely to take part in several activities within a given cluster of activities than in those that fall into different clusters (Burton, 1971; Proctor, 1962; Moss and Lamphear, 1970).

Five factors were specified with no theoretical justifications given for the activity selection. Therefore, the data provided the initial clustering of factors. A cutoff factor loading value of 0.4 was specified for initial retention of the activity on the factor. If an activity loaded on more than one factor, it was permitted to remain on all factors provided it met the criteria. Initially, 35 of the 45 activities met the minimum 0.4 requirement on one or more of the factors. The original 35 items meeting minimum criteria, and their respective factor loadings, are presented in Table IV. Further considerations of inter-item correlations, item-to-total correlations, and logical fit among the items reduced the clusters to 9, 6, 7, 4, and 4, respectively.

*The Factors*

Each factor has a fairly homogeneous grouping of activities. Factor I *(games and sports)* consists of nine activities composed of physically active pursuits. A possible exception is spectator

## Table IV
### Factor Analysis Cluster of Outdoor Recreation Activities Based on Five Factors

| | Factor Loading | | Factor Loading |
|---|---|---|---|
| **Factor I—Games and Sports** | | **Factor III—Hunting and Fishing** | |
| *Bicycling | 0.530 | *Gathering specimens | 0.437 |
| *Baseball and softball | 0.645 | *Archery | 0.587 |
| *Football | 0.647 | *Trap or target shooting | 0.489 |
| *Basketball | 0.676 | *Hunt small game | 0.732 |
| *Swim—outdoor pool | 0.603 | *Hunt waterfowl | 0.654 |
| *Motorbike—motorcycle | 0.546 | *Fishing | 0.509 |
| *Spectator sports | 0.466 | *Ice fishing | 0.515 |
| *Ice skating | 0.566 | Hunt big game | 0.443 |
| *Sliding, sledding, tobogganing | 0.578 | | |
| Horseback riding | 0.443 | **Factor IV—"Motorized" Activities** | |
| Golf—regular | 0.435 | *Powerboating and water-skiing | 0.465 |
| Golf—miniature | 0.434 | *Snowmobiling | 0.648 |
| Swim—natural environment | 0.411 | *Swim—natural environment | 0.448 |
| Tennis | 0.440 | *Camp (wheeled vehicle) | 0.464 |
| **Factor II—Nature Appreciation** | | **Factor V** | |
| *Hiking or walking for pleasure | 0.539 | *Outdoor exhibits | 0.475 |
| *Nature walks | 0.549 | *Camp—tent | 0.558 |
| *Bird watching | 0.557 | *Camp—group | 0.555 |
| *Nature photo—outdoor painting | 0.603 | *Canoe | 0.441 |
| *Drive for pleasure—sightseeing | 0.572 | | |
| *Family picnic—small group picnics | 0.510 | | |

*Indicates items accepted for analysis.

sports. However, if one is interested in participating in active sports he probably will have an interest in observing others participate in these same activities. Participation in these activities is relatively inexpensive, and to some extent is undertaken within a team or club setting, with the possible exception of motorcycling. All activities, except cycling, are usually undertaken in an urban, manmade environment.

Factor II *(nature appreciation)* consists of six relatively passive outdoor activities. They involve unorganized pursuits that take place in a "natural" environment. They can be either individual or group activities, and do not require a specified "playground." Participation requires little physical skill or expense.

Factor III *(hunting and fishing)* is a homogeneous group of seven activities that involve some form of hunting or fishing during all seasons of the year. Though skill is an advantage to the participants, it is not necessary for participation. All these activities, except gathering specimens, require some equipment and are usually inexpensive to moderately expensive.

Factor IV *("motorized" activities)* consists of four activities. With the exception of swimming, these activities are quite expensive, involve mechanization, and have considerable status attachment. All require some skill. They can be participated in alone, but are usually group activities.

Factor V contains four activities and is a more heterogeneous cluster than the others. "Outdoor exhibits" does not fit well into the camping-canoeing category, except that it can be participated in while camping. Individuals or groups can take part in these activities, though there is a risk of attaching too much significance to this factor.

After the factors were produced and the 0.4 criteria established, further analysis was performed to develop recreation types that statistically and logically fit together. A number of statistics were computed to determine internal consistency. These included: (1) a comparison of the minimum acceptable item-total correlation coefficient and the calculated coefficients of each scale based on the field sample, (2) determination of the coefficient of reliability by means of coefficient alpha (Cronbach, 1951; Bohrnstedt, 1969) and (3) determination of the average intercorrelation among items of each scale (Warren, *et al.* 1969).

All item-total correlations except snowmobiling (Factor IV) were greater than the acceptable minimum, with average $r_{it}$ greater than the minimum by 0.281, 0.198, 0.214, 0.130, and 0.136, respectively (see Table V). By using coefficient alpha as a measure of internal consistency, values of 0.809, 0.661, 0.675, 0.519, and 0.506 were obtained. Average intercorrelation coefficients of 0.329, 0.248, 0.258, 0.211, and 0.218 were obtained. In Factors I through V, respectively, 100, 93.3, 76.2, 66.7, and 66.7 per cent of the intercorrelation coefficients were significant at the 0.001 level, and only one intercorrelation of all factors was not significant at the 0.05 level. All were in the same direction within each factor. On the basis of these data and the magnitudes of quantity obtained, a reasonable case for linearity of the factors has been presented; therefore, the scalability of the factors is claimed. More complete information is presented in Table VI.

## Table V
### Correlations and Reliability Coefficients for the Five Factors

| Activity | Item-Total Correlation | | | |
|---|---|---|---|---|
| *Factor I* | | | | |
| Bicycling | 0.6010 | | | $\bar{r}_{it} = 0.6344$ |
| Baseball and softball | 0.7023 | | | |
| Football | 0.7005 | meaningful | | $r_{it} = 0.3533$ |
| Basketball | 0.6654 | | | |
| Swim—outdoor pool | 0.6606 | | | $\bar{r}_{ij} = 0.3293$ |
| Motorbiking & motor-cycling | 0.5476 | | | Alpha Coefficient = 0.8089 |
| Spectator sports | 0.5393 | | | |
| Ice skating | 0.6242 | | | |
| Sledding, sliding, toboganning | 0.6687 | | | |
| *Factor II* | | | | |
| Hiking or walking for pleasure | 0.7088 | | | $\bar{r}_{it} = 0.6058$ |
| Nature walks | 0.5819 | | | |
| Bird watch | 0.4855 | meaningful | | $r_{it} = 0.4082$ |
| Nature photo—outdoor painting | 0.5314 | | | $\bar{r}_{ij} = 0.2478$ |
| Drive for pleasure—sightseeing | 0.6525 | | | Alpha Coefficient = 0.6614 |
| Family picnics—small group picnics | 0.6749 | | | |
| *Factor III* | | | | |
| Gathering specimens | 0.6017 | | | $\bar{r}_{it} = 0.5916$ |
| Archery | 0.5191 | | | |
| Target or trap shooting | 0.5393 | meaningful | | $r_{it} = 0.3780$ |
| Hunting small game | 0.7425 | | | |
| Hunting waterfowl | 0.6031 | | | $\bar{r}_{ij} = 0.2582$ |
| Fishing | 0.6916 | | | |
| Ice fishing | 0.4445 | | | Alpha Coefficient = 0.6749 |
| *Factor IV* | | | | |
| Swim—natural environment | 0.7486 | | | $\bar{r}_{it} = 0.6297$ |
| Camping (wheeled vehicle) | 0.6236 | | | |
| Power boating and water skiing | 0.7044 | meaningful | | $r_{it} = 0.5000$ |
| Snowmobiling | 0.4425 | | | $\bar{r}_{ij} = 0.2015$ |
| | | | | Alpha Coefficient = 0.5191 |

## Table V (Cont'd)

| Activity | Item-Total Correlation | | |
|---|---|---|---|
| *Factor V* | | | |
| Outdoor exhibits | 0.6827 | | $\bar{r}_{it} = 0.6360$ |
| Camp—tent | 0.7189 | | |
| Camp—group | 0.5379 | meaningful | $r_{it} = 0.5000$ |
| Canoe | 0.6044 | | |
| | | | $\bar{r}_{ij} = 0.2176$ |
| | | | Alpha Coefficient $= 0.5061$ |

*Socioeconomic Characteristics Related to Recreation Types*

A number of socioeconomic characteristics were correlated with the total scores of each of the five recreation types (Table VII). For most characteristics, all correlations were significant with all factors, though the magnitude of the correlations differed considerably. Age is inversely related to each factor, with the *games and sports* factor indicating the greatest magnitude. Young people participate far more in *games and sports;* males participate more than females in all factors except *nature appreciation;* and males participate most in *games and sports* and *hunting and fishing.*

Family size is directly related to participation in all recreation types. The larger the family size, the greater the participation in each recreation type. Again, the greatest magnitude is found in *games and sports* and *hunting and fishing.*

Residence has been another characteristic used to delineate participation in recreation activities. The respondents were asked to indicate their residence during childhood (ages 12-17). Statistically significant results are found for *games and sports* and Factor V *(camping, canoeing, outdoor exhibits)*, although the magnitude of the correlations is low. The findings indicate that those who lived in urban areas during ages 12-17 were more likely to have participated in more of the activities in each of these two factors than those who lived in rural areas during ages 12-17. Present residence has a different impact on use, being statistically significant only with *hunting and fishing.* Rural residents take part in a greater number of the activities in *hunting and fishing* than do urban residents.

The education of the respondent is significantly related to *games and sports, nature appreciation,* and *hunting and fishing,* but in

## Table VI
### Correlation Matrix of Activities in Factor I

| | Bicycling | Baseball Softball | Football | Basketball | Outdoor Pool | Motorbiking Motorcycling | Spectator Sports | Ice Skating | Sledding Sliding Tobogganing |
|---|---|---|---|---|---|---|---|---|---|
| Bicyling | — | | | | | | | | |
| Baseball-softball | 0.3685 | — | | | | | | | |
| Football | 0.3146 | 0.5810 | — | | | | | | |
| Basketball | 0.2738 | 0.5443 | 0.4728 | — | | | | | |
| Outdoor pool | 0.3909 | 0.3051 | 0.3716 | 0.3145 | — | | | | |
| Motorbiking-motorcycling | 0.2041 | 0.2610 | 0.3740 | 0.2933 | 0.2329 | — | | | |
| Spectator sports | 0.2203 | 0.2557 | 0.2106 | 0.2778 | 0.2550 | 0.2207 | — | | |
| Ice skating | 0.2203 | 0.3635 | 0.3993 | 0.4188 | 0.3617 | 0.3613 | 0.2149 | — | |
| Sledding, sliding tobogganing | 0.4014 | 0.3408 | 0.3497 | 0.2999 | 0.4509 | 0.2999 | 0.2481 | 0.3128 | — |

different directions. *Games and sports* and *hunting and fishing* are negatively related, indicating that the higher the number of years of schooling attained the lower the participation score for the factor. *Nature appreciation* is positively related to years of education attained. The higher the educational attainment, the greater the number of *nature appreciation* activities in which the respondents participated.

Income is also related to participation. Factor V *(camping, canoeing, and outdoor exhibits)* is the only factor that does not have statistical significance. For the other factors, the higher the income, the greater the number of activities in which the respondents participated. A summary of the characteristics related to the factor scores is given in Table VII.

### Table VII
Relationship of Socioeconomic Characteristics to Five Factors

| Socioeconomic Characteristics | Factor I | Factor II | Factor III | Factor IV | Factor V |
|---|---|---|---|---|---|
| Age | −0.6196** | −0.2864** | −0.2563** | −0.3422** | −0.2915** |
| Sex | −0.2277** | 0.0604 | −0.4214** | −0.1578* | −0.0199 |
| Family size | 0.4083** | 0.1872** | 0.3025** | 0.1257* | 0.1751** |
| Residence ages 12-17 | 0.1404* | 0.0370 | −0.0598 | 0.0401 | 0.1008* |
| Present residence | 0.0359 | −0.0572 | 0.1466* | −0.0058 | −0.0381 |
| Education | −0.1704* | 0.1763** | −0.1429* | 0.0945 | 0.0684 |
| Income | 0.2712** | 0.2518** | 0.1498* | 0.2716** | 0.0547 |

*0.05 level of significance.
**0.001 level of significance.

## SOME RESOURCE MANAGEMENT IMPLICATIONS

Clustering of activities in terms of participation by particular people has important implications for development and modification of recreation facilities. First, it provides at least a partial basis for estimating probable response to new kinds of recreation facilities in a given geographic region. This is an extremely important factor in planning new facilities that cannot be estimated directly from current use-patterns and conventional projections. Clustering implies that new kinds of facilities will be used primarily by those already participating in other activities in the same cluster. For example, new facilities for powerboating and water-skiing will be used primarily by people already participating in snowmobiling, vehicle camping, and natural environment swimming, or boating at some other location. Direct estimates of participation in other activities can be used as a basis for roughly estimating probable participation.

At Red Rock Reservoir, which was referred to previously, a preconstruction survey showed that a relatively small percentage of respondents in the adjacent region were participating in power boating and related activities. Therefore, it was reasonable to expect relatively modest participation in these activities at the new facility, which proved to be the case. Only modest changes occurred in the individual's recreation patterns as a result of the new facilities. In another region with heavy participation in snowmobiling, vehicle camping, etc., a much greater response would probably occur. The major point is that clustering makes it possible to use participation figures for related activities to obtain crude, but useful, estimates of probable participation in new activities.

Second, clustering provides a partial basis for decisions about the specific activities to be provided at particular recreation sites. Two quite different situations can be considered to illustrate these possibilities. One is a relatively isolated site intended to serve the needs of the total population of the area it surrounds; the other is a regional system of sites which are intended to serve such needs.

The single facility might best provide for compatible combinations of activities from several clusters. Compatibility would involve both relations among user-groups and the physical and ecological characteristics of the site. Simplifying considerably, a given facility might be developed to provide for the following activities:

| | |
|---|---|
| Bicycling | from Factor I |
| Nature walks and family picnics | from Factor II |
| Fishing | from Factor III |
| Swimming | from Factor IV |
| Tent camping | from Factor V |

Such a combination would provide a more useful single facility than would heavy concentration of activities from the same cluster, *e.g.*, bicycling, baseball, basketball, and swimming; or archery, trap shooting, and fishing.

A quite different approach seems feasible in developing a regional system of facilities. Modest specialization of individual facilities in patterns suggested by the clusters seems potentially promising. For example, one facility might provide for bicycling, baseball, basketball, and swimming in a pool (all from Factor I), while another might provide for archery, trap shooting, fishing, etc. (all from Factor III). Other possibilities might include facilities focused on hiking, bird watching, nature photography, and nature walks; and facilities focused on "motorized" equipment involved in such activities as powerboating and snowmobiling with highly developed camping facilities.

Such specializations would necessitate the locations being in close proximity in order to serve the entire population realistically, and they would depend on the characteristics of particular sites. But, having met these tests, specialization might have several advantages. Specific population groups would find several of their interests met at one site, and user-groups with quite different preferences would be less likely to interfere with one another's enjoyment. Specific sites could be designed to take advantage of complementary facility needs among specific activities. For example, roadways to boatramps also could serve as snowmobile trails with those trails continuing on the ice surface of the river or lake to another ramp.

Specific management of facilities could be undertaken to meet the needs of one set of activities with less interference and/or damage from other incompatible activities. As an example habitat management could be undertaken at a facility devoted to hiking, nature walks, bird watching, and nature photography. This type of plan could be carried out on a much more intensive basis here than at a general-use site where incompatible uses might destroy delicate vegetation.

None of these ideas for combining activities is radically new. But the clustering of activities developed in this study does provide a firmer basis for systematically making decisions in the development of recreational facilities. As more recreation facilities are made available to local residents, resource planners must consider the entire range of consequences of particular alternative development plans. If appropriate consideration is given, the quality of life of the community residents can be improved.

## ACKNOWLEDGMENT

Journal Paper No. J-7556 of the Iowa Agriculture and Home Economics Experiment Station, Ames, Iowa. Project No. 1949. I would like to thank Dr. Richard D. Warren for his statistical consultation and Dr. Henry Webster for his helpful comments on earlier drafts.

## REFERENCES

Bohrnstedt, G. W. "A Quick Method for Determining the Reliability and Validity of Multi-item Scales," *Amer. Soc. Rev.* **34**, 542 (1969).
Burton, T. L. *Experiments in Recreation Research* (Totowa, N.J.: Rowman and Littlefield, 1971).
Burton, T. L. "Identification of Recreation Types through Cluster Analysis," *Soc. Leisure* **1**, 47 (1971).
Clark, R. N., J. C. Hendee, and F. L. Campbell. "Values, Behavior and Conflict in Modern Camping Culture," *J. Leisure Res.* **3**, 143 (1971).
Cronbach, L. J. "Coefficient Alpha and the Internal Structure of Tests," *Psychometrika* **16**, 297 (1951).
Ferriss, A. L. "The Social and Personality Correlates of Outdoor Recreation," *The Annals* **389**, 46 (1970).
Harmon, H. H. *Modern Factor Analysis,* 2nd ed. (Chicago: University of Chicago Press, 1967).
Holme, A., and P. Massie. *Children's Play: A Study of Needs and Opportunities.* (London: Michael Joseph, 1970).
Lime, D. W. "Behavioral Research in Outdoor Recreation Management: An Example of How Visitors Select Campgrounds," in *Environment and the Social Sciences: Perspective and Applications,* J. F. Wohlwill and D. H. Carson, Eds. (New York: American Psychological Association, 1972) pp. 198-206.
Lime, D. W., and G. H. Stankey. "Carrying Capacity: Maintaining Outdoor Recreation Quality," *Recreation Symposium Proceedings,* Northeastern Forest Experiment Station, Upper Darby, Pa. (1971) pp. 174-184.
Lucas, R. C. "The Status of Recreation Research Related to Users," *Soc. Amer. Foresters Proc.* (1963) pp. 127-130.

Moss, W. T. and S. C. Lamphear. "Substitutability of Recreational Activities in Meeting Stated Needs and Drives of the Visitor," *J. Environ. Educ.* 1, 129 (1970).

Nunnally, J. C. *Psychometric Theory* (New York: McGraw-Hill, Inc., 1967).

Proctor, C. "Dependence of Recreation Participation on Background Characteristics of Sample Persons in the September 1960 National Recreation Survey," in *National Recreation Survey*, Abbott L. Ferriss, *et al.*, Outdoor Recreation Resources Review Commission, Report No. 19, Washington, D.C. (1962) pp. 77-94.

Warren, R. D., G. E. Klonglan, and M. M. Sabri. "The Certainty Method: Its Application and Usefulness in Developing Empirical Measures in Social Sciences," Iowa State University, Rural Sociology Report No. 82 (1969).

# 12. Economic Impact of Outdoor Recreation: What Have We Learned?

**H. H. STOEVENER, R. B. RETTIG, AND S. D. REILING**

## INTRODUCTION

The following item appeared in *The Oregonian* on Friday, April 6, 1973:

> Vancouver, Wash.—Developers of Vancouver Mall filed Clark County's first environmental impact statement Thursday.
>
> And, so far, no one is certain what to do with it.
>
> The statement is required by state law, but beyond preparation, there appears to be a gray area as to what to do with it.
>
> Zone changes for the center, which developers say eventually will rival Portland's Lloyd Center, already have been made. The Planning Commission has little use for the study now.
>
> There also appears to be little in the law as to what an environmental impact statement should contain on such a project.

While the newspaper story is about a shopping center, the same confusion of decision-makers exists for many of the environmental impact studies that have been developed since the National Environmental Policy Act created the requirement. Why do the environmental studies have to be made? If these studies are needed (and many would argue that they are), why aren't they more useful for local resource decisions?

A great deal has been learned about the economic impact of

outdoor recreation, but many lessons will gather dust on a shelf in a planner's office if they are lucky enough to miss his waste basket. Consequently, only those findings that are useful to those responsible for decisions relating to a community, or that could be useful if additional research would fill in critical gaps in knowledge, will be discussed here.

Recall the tale of the six blind men and the elephant. The first blind man felt the elephant's side and believed that the elephant was a wall. Another felt a knee and perceived the beast to be a tree. The one grasping the trunk believed he had found a snake. The man feeling an ear thought the elephant was a fan, while his tusk-holding colleague was sure spears were involved, and the man left holding the tail was equally sure that they were dealing with a rope. There is a little bit of those six blind men in everyone. Images of reality depend critically upon mental constructs. For example, how many of us have taken a guided nature walk and have seen things that we had not seen before the naturalist pointed them out? There is nothing innately wrong with different images. However, when the six blind men fall into a bitter fight about the nature of the elephant, or when a group policy choice depends upon the perception of reality, a problem arises that is frequently called a "communication gap."

In *The Image,* Boulding (1956) states that there are basically two types of images. So far, we have been talking about the first image, that which we know or think we know the facts to be. The second image is the value image, an evaluation of what we believe exists.

Returning to the newspaper story concerning the environmental impact statement, we would argue that such statements are required by Washington state law so that a richer or more complete image of the real facts can be obtained. The desire for more facts, in turn, arises from a difficulty in aggregating a social value image from individual value images. In other words, it was believed that public decisions reconciling divergent points of view can be more readily reached if perceptions of reality were based on similar descriptions of facts. The six blind men may more easily agree on their evaluation of the problematic elephant if each is forced to touch tail, tusks, ear, knee, trunk, and body.

For the purposes of this chapter, community development is defined as the process by which a community creates an expansion of choices and opportunities for the people as they seek to satisfy their personal and group goals. In the following discussion we take a decided "community" point of view. The main focus is on the impacts borne, individually and collectively, by residents within commuting range of the recreational resource in question.

Public or community decision-makers are those who speak for a particular community. They may be responsible for investment projects for the development or preservation of recreational resources. More frequently, they are the individuals called on to represent the social viewpoint when private decisions are made that impinge upon the availability of outdoor recreation activities. Or, they may be the spokesmen who are expected to articulate local concerns when such decisions are made at higher levels in the governmental structure.

It is the authors' opinion that the definition of community development stated herein correctly implies that community decision-makers are not, and should not be, directly concerned with the economic value of the recreational facility, a value that may be comprised largely of the net willingness of individuals outside the local community to pay for the facility. Therefore, it should not come as a surprise that many of the studies done in the area of outdoor recreation have become "dust collectors" in the offices of community planners. One may ask, then, what the local decision-maker is concerned with. The above definition suggests that local planners and decision-makers are concerned with how the recreational development affects the residents of the local community. At the very minimum, community decision-makers are interested in knowing to what extent local people will participate in the recreational opportunity in question.

## DIRECT AND INDIRECT IMPACTS

Two types of economic benefits are usually generated by the development or preservation of outdoor recreation. First, the population of users captures the primary or direct recreational benefits made possible by the action. The degree to which the local community is benefited depends upon how intensively the residents of the community use the recreational facility. Unless a unique recreational opportunity is provided, these benefits are measured by the lower time and money costs with which the recreationist can reach this facility compared to another, more distant, facility.

The second type of economic benefit arises from the stimulation of economic activity in the community due to the increase in outdoor recreational activities. As recreationists are attracted to the area by the recreational development, they will purchase goods and services from the local economy. These expenditures will have a multiplier effect and will eventually result in larger incomes for the households in the local community. These are some of the secondary or indirect benefits associated with the development. Moreover, the public sector is likely to be affected, both in terms of increased property tax receipts and the demand for public services. Increased economic activity, in general, may lead to additional rounds of environmental impacts. These effects will be considered in greater detail from the perspective of the local community in a later section.

**Some Direct Benefits**

Recreational benefits, as defined here, exist only if there is a viable demand by local residents for the recreational opportunities provided by the development (see Stoevener, 1972, Chapter 8). In an attempt to provide relevant information of the type that is of interest to community decision-makers, data collected for three recreation studies conducted in Oregon were analyzed.

The three studies utilized in the analysis are: (1) the Yaquina Bay study (Stoevener, *et al.* 1972), which dealt with a water use conflict involving recreational use of the estuary, (2) the Klamath Lake study (Reiling, *et al.*, 1973), which estimated the economic value of Upper Klamath Lake, assuming various degrees of water quality improvements, and (3) the study of the Bend Ranger District of the Deschutes National Forest in Central Oregon (Guedry and Stoevener, 1970), which measured the value of recreational facilities according to levels of remoteness.

These studies were undertaken for purposes quite different from those of this chapter. Yet they cover a wide range of the recreational opportunities available in the Pacific Northwest. The Yaquina Bay study evaluated oceanic and estuarine recreational activities, while the Bend Ranger District study was concerned with forest recreation and water-related activities available within the district. The Klamath Lake study evaluated four lakes in Oregon that vary significantly in terms of water quality. The diversity of recreational opportunities offered by these resources is both a benefit and a detriment for the purposes of the analysis considered here. The wide variation in resource types makes it difficult to determine whether the variability in the data discussed below is due to the different characteristics of the facilities or to differences in the local communities near the recreational facilities. On the other hand, this diversity offers an opportunity to make observations about community impacts associated with these different types of outdoor recreation resources.

Data for the three studies were analyzed to determine how intensively the recreational facilities were used by local residents. The results are summarized in Table I. The numbers in the last column of the table indicate that the extent to which local residents use the recreational facilities varies significantly, ranging from 0.11 recreation days per local resident for the clam fishery at Yaquina Bay to 1.91 recreation days per local resident for the Bend Ranger District of the Deschutes National Forest. Although it is difficult to draw any general conclusions from the results, we can identify a few factors from these data that may be important. The Bend Ranger District will be considered first.

The District covers a land area of approximately 540,000 acres and contains 59 designated summer recreation sites. The level of development (man-made improvements) among these sites varies considerably. Therefore, the facility is well-suited for a wide range of recreational activities, ranging from back-packing in a wilderness area to relaxing on the patio of a resort. The range of recreational activities available within the District is probably an important factor in explaining the high local participation rate at the facility; the District can be used by people with a variety of outdoor recreational interests.

Another factor that may be related to the local participation rate in the Bend Ranger District is the high proportion of recreational opportunities available to the local community. The District contains a larger number of recreational sites than the other facilities considered here. So the quantity, as well as the diversified types, of recreational sites may be an important determinant of the local use rate.

The location of the recreation facility relative to the population center of the community may also be important. For example, the southern tip of Upper Klamath Lake lies within the city limits of Klamath Falls. Consequently, the lake is a readily accessible and inexpensive recreational site. The convenience and low cost partially explain the high local participation rate at the lake. This

## Table I

Total Recreation Days or Visits Per Year, Local Resident Recreation Days or Visits Per Year, and the Population of the Local Community for the Bend Ranger District, Yaquina Bay, and the Klamath Lake Study Area

| Study Area | Total Recreation Days or Visits/Year | Local Recreation Days or Visits | Local as a % of Total Recreation Days or Visits | Population of Local Community | Recreation Days or Visits/Local Resident/Year |
|---|---|---|---|---|---|
| Bend Ranger District[a] (Rec. days) | 1,174,100 | 89,349 | 7.61 | 46,800[d] | 1.91 |
| Yaquina Bay (Rec days)[b] | | | | | |
| Bottomfish | 31,855 | 8,524 | 26.76 | 24,635[e] | 0.35 |
| Salmon | 10,914 | 2,965 | 27.17 | 24,635 | 0.12 |
| Clam | 6,606 | 2,755 | 41.70 | 24,635 | 0.11 |
| Klamath Lake Study (Visits)[c] | | | | | |
| Odell Lake | 180,304 | 55,769 | 30.93 | 200,700[f] | 0.28 |
| Lake of the Woods | 267,327 | 136,328 | 51.00 | 140,900[g] | 0.97 |
| Upper Klamath Lake | 146,491 | 88,305 | 60.28 | 49,600[h] | 1.78 |
| Willow Lake | 109,471 | 58,187 | 53.18 | 91,300[i] | 0.64 |

[a] Guedry, 1970, adapted from Table 3, pp. 71-72.
[b] Stevens, 1966, adapted from Table 7, p. 56, and Table 8, p. 57.
[c] Reiling, et al., 1973, Table 3, p. 46.
[d] The "local community" is defined to be Deschutes, Crook, and Jefferson Counties.
[e] The "local community" is defined to be Lincoln County.
[f] The "local community" is defined to be Lane County.
[g] The "local community" is defined to be Jackson and Klamath Counties.
[h] The "local community" is defined to be Klamath County.
[i] The "local community" is defined to be Jackson County.

COMMUNITY AND LEISURE 241

high local use rate exists in spite of very poor water quality conditions.

Whether or not other similar recreational resources are available, another factor must be considered in evaluating how the local community may view a recreational facility. The natural resources of the Pacific Northwest are easily adapted to offer a wide range of recreational services. Many recreational facilities are substitutes for other facilities. This is true for the three areas analyzed. They do not offer what most recreationists would call truly "unique" services. The price elasticities calculated from the demand equations for the different levels of remoteness in the Bend Ranger District illustrate this point. The demand curves become more inelastic as the level of remoteness increases. The price elasticities range from $-2.13$ for the easily accessible sites to $-0.291$ for the most remote sites. This is consistent with the expectation that the price elasticity of demand is greater for recreational sites for which substitutes are readily available. If a particular facility is to capture a very large share of the recreation time spent by local residents, it must possess some characterstic that is desirable to local recreationists, such as location or fishing success.

The above examples illustrate that the characteristics of the recreational resource itself are important in determining the local participation rate. Some characteristics of recreationists also appear to be important. For example, Table II illustrates that the level of income seems to be important in the studies. The Yaquina Bay data suggest that salmon fishing at Yaquina Bay is a rich man's activity when compared to bottomfishing and clamming. Local families with incomes of less than $6,000 accounted for 71.3 per cent and 74.4 per cent of local resident recreation days of clamming and bottomfishing, respectively, but only 26.2 per cent of the local resident recreation days of salmon fishing. About 64 per cent of the local families had incomes less than $6,000. This divergence does not exist in the population of nonlocal fishermen with incomes less than $6,000, who accounted for approximately equal proportions of the nonlocal recreation days of clamming (33.16 per cent), bottomfishing (36.15 per cent) and salmon fishing (35.22 per cent).

The income elasticities of demand for the three fisheries at Yaquina Bay are consistent with expectations based on the local resident data. Income elasticity of demand for the salmon fishery is positive ($+1.38$), while income elasticities for bottomfishing

### Table II
Distribution of the Local Population by Income Groups, and Percentage of Local Recreation Days by Income Groups, for Yaquina Bay and the Bend Ranger District

|  | Family Income Group | | | | |
|---|---|---|---|---|---|
|  | Less than $4,000 | $4,000 – $5,999 | $6,000 – $9,999 | $10,000 – $14,999 | $15,000 – $24,999 |
| *Yaquina Bay* | | | | | |
| Percentage of local population in income group[a] | 34.98 | 28.60 | 26.72 | 6.43 | 3.29 |
| Percentage of local bottomfishing recreation days, by income group[b] | 41.80 | 32.60 | 31.80 | 3.80 | — |
| Percentage of local clamming recreation days, by income group[b] | 56.90 | 14.40 | 27.70 | 1.00 | — |
| Percentage of local salmon fishing recreation days, by income group[b] | 8.50 | 17.70 | 57.80 | 9.90 | 6.70 |
| *Bend Ranger District* | | | | | |
| Percentage of local population in income group[a] | 25.79 | 16.13 | 35.72 | 16.12 | 6.24 |
| Percentage of local recreation days, by income group[c] | 42.26 | 11.80 | 25.46 | 15.21 | 5.27 |

[a] May not sum to 100 per cent, due to rounding error.
[b] Stevens, 1966, p. 59.
[c] Guedry, 1970, p. 71.

(–0.24) and clamming (–0.8) are negative. Both population growth and the secular increase in per capita income tend to increase the demand for the salmon fishery. In the clam and bottomfish fisheries, however, the negative income effects would partially offset the increased demand brought about by population growth.

Analysis of the Bend Ranger District data reinforces the conclusions reached with the Yaquina Bay data. Local residents with incomes of less than $4,000 accounted for 42.26 per cent of the local resident recreation days, while making up only 25.8 per cent of the local population. Unfortunately, the sample size for local recreationists at Klamath Lake was too small to provide a meaningful distribution of recreation days by income groups. However, the average income for local recreationists ($8,907) was significantly lower than the average income of nonlocal recreationists ($11,550) at the lake. These results parallel, and are consistent with, those reached in the other studies.

Two factors seem to be important in explaining the high participation rate for low-income families at Yaquina Bay and the Bend Ranger District. First, a significant segment of the low-income families is composed of retired people with more leisure time to pursue recreational activities. Second, since the facilities are relatively near the population centers of the two areas, they are less costly in terms of travel time and money, making the sites more attractive to low-income residents.

If these findings about higher participation rates of low-income recreationists in local recreational sites could be replicated elsewhere, there might also be important national implications. To the extent that national policy considers it meritorious to provide recreational opportunities for the less affluent, a dispersal of national effort to make available recreational services at numerous locations close to the poor (both urban and rural) may be called for. This is in contrast to concentrating the national effort in a few locations that may be accessible only to the relatively affluent.

The negative income effect for two of the three fisheries at Yaquina Bay and another unpublished study (Edwards, *et al.*) utilizing the Bend Ranger District data suggest that additional research on income effects on recreation would be useful. Most economic studies of outdoor recreation have proceeded under the assumption that recreation is a normal good, *i.e.*, that the income effect is positive. However, there is some indication that this may not be true for all forms of outdoor recreation. Particular forms of recreation or recreation at specific sites may indeed be inferior goods. An in-depth analysis of the effect of income changes on different types of outdoor recreation should be high on the economist's list of priorities because of the long-run implications it may have with respect to the recreation-oriented community as well as on broader policy decisions.

From the above analysis it can be concluded that, if the three areas studied are representative of other recreational facilities in the Pacific Northwest, local recreational facilities are not intensively used by the local community. The highest local participation rate observed at the three facilities was less than two recreational days per local resident each year. Characteristics of both the recreational facility and the recreationists appear to be important determinants of the local use rate. However, this information does not provide the local decision-maker with an adequate answer to his question. This analysis clearly illustrates a lack of knowledge as to why people recreate in a particular manner.

This should not be surprising since most of the work done on the evaluation of the direct economic benefits of outdoor recreation has not been oriented to the local community viewpoint. A new research perspective that analyzes the problems of interest to the local community will be necessary if we are to be of greater help to the local decision-maker.

**Indirect Benefits**

Another section of this book is concerned with the general interrelationships between water resources and regional development. Some of the studies referred to earlier were also directed at the secondary or indirect economic impact of outdoor recreational development. These impacts are especially important given the community focus being taken. In the Pacific Northwest many communities are looking to recreational developments as a means to achieve economic growth. Most areas have already taken advantage of their opportunities in the development of other activities based on natural resources, primarily through the agricultural and forest industries.

While further opportunities are likely to open up in selected areas of the region, technological changes generally, and declining timber supplies in some areas, have had negative effects on many local communities. In addition, given the seasonal and cyclical variations in the activities of these industries, it is not surprising that many communities have sought to broaden their economic bases. Recent increases in tourism and outdoor recreation have become natural candidates for many communities' consideration as additional or alternative economic bases. This became apparent when it appeared that recreation might occur throughout the entire year, or might have different seasonal peaks from other local activities utilizing the same resources.

Lessons have been learned about the local economic impacts of outdoor recreation that go beyond those felt by the participating recreationists. In part they arise from expenditures made in the community by recreationists. Even though these expenditures are made largely in the service sectors of the economy, they are often viewed as playing a role similar to the sectors more commonly thought of as constituting the economic base of the community. Given the resource configuration of the Pacific Northwest, recreational services result primarily from production processes involving natural resources. To the extent that expenditures are made by nonresidents of the community in question, these money flows represent payments for goods and services "exported."

Table III summarizes the magnitude and distribution of recreation expenditures in three areas studied in Oregon. Observing the different purposes for which the three studies were undertaken, the numbers in the table are not fully comparable. Yet they give a general indication of the role that recreational expenditures have played in the economies of these three communities.

**Table III**

Annual Recreationists' Expenditures, by Economic Sector, Total Recreation Days, and Local Household Incomes, in Three Oregon Areas

|  | Yaquina Bay Sport Fishing | Klamath Lake | Grant County Big Game |
|---|---|---|---|
| Total expenditures | $ 154,550[a] | $ 837,292[d] | $ 537,455[g] |
| Lodging | 23,995 | 132,292 | 16,945 |
| Marinas & resorts | 47,461 | 12,811 | — |
| Cafes & taverns | 25,346 | 75,859 | 96,682 |
| Service stations, automotive purchases | 19,319 | 403,658 | 208,228 |
| Other product purchases | 34,465 | 212,672 | 164,529 |
| Other service purchases | 3,864 | — | 61,071 |
| Total recreation days | 49,375[b] | 288,587[e] | 95,163[h] |
| Expenditures/recreation day | $ 3.13 | $ 2.90 | $ 5.65 |
| Local household income | $24,808,000[c] | $95,449,000[f] | $19,176,000[i] |
| Recreation expenditures as percentage of household incomes | 0.63 | 0.88 | 2.81 |

[a] Stoevener, et al., 1972, Table 3.6, p. 26.
[b] Stevens, 1966, Table 8, p. 57.
[c] Stoevener, et al., 1972, Table 3.1, p. 18.
[d] Reiling, et al., 1973, Table 15, p. 90.
[e] Reiling, et al., 1973, p. 89.
[f] Reiling, et al., 1973, Table 8, p. 77.
[g] Brown, et al., 1973, Table 25, p. 57.
[h] Brown, et al., 1973, p. 54 and Table 32, p. 95.
[i] Haroldsen and Youmans, 1972, Table 5, p. 9.

It is difficult to react to the numbers in Table III for total recreation expenditures and total recreation days, although the latter numbers will appear impressively large, at least to some observers. Similarly, it is difficult to interpret local expenditures per recreation day, which is a range from $2.90 to $5.65. These numbers become more meaningful when viewed relative to the magnitude of local economic activity. This is accomplished by expressing local recreation expenditures as percentages of local household incomes. We note that for Grant County this percentage is less than three, and for the other two areas it is less than one. Assuming that about 25 per cent of the sales made by businesses serving recreationists goes directly into factor payments, the likely direct impact of these expenditures on the incomes received by local residents is a fraction of one per cent. (For the Grant County area, direct purchases by sectors ranged from 9¢ to 40¢ per dollar of sales; see Haroldsen and Youmans, 1972.) Hence, this type of impact must be judged to be minimal.

Proponents of the view that this type of recreation expenditure has a more significant local economic impact than reflected by the numbers in Table III will be quick to point out that these numbers do not include their multiplier effects on local economic activity. Therefore, impacts are understated, possibly very significantly. The studies that were conducted in Oregon are well-designed to bring empirical evidence to bear on this question. The economic structures of several communities were analyzed in considerable detail through the use of small area interindustry models. All of these studies are patterned after Leontief's suggestion for studying interrelationships in the national economy. See, for example, Leontief, 1970. The models provide the soundest conceptual base for the empirical estimation of the types of multipliers under consideration in this discussion.

Table IV presents output multipliers for the sectors listed in Table III, again for the same three communities. The multipliers for the Klamath County sectors are consistently lower than for those in the other two areas apparently because of the exclusion of the effects induced by local household consumption. These effects are, in turn, the result of income flows to the household sector associated with the recreational expenditures. In other words, in contrast to the other two studies, the Klamath County analysis did not consider the household sector as a part of the interindustry economic structure.

The overall impact of recreation expenditures on the levels of economic activity in the three areas is best illustrated by the multipliers shown in line (7) of Table IV. Output multipliers of approximately 2.0 refute the hypothesis that receipts generated from sales to recreationists are "spent many times over" in the local community.

Certainly more important from the point of view of local residents is the impact that recreational expenditures have upon fac-

### Table IV
Output Multipliers and Income-Output Coefficients, Selected Economic Sectors, and Weighted Average for Three Oregon Communities

|  | Yaquina Bay[a] | Klamath County[b] | Grant County[c] |
|---|---|---|---|
| (1) Lodging | 3.06 | 1.46 | 2.26 |
| (2) Marinas & resorts | 2.10 | 1.50 | — |
| (3) Cafes & taverns | 2.18 | 1.70 | 2.51 |
| (4) Service stations, automotive purchases | 1.40 | 1.20[d] | 1.49 |
| (5) Other product purchases | 1.51 | 1.18[e] | 1.34 |
| (6) Other service purchases | 2.54 | — | 2.14 |
| (7) Weighted output multiplier | 2.06 | 1.36 | 1.72 |
| (8) Weighted income-output coefficient | 0.39 | 0.28 | 0.23 |

[a] Stoevener, et al., 1972, p. 23, p. 27 for line (7), pp. 26-27 for line (8).
[b] Reiling, et al., 1973, p. 84, p. 92 for lines (7) and (8).
[c] Haroldsen and Youmans, 1972, Table 2, lines (7) and (8) computed from the same table, and pp. 56-57 in Brown, et al., 1973.
[d] Pertains only to service stations in Klamath County model. Multiplier for separate automotive sector is 1.13.
[e] Does not include grocery purchases in Klamath County model. Multiplier for separate grocery sector is 1.51.

tor payments. The entries in line (8) of Table IV reflect the effect of a one-unit change in recreationists' expenditures upon local household incomes. Approximately one-third of the value of recreational expenditures accrues as payments to households in the local area, after the interindustry effects portrayed by this method of analysis have been taken into account.

The above discussion focused upon the effects of recreational developments that can be studied by the use of a traditional analytical tool: interindustry analysis. Some extensions of this analysis have been made to broaden the scope of this type of study. Two extensions are based on the realization that market transactions portrayed in traditional input-output models do not reflect some important developmental consequences to the affected community.

*Public Sector Impacts*

Collin (1973) incorporated into the input-output model 12 local government service sectors. In so doing, the assumption was made that the levels of local government service sales (as measured by local tax receipts of these units), like the output levels of the commercial sectors in the economy, are a function of the general level of activity of the economy under study. The realism of this assumption must be questioned. There are two principal determinants of local tax receipts: the local property tax base and the tax rate. The political determination of the latter is only partly influenced by economic considerations, especially those portrayed by input-output models.

Static input-output models do not concern themselves with the explanation of changes in the capital stock, which would be required to explain changes in the property tax base. Nevertheless, it may be possible to gain insight into the impacts of developmental changes on local economies by treating local government in the way Collin did. While property tax payments will not respond to sectoral output changes in the manner required for current account transactions, one can expect such a relationship to exist over the longer run. Furthermore, because small area interindustry analysis is based primarily on trade rather than technological relationships, not regarding local government transactions as part of the local economic structure fails to account for an important local economic interdependence and overestimates the amount of "leakages" in the economy.

Unfortunately for the purposes of this chapter, Collin's work was not concerned with the impact of a recreational development. Instead, the Clatsop County study dealt with the analysis of the impact of a proposed aluminum plant. The developed methodology would, however, be readily applicable to other situations. If one assumes the tax structure to remain fixed, the following question can be answered: After the interdependencies in the local economy have been taken into account, what is likely to be the long-run change in local government receipts, given the distribution of these receipts among the various services? In the Clatsop County case, the direct contribution of the aluminum plant to local tax receipts was estimated as $1,427,000. However, this quantity would rise to $1,594,000, taking into account the interindustry effects. Furthermore, knowing that out of this total $1,039,000 would be allocated to education, $53,000 to law enforcement, etc. (Collin, et al., 1973), the community is better equipped to cope with the development decision. The derived estimates of receipts need to be confronted with the projections on expenditures. Local government is better equipped to obtain these estimates than those that resulted from the Collin work.

## Environmental Consequences

A second important extension of traditional input-output analysis was pioneered by Leontief (1936) and Isard (1972) in order to shed light on an important class of consequences usually referred to as environmental impact. Laurent and Hite (1971) made a novel adaptation that appears to be very useful as a supplement to input-output models of small economies.

We are all becoming aware of the impact of our actions upon the environment. If we drive our automobiles emissions occur and we contribute to the energy crisis by dwindling oil reserves. However, there is another way that we affect the environment about which there is less general awareness. Suppose a "clean" industry is introduced into an unpolluted area, perhaps a "think tank" that conducts only research. It must be realized that this industry is not totally clean because solid wastes of scratch paper are produced. In addition to such direct effects upon the environment, there are indirect alterations of the environment by all the industries that expanded when the think tank was introduced.

The first step in examining total environmental impact is to study the direct environmental impact of industries within a small economy. To illustrate, another recent study of Clatsop County, Oregon (Roberts, 1973), showed that 0.509 pounds of 5-day biochemical oxygen demand (BOD) was emitted for every dollar of gross output from the lumber industry, and 0.005 pounds of 5-day BOD accrued per dollar output of fish processing. The other 28 sectors were assumed to contribute virtually none of this particular emission. Similar calculations were made for several other environmental parameters. By post-multiplying an environmental matrix summarizing the direct environmental impact by the Leontief matrix, one gets a matrix summarizing direct and indirect environmental impact per dollar delivery to final demand. One can see that the direct impact of increasing lumber sales by one dollar is 0.509 pounds of 5-day BOD, and that the direct and indirect effect of increasing final demand of lumber by one dollar is 0.551 pounds of 5-day BOD. Of more interest is that no direct effect is measured for BOD from increasing economic activity in sectors such as lodging, but when one examines the expansion of the economy one sees that for an increase in final demand for lodging, an increase of 0.001 pounds of 5-day BOD per dollar takes place. In fact, increasing final demand in any sector will increase BOD.

Table V summarizes direct and indirect effects for one economic sector, lodging, and selected water data.

### Table V
### Ecologic Linkage to Lodging Sector in Clatsop County, Oregon

| Impact in Terms of | Direct Effect Per Lodging Dollar of Gross Output | Direct and Indirect Effect Per Lodging Dollar Delivery to Final Demand |
|---|---|---|
| Water intake (gal) | 0.196 | 7.042 |
| Water discharge (gal) | 0.157 | 5.669 |
| 5-day BOD (lbs) | — | 0.001 |
| Suspended solids (lbs) | — | 0.120 |

There are two important lessons to be learned. First, the total environmental impact of introducing a new industry or expanding a current industry is different from direct environmental impact. One may even doubt whether there are any clean industries. Secondly, the contribution to environmental change of one industry relative to others is not necessarily what it appears to be. For example, in Clatsop County measurement of direct effects suggests that the fish processing sector ranks second in contributing BOD (0.005 pounds of 5-day BOD per dollar of gross output, as compared to 0.509 pounds for the lumber sector). When one considers indirect environmental effects due to expansion of the economy, fish processing falls to third (0.005 pounds of 5-day BOD per dollar delivery to final demand, as compared to 0.007 pounds for the communications and transportation sector and 0.551 pounds for lumber). The economic expansion by the predominant BOD contributor, lumber, due to an expansion by communications and transportation now causes exogenous changes in that sector to have more BOD impact than the higher direct contributor, fish processing.

## A NEGLECTED ISSUE

To this point conventional input-output models and derived implications for the flow of products, incomes, and environmental goods have been discussed. While this information is highly important, we choose to end noting the shortcomings of our work and point the way toward useful future research. The key issue of neglect is, in a word, stocks.

When concentration of mercury in halibut exceeds a certain percentage, these halibut are banned from sale. However, harm caused by human ingestion of mercury is due not only to the rate of intake, but also the total stock already accumulated in the body. The point is that marginal impact is largely determined by the accumulated stock.

This same point is true for conventional economic goods as well as environmental goods (and "bads," such as the mercury). Even when the generation of income in local communities is of relatively modest size, local interests may be quite concerned about a rise (or fall) in land values.

That recreational opportunities have a significant impact upon land values has been demonstrated in the early work of Knetsch (1964), and a more recent study in Florida (Conner, et al., 1973). This oversight is highly significant. Environmentalists become distressed by the participation of realtors on any local planning agency. If studies of community impact sought more directly to predict changes in value of assets, including land, the structure of local input could be interpreted more fairly. If realtors are conspiring against the public interest, such information should allow the public to fight back. On the other hand, if realtors making strong stands on particular projects are simply stating the position of the community at large, information on the distribution of capital gains from recreational development can clear the air, reduce local bickering, and allow more democratic determination of local interest.

Sociologists will quickly point out that a similar oversight is committed when we consider only the changing asset values of natural resources. Are there effects upon the human resource or upon the local social system that are overlooked? It has been hypothesized that the benefits accruing to individuals from participation in certain outdoor recreational endeavors are analogous to the investment in human capital made through education. The absence of recreational opportunities has been identified as one of the possible causes for urban unrest. Research on these issues has not been very extensive. Nor is this an assignment for economists to tackle. The primary input will have to be made by other behavioral sciences. But if the contribution of such studies is to be of the "nondust-collecting" kind, it is likely that close, truly interdisciplinary cooperation is required among such disciplines as psychology, sociology, anthropology, economics, and political science. This is no easy assignment, but its accomplishment may be a necessary condition for the application of research results to community decision-making.

## CONCLUSION

In the introduction to this chapter, it was noted that many groups who file and/or read environmental impact statements do not know exactly what to put in the statements, or how to use the information as it becomes available. The community of Vancouver is not the first group to file away an environmental impact statement because they did not know what to do with it.

Studies of project effects cannot be expected to alter decisions on projects unless they alter the image of reality (*i.e.*, decision-makers' understanding of what will physically occur) or the value image (*i.e.*, decision-makers' understanding of the evaluation to be placed upon what will occur). Apparently many environmental studies just contribute to background noise (those facts that never really reach our consciousness because they don't fit into the image of reality upon which our value image is based).

The first step is to view an economic system and an environmental system with feedback that can converge iteratively to a new balance or equilibrium, or can first "explode," then converge to an unexpected outcome, as when a biological unit is destroyed or when an economic activity leads to its own demise through resource dissipation.

The conceptualization of interdependent systems is only a first step because it leads to analysis that man, with his current limits to knowledge, does not know how to follow. Some analysts have moved from such a sweeping conceptualization to highly aggregative studies, the most popular one of which today is *The Limits to Growth* (Meadows, *et al.*, 1972). Other investigators have chosen to look at parts of the whole system. This study has been of the second type.

The first involvement was the multidisciplinary study of the community impact of a new pulp mill in Yaquina Bay. In that study engineers postulated changes in water quality due to certain effluent discharge alternatives. Fishery biologists then estimated changes in fishery resources and recreational fishing success due to water quality change. Economists related changes in fishing success to reduced demand for fishing as a recreational activity and estimated the impact upon the local community by tracing the altered recreational expenditure through an input-output model.

In the Klamath Lake study discussed earlier, a change in environmental quality was hypothesized; eutrophication was to be reversed in Upper Klamath Lake. Changes in recreational activity were then estimated, and the community impact of the new activity was traced.

One step that had been omitted in the studies above was to allow feedback of the community economic impact back into the environment. This step was used in the Clatsop County study discussed above. When an extension specialist was discussing the study on community impact of a new aluminum plant, he found much local concern about the impact upon the environment. A vague image existed in the local community that statements about environmental impact did not explain the whole story. Thus, there appeared a need for the study of direct and indirect environmental impact.

What next? Some would seek to build more beautiful models, models that would trace out more feedbacks. There is good reason to be skeptical of this process. The informational requirements are likely to be so severe that it would be necessary to make even more tenuous assumptions than were made in earlier work. Such models also place an excessive judgment burden on the researcher as to how to economize in the information gathering.

Instead, turn again to how these studies relate to the image used by decision-makers. The Yaquina Bay study went from change in economic activity to change in the environment to change in economic activity and its community impact because in the community there was an image that such a relationship existed, was important, and needed more careful estimation. The Klamath Lake study went from environmental change, to change in economic activity, to community impact because the community felt there were dollars to be earned by cleaning up their lake. Direct and indirect environmental impact of the new aluminum plant was studied because there was a fuzzy image that something was happening to the environment. It is suggested that research be designed to integrate environmental-economic interaction with community impact, keeping in mind some of the questions framed by relevant decision makers.

Finally, it should be pointed out that most decisions are, and should be, based on uncertainty and entered into with caution, and that sophisticated computational results may give a feeling of certainty of outcome where such does not exist.

## ACKNOWLEDGMENT

This paper was prepared as Oregon Agricultural Experiment Station Technical Paper No. 3614, and was supported in part by the National Oceanic and Atmospheric Administration (maintained by the U.S. Department of Commerce) Industrial Sea Grant 04-3-158-4. We are indebted to Emery Castle, Jim Fitch, and Russ Youmans for comments on an earlier draft of this chapter.

## REFERENCES

Boulding, K. E. *The Image*. (Ann Arbor: The University of Michigan Press, 1956).

Brown, W. G., F. H. Nawas, and J. B. Stevens. "The Oregon Big Game Resource: An Economic Evaluation," (Corvallis: Oregon Agricultural Experiment Station Special Report 379, 1973).

Collin, T., R. Youmans, and H. Stoevener. "Impact of a Major Economic Change on a Rural Coastal Economy: A Large Aluminum Plant in Clatsop County, Oregon," (Corvallis: Oregon Agricultural Experiment Station Bulletin 614, 1973).

Conner, J. R., K. C. Gibbs, and J. E. Reynolds. "The Effect of Water Frontage on Recreational Property Values," *J. Leisure Res.*, to be published (1973).

Edwards, J. A., K. C. Gibbs, L. J. Guedry, and H. H. Stoevener. "The Demand for Non-Unique Outdoor Recreational Services: Methodological Issues," Oregon Agricultural Experiment Station Technical Paper, to be published.

Guedry, L. J., Jr. "The Role of Selected Population and Site Characteristics in the Demand for Forest Recreation," unpublished Ph.D. thesis. (Corvallis: Oregon State University, 1970).

Guedry, L. J., and H. H. Stoevener. "The Role of Selected Population and Site Characteristics in the Demand for Forest Recreation," in *An Economic Study of the Demand for Outdoor Recreation: Conference Proceedings of the Cooperative Regional Research and Technical Committee*, Report No. 2, Reno (1970).

Haroldsen, A., and R. Youmans. "Grant County, Oregon: Structure of the Local Economy," (Corvallis: Oregon State Cooperative Extension Service Special Report 358, 1972).

Isard, W., C. L. Choguill, J. Kissin, R. H. Seyforth, and R. Tatlock. *Ecologic-Economic Analysis for Regional Development* (New York: The Free Press, 1972).

Knetsch, J. L. "The Influence of Reservoir Projects on Land Values," *J. Farm Econ.* **46**, 231 (1964).

Laurent, E. A., and J. C. Hite. "Economic-Ecologic Analysis in the Charleston Metropolitan Region: An Input-Output Study," Water Resources Research Institute, No. 19 (Clemson: Clemson University, 1971).

Leontief, W. W. "Quantitative Input-Output Relations in the Economic System of the United States," *Rev. Econ. Stat.* **18**, 105 (1936).

Leontief, W. "Environmental Repercussions and the Economic Structure: An Input-Output Approach," *Rev. Econ. Stat.* **52**, 262 (1970).

Meadows, D. H., D. L. Meadows, J. Randers, and W. W. Behrens, III. *The Limits to Growth.* (New York: Universe Books, 1972).

Reiling, S. D., K. C. Gibbs, and H. H. Stoevener. "Economic Benefits from an Improvement in Water Quality," Socioeconomic Environmental Studies Series EPA-R5-73-008, Office of Research and Monitoring, U.S. Environmental Protection Agency, (Washington, D.C.: U.S. Government Printing Office, 1973).

Roberts, K. J. "Economic and Environmental Trade-offs in an Estuarine Based Economy: A Modified Input-Output Model of Clatsop County, Oregon," unpublished Ph.D. thesis (Corvallis: Oregon State University, 1973).

Stevens, J. B. "A Study in Conflict in Natural Resource Use: Evaluation of Recreational Benefits as Related to Changes in Water Quality," unpublished Ph.D. thesis (Corvallis: Oregon State University, 1966).

Stoevener, H. H., J. B. Stevens, H. F. Horton, A. Sokoloski, L. P. Parrish, and E. N. Castle. "Multi-disciplinary Study of Water Quality Relationships: A Case Study of Yaquina Bay, Oregon," (Corvallis: Oregon Agricultural Experiment Station Special Report 348, 1972).

# Part V

# Environmental Demands on Water

# About the Contributors

*Thomas Crocker,* a native of Maine, received his PhD from the University of Missouri-Columbia and has taught at the University of Wisconsin. He is now an Associate Professor of Economics at the University of California, Riverside. Resource and environmental economics with a particular emphasis on air pollution has been his major research interest.

*Thomas A. Heberlein* is Assistant Professor of Rural Sociology at the University of Wisconsin, Madison, where he also received his PhD. Research interests involve the effects of attitudes, norms and roles on behavior related to the natural environment. Dr. Heberlein's publications are in the areas of methodology and environmental attitudes. He serves as Associate Editor of *Sociological Methods and Research.*

# Part V
# Environmental Demands on Water

The emergence of a broad public interest in the environment scarcely requires documentation. In a relatively short time, public awareness of conflicting environmental demands has grown from what was previously the concern of a few conservation societies to a developing national ethic. The Environmental Policy Act of 1969 along with specific legislation for water and air quality represent some of the results. The National Water Commission, mentioned frequently in this book, gave high priority to water quality. As a public issue, however, it has been difficult to sharply define the issues and develop possible solutions which are simultaneously effective and easily understood.

Causes of environmental problems have been exhaustively identified and classified, but few have been modified. Increasing population, modern technology, high incomes, three-car families, built-in obsolescence, and failure of economic and social institutions are among the frequently cited factors. It is commonly easier to tinker with symptoms, however, than to undertake fundamental reform of institutional structures which influence human behavior. This accounts for some of the frustration and conflict over environmental objectives as well as alternative solutions.

Both Heberlein and Crocker examine the issue of institutional change, but from quite different perspectives. In the search for answers to environmental decay there are three major categories of proposals. Technology, while in some cases the villain which caused the problem, is often looked to as the solution. Proponents of a technological solution suggest that if we resist impatience, the advances in technological achievement will help get us out of the mess. Heberlein shows that this approach may carry the seeds of its own destruction. A second category is that of changing human behavior through voluntary action, but this has some limitations in practice. The third category is to change social or economic institutions which influence group and individual behavior. Heberlein discusses these general approaches and presents a new look at their respective advantages and disadvantages.

Crocker approaches institutional change through an economic framework. The issue of transaction costs has been largely neglected by economists, and even when acknowledged has been lightly dismissed. He identifies the nature and sources of transaction costs (he calls them coordination costs) and goes on to construct a model for assessing them. His conclusions should be of considerable interest to both scholars and policymakers.

# 13. Water and the Economics of Implementing Environmental Objectives

### THOMAS D. CROCKER

It is again becoming acceptable in economic analysis to look explicitly at institutional factors. The economics of institutional design are being analytically refurbished after having been relegated to the dustbin of professional disrepute after World War II. Within the general analytical framework of preference rankings, endowments, and production and exchange possibilities, the latter are no longer viewed as invariant with respect to institutional arrangements.

Until recently the failure to give little more than lip service to institutional considerations probably rests on more than intellectual conservatism. A basic reason appears to be that institutional factors have been presented as appendages to a received theory beginning with the fundamental assumption of costless exchange. An abstract theory of institutional choice permitting received theory based on costless exchange to be viewed as a special case simply has not existed and does not now exist. Most attention given to institutional considerations has pointed out the inefficiency of actual institutions, relative to the efficiency achieved by the central manager/owner of the organizational unit in the standard analytical apparatus. In treating organizations and individuals as equivalent units of analysis, economic analysts have found that a system employing only prices as means of allocation will provide information and incentives necessary to maximize the aggregate value of all economic agents' activities (Arrow and Hahn, 1972).

One merely begs the question by making a set of assumptions inexorably leading to the conclusion one desires. By initially assuming that institutions compatible with costless exchange are the only forms of economic cooperation that lead to efficient outcomes, one must realize that the conclusions reached from this assumption will have been preformed. This assertion insists that reality conform to a state that is economically unfeasible in most circumstances. What constitutes "efficient" outcome has been prejudged.

Examples of the above attitude are as frequent in water resources literature as they are elsewhere. In their encyclopedic volume on the northern California water industry, Bain, et al. (1966) assert that "the pricing rules of some agricultural water districts reveal no apparent economic logic." This is probably true if one identifies economic logic only with equating the intradistrict price of water to the district's marginal costs of supply and delivery. Any failure to employ the decision rules of the all-powerful, central owner/manager of textbook economic theory is to be taken as prima facie evidence of sloppy decision-making. Yet it is clearly possible that any number of alternative decision rules may yield the district a net gain if the reduction in the value of the resources necessary to implement the allocations caused by the rules outweighs the value of any losses in efficiency.

The point of the preceding is that there is very little economic theory presently available to provide a consistent basis for discussion of the economics of implementing environmental objectives related to the water resource. If one insists that explanations of real world phenomena are insensitive to the assumption of costless allocation, then the implementation problem appears economically trivial because it is not consumptive of valuable resources. On the other hand, if one suspects these explanations are sensitive to the assumption, he must approach a discussion of implementation problems in a state of theoretical near-nakedness. The discussant might not be arrested for indecent exposure but would certainly attract sour looks from all purists on the beach. In spite of such dangers, an attempt is made in this paper to describe a framework suggesting one manner in which the problem of choice among alternative means of implementing environmental objectives might be approached.

## THE NATURE OF THE IMPLEMENTATION PROBLEM

The implementation problem consists of coordination of economic activities of interdependent economic agents. Consider a set of resource owners who are price takers in all relevant economic modes of cooperation. That is, they do not engage in any strategic behavior although they are permitted to act upon their awareness that consequences of their activities depend upon activities of other owners. Assume these owners are considering combining their resources to produce an output, the returns from which they intend to share in some mutually agreeable but unspecified fashion. For example, the owners may cause and suffer from water pollution, but they are considering ways of allocating the waste disposal abilities of a watercourse. The method of allocation is presumed to be a matter of indifference to them; they evaluate alternative methods differently only because variant methods are thought to yield different results.

Several alternative modes are available to the owners for coordination of their activities. Nevertheless, whether the adopted mode consists of a multitude of bilateral exchanges or a completely centralized authority acting as a residual claimant (Knight, 1965; Niskanen, 1971; and Peltzman, 1971), owners will incur costs in attempting to coordinate their activities. Coordination is not free. No matter how skilled resource owners are at innovating institutional forms, positive quantities of some valuable resources must be expended on the process. These will consist of the costs of establishing agreement to undertake a joint enterprise and the expenditures necessary to ensure realization of the terms of agreement. They include costs of negotiating the agreement as well as costs of monitoring the contributions of resource owners and the rewards they receive. Coordination costs also include the costs of determining how rewards and costs will be assigned to resource owners responsible for changes in output, in addition to costs of ensuring they are assigned in the agreed-upon manner. Included also are circumstances in which an individual adopts obligations. Since an obligation implies contingent or uncontingent commitment to a course of action, the owner's opportunity to specify the set of alternatives he is willing to consider and his opportunity to choose from among a given set of alternatives is reduced. He thus foregoes self-discretion, a facet of human existence to which people generally attach a positive value.

Costs of information and search are not considered components of coordination costs in this instance. It is assumed that the individual does not have the opportunity to convert available but unfeasible choices into feasible choices. He deals only with the choice problem that exists given the *a priori* decision not to allocate additional resources to search. This assumption is made partly because, in the absence of knowledge about the consequences the owner desires, it is not apparent exactly what constitutes "more" information. To a water polluter who wants to know only whether he will be permitted to increase or decrease his effluent, knowledge that his permissible discharges will, with equal probability, either be a maximum of ten per cent more or ten per cent less is of no value whatsoever. Less detailed information specifying whether the permissible discharges will be increased or reduced would be of greater value. In fact, any information, no matter how detailed, not enabling this polluter to distinguish between the signs of changes in permissible discharges must be less valuable than information specifying only the sign of the change.

Another reason for distinguishing between search and coordination costs involves the difference between completeness and accuracy of flows of information, and the incentive to provide this information. Radner (1969) and Stigum (1969) have expounded on the problem faced by a seller trying to provide information that a potential buyer is unable to evaluate until he receives adequate information. Upon disclosure, the proprietorship of the seller in the information is dissipated. However, one can imagine the buyer signaling his informational requirements so that the seller responds to the signal, presuming that terms of provision are mutually satisfactory. The seller is thus provided with an incentive to supply the information. Establishing and maintaining these incentives is a problem of coordination rather than search.

Given the assumption that all owners are price takers and therefore do not exhibit a purely pecuniary interdependence, coordination costs have three sources. First, nonseparable effects among owners may exist so that each owner's contribution to enterprise output is dependent on the contributions of other resource owners. Thus a change in the resource contributions of any one owner can affect the output for which all other owners are responsible, even when the resource contributions of these other owners are unchanged. Exact assignment of rewards according to the responsibility for enterprise output requires that rewards be recalculated each time the contribution of one owner changes. A requirement that this exact assignment be fulfilled would obviously impose severe demands on enterprise coordination. Under these circumstances, some alternative indicator of owner output responsibility will probably be adopted. For example, the owner's input contributions might be made the basis for calculating his earned rewards (Alchian and Demsetz, 1972).

A second source of coordination costs occurring in the absence of pecuniary interdependence is the cost of monitoring input and/or output contributions in a production process, or the goods traded in an exchange process. This source is relevant even when there are no nonseparable effects. Many inputs are simply hard to count. Writing a research paper on environmental concerns in water resources is certainly a separable activity; but measuring the effort the writer devotes to the composition is no easy matter. It is possible that the writer spent a great deal of time daydreaming while supposedly working on the manuscript. For most of the inputs and outputs used as textbook cases for the operation of the price system, these costs of measurement are trivial. Nevertheless, there is nothing in the literature attempting to explain why water consumption is sometimes measured by the acre foot and at other times by cubic feet per second, or why cabbages are usually measured by the head rather than by mass.

On the other hand, the informational content of the same measure may differ among resource owners. The coliform count in a body of water may be highly meaningful to an epidemiologist but meaningless to the lay person. For the latter, the relative turbidity of the water body is more likely to indicate its degree of purity. Unless each individual can be shown exactly how turbidity and coliform counts are related, a common measure cannot be defined. The two measures are noncomparable.

Finally, when a purely pecuniary interdependence does exist, coordination costs may be introduced because some owners derive particular advantage from one measure of the same phenomenon rather than another. Consider the likely difference in pollution concentrations obtained from a monitoring station located at the outfall of a polluter, as opposed to a station located a mile downstream. Both stations could be located on a portion of the stream bordered by the polluter's property. Yet the location of the monitoring station would usually make a substantial difference in calculated pollution discharges. Establishment of a sampling location mutually acceptable to the sampling agency and the polluter requires that both parties expend valuable resources. If agency and polluter have agreed to monitor the polluter's waste loading and have further agreed on the basis for stream management, the decision problem is no longer the quantity of waste to permit in the stream but instead the values to be given to the parameters of the management model. Monitoring data is required to estimate the values of these parameters. The means by which this data is accumulated can be more or less costly to the polluter and the agency depending on the waste loading at any point removed from the monitoring station.

Prices, by themselves, work well where resource contributions are easily ascertained and reciprocated by rewards. For example, the spot exchange of two currencies requires no statement of terms other than exchange ratio. When cardinally measurable and perfectly homogeneous commodities such as currencies are exchanged, the parties to the enterprise need only count the quantities exchanged to establish what they have obtained. However, there are many commodities, including water pollution control, for which the implicit assumption of trivial measurement costs seems to be questionable, especially when considering policy questions. There can be harsh impediments to tracing the parties initially responsible for the water pollution, unraveling what is being called "water pollution," and finally, monitoring the contributions of each polluter.

It is now widely known that in a world of costless coordination where nonseparabilities are present the sum of owner utilities will be maximized if the marginal effect of an activity on an owner's income is equal to the marginal effect of that same activity on the sum of the incomes of all other owners. In less pompous language this is simply requiring marginal private gain to be equal to marginal social cost. It is the old problem of making the private optimum compatible with the collective optimum. Even in a world of costless coordination, a set of prices alone is not sufficient to assure compatibility between collective and private optima (Baumol and Fabian, 1964). In the separability case, as has been noted earlier, when there is no consensus on standards for measuring flow of resources, prices by themselves will be insufficient.

When coordination costs exist, the economic structure itself becomes a variable of the decision problem. The problem can be viewed as finding a set of obligations for owner behavior so that the resource owner's costs and rewards are made less dependent on his joint relations with the other resource owners in the enterprise. Rules of evidence and procedure are established for all participants in the joint enterprise. Likely and important contingencies will be specified and appropriate responses will be stipulated. In short, a mode of coordination other than the decentralized market in which observed price is the sole coordinating device is likely to be adopted. Objective, easily measured performance standards will be formulated. These standards may not always be consistent with maximizing the value of joint output under conditions where the coupling of output responsibility and rewards poses only trivial measurement problems. Nevertheless the standards serve to introduce a greater degree of separability, and thus make the rewards of the resource owner from production of the enterprise at least partly independent of activities imposing costs upon his fellows. If each owner tries to maximize his rewards subject to the constraints imposed by his obligations, the expected value of the enterprise output is maximized (given the owners' stock of information about the state of nature and their utility functions). These obligations serve to make a set of owners behave as a team. Regularity, coherence, and predictability about the behavior of all owners is introduced. The limits within which owners and their custodians may operate without fear of penalty are defined. By defining the activities owners may undertake with respect to property objects, their behavior with respect to each other is specified. Who has to obtain permission from whom for an activity to be performed, the form the permission must assume, and stipulations as to time, place, and conditions of use, exclusion, and alienation are specified. These terms of cooperation are specifications of acceptable conditions serving to narrow the set of possible outcomes. In effect, the owners state the conditions for a satisfactory outcome and mutually accept any realized outcome. The choice among alternative combinations of conditions (that is, the choice among alternative modes of coordination) is made in order to select the combination yielding the most efficient set of activities for the given set of resource owners.

## OUTLINE OF A FRAMEWORK FOR ASSESSING MODES OF COORDINATION

Given the frequently long time lag between environmental degradation and the recognition of it by owners possessing some discretion about the manner in which the environment is used, it is not possible to view an environmental state at time $t$ as independent of the efforts made to coordinate owners' activities in previous periods. This is true even in a quasi-static analytical world where signals about environmental states are changing and the owner must adapt to situations that occur with stochastic regularity. These situations are therefore predictable but precise advance knowledge of the state to be realized is not feasible. As is true for any type of economic activity, the set of coordination activities currently adopted will depend on the relative prices of inputs necessary to undertake them. The current relative prices of coordination inputs help to determine the environmental states that will ultimately be realized. If an index of current prices of coordination inputs rises, owners will be satisfied with less precise understanding of the alternatives available to them, cruder efforts at coordination, and, in general, reductions in the amount of activity relating to predicting and controlling environmental states. Similarly, if the cost of monitoring current environmental states increases relative to the cost of monitoring activities of individual owners, more emphasis will be placed on monitoring the activities of other owners. Determining contributions of individual owners to current states will be less costly, but identifying these states will be more costly. This change in relative prices of coordination inputs will affect the form of future states. Therefore, it is important to disassociate the level of use of coordination inputs from current environmental states if an analysis is to have the kind of dynamic structure that the nonstatic problem of coordination requires. Equivalently, the relation between the use of coordination inputs and current environmental states must be mediated by the introduction of another element.

In basic economic theory, this kind of problem is typically managed by positing a production function which is intermediate between inputs and results. The analytical value of the production function is that a technically efficient set of input combinations can be determined, and the selection of the most valuable combination can be made from within this more restricted domain. The economically efficient combination is then determined as a function of the prices of the inputs and the values of results. A similar procedure for designing modes of coordination is adopted here. This will be done by posing an output referred to as earlier "rules" or obligations defined independently of prices of coordination inputs. Those realizable obligations compose an individual owner's claim on a particular resource. Obligations are made realizable by application of a set of coordination inputs. The obligations specify what the owner can do with the resource and what will happen to him if he fails to fulfill his obligations. In short, the obligations represent the means that various owners employ to coordinate their activities. For example, if the resource is the water in a particular watercourse and the owner is a water polluter, obligations might be agreements the owner has reached with others specifying the timing and character of his waste discharges. If the owner fulfills his obligations, the other parties will be able to predict his waste discharges and will be better able to formulate their own plans. They will not have to endure the cost of preparing contingent plans and adopting contingent technologies for a variety of potential polluter waste discharges.

Obligations can be described by a scaler measure. For example, an effluent standard clearly can be viewed as a scaler, and a deadline bringing the time for installing pollution control equipment closer to the present can be treated as an increased obligation and measured as the inverse of the time interval still available for meeting the deadline.

For our purposes, an institution is defined by the obligations or rules to which a group of individuals adhere in their interdependent activities. An equilibrium mode of coordination or institutional structure is one in which knowledge of the internal observable exchange price for a valuable entity by the members is sufficient to ensure that each individual owner's optimum is compatible with the collective optimum. That is, no one owner who has committed his resources to the institution desires to alter his obligations. Reciprocal economies that owners create by coordinating their activities are at the margin exactly offset by the losses the owners sustain by foregoing self-discretion and expenditures on coordination inputs.

If a mode of coordination or institution is defined by the realizable reciprocal obligations its participant owners have, the coordination inputs can be mapped into the space of obligations. Each set of obligations is associated with one or more coordination inputs. Analysis of modes of coordination may then proceed using the space of obligations in a framework quite similar to that in indifference curve analysis, without a need to directly consider the institutional objective.

Elsewhere decision criteria have been derived for an individual owner who agrees to join several alternative institutions, each of which differs in the self-discretion he is required to forego, and the realizable obligations to him the institution is willing to assume

(Crocker, 1973). That is, in order to have an institution accept these obligations he must accept obligations to the institution. The individual is assumed to be a pecuniary maximizer. His objective is to maximize the difference between his gross money income and his outlays on inputs of the customary sort and coordination inputs.[1] Money value of the outlays on coordination inputs is made a function of the number of realizable obligations, the magnitude of each obligation realized, and the quantity of objective output the individual produces. (By "objective output" is meant a physical output the physical attributes of which will be perceived identically by any individual.) The latter is included to account for the possibility that unit coordination costs may differ according to the number of units of output involved in the coordination effort. The selling or offer price of an output is made a function of the obligations attached to it and the quantity demanded or supplied. As stated earlier, realizable obligations are conceived as being produced by coordination inputs, each of which has a price attached. The system of equations implicit in the statement of this paragraph is then solved to yield the following three decision criteria.

> (1) For a given combination of obligations and a given objective output level, the relative prices of the coordination inputs must be set equal to the negative of the rate at which the coordination inputs can be substituted for each other.
>
> (2) For a given level of objective output, the rate at which one obligation can be transformed into another obligation while maintaining constant total revenues must be set equal to the rate at which one obligation can be substituted for the other while maintaining constant total coordination costs.
>
> (3) For any given combination of obligations, the marginal cost of coordination (the marginal cost of realizing the obligations) must be equated to the marginal revenues that the obligations generate.

The first criterion corresponds to the standard decision rule regarding relative input prices and marginal rates of substitution. The second criterion is the decision rule for coupling obligations. The third criterion clearly corresponds to the familiar marginal cost-marginal revenue rule employed to determine net revenue

---

1. This objective is selected not because it is thought that it is the only objective worthy of consideration in environmental questions. Its use here is simply a means of avoiding the difficult question of weights to be assigned alternative "social indicators." It in no way influences the basic points of the paper.

maximizing level of output in the theory of the firm. However, in this case it is coordination costs that vary with the level of output. If, after some output level, marginal control costs are monotonically increasing, they correspond to the "control loss" phenomenon in which increasing coordination difficulties set limits to the organization size (Williamson, 1970). This third criterion implies that for a given combination of obligations, the marginal value of the coordination costs equals the marginal value of the returns from producing a given objective output under that institutional form.

## SOME IMPLICATIONS

It is the second decision criterion in the previous section that is of greatest interest. The function representing constant total revenues corresponds to what is usually termed an isorevenue function. Similarly, the function representing constant total coordination costs can be termed an isocost function. Figure 1 depicts the second criterion in a situation where we assume a river basin management agency is limited by legislative charter to choose from among three combinations of two obligations to control the waste disposal activities of polluters. The pair of obligations shown here allow the authority to impose various combinations of effluent standards and effluent charges upon polluters.

The line ADBEC in Figure 1 represents the isocost function; it shows the rate at which one obligation can be transformed into another with the availability of a given stock of coordination inputs at given prices. Thus, each combination of the two obligations in Figure 1 within the feasible region of ADBEC is realizable only by application of a given quantity of coordination inputs having given prices. However, a variety of combinations of inputs could yield the particular combination of obligations, although there will generally be a unique input combination that is less costly than alternative combinations.

If the stock of coordination inputs is finite and/or the river basin authority has a budget constraint, the isocost or transformation function shows the maximum quantity of one obligation that can be realized for a given realization of the other obligation. That is, the line ADBEC represents the obligations attainable if the authority's whole budget is spent on realizing the two obligations. Assuming that the "production function" for obligations is always linear and homogeneous so that a doubling of the least

## 272 WATER AND COMMUNITY DEVELOPMENT

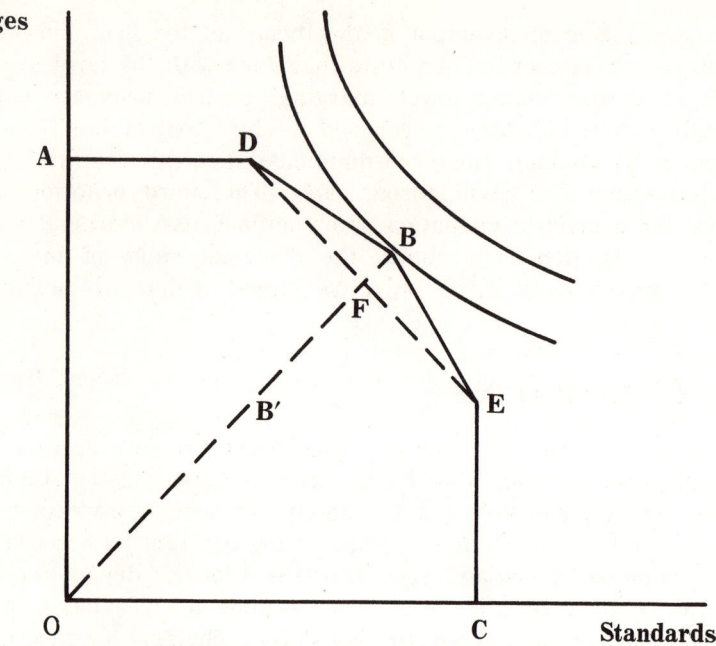

*Figure 1.* Linear depiction of decision criteria.

costly combination of coordination inputs yields a doubling of intensity of each obligation, then the maximum intensity of each obligation that can be realized is given by the end point of a vector whose length is determined by the authority's budget constraint and prices of coordination inputs. The set of these vector end points and their linear combinations form the line ADBEC. For example, point B lying on the transformation function is the end point of the vector OB.

Now suppose the cost of coordinating the organizational structure represented by the combination of obligations at B increases and the cost of the alternative institutional structures remains constant. In Figure 1, this increase in cost is represented by a shift of the end point of the OB vector from B to B'. The isocost function would now become ADEC because the obligation proportion represented by the OB vector is no longer efficient. Given no change in the isorevenue surface represented by the convex curves, the efficient organizational structure will be a combination of obligation combinations at E and D. The proportion in which the two obligations are combined will be identical to the proportion depicted in the OB vector. However, the organizational structure differs from that implied by the OB vector because structures associated with OD and OE retain their individual identities and operate "in parallel" with one another. In the case of the river basin, this can mean that there are now two authorities having jurisdiction over the uses to which water resources can be put. A somewhat more obvious example might be a firm that decentralizes authority by breaking up a division into two autonomous units having the same obligations in different proportions, or a geographic area broken up into various jurisdictions, *e.g.*, central cities and suburbs.

It is obvious from Figure 1 that different organizational or institutional structures can be made to emerge by varying the pattern of coordination costs. If the coordination inputs used to produce obligations differ in proportion or kind, changes in the relative prices of inputs can cause substantial changes in organizational structures. It follows that there is no such thing as a universally preferable mode of economic coordination whether one is dealing with water or any other resource. Even with a single-valued objective function such as gross national product, it is easy to establish that a wide variety of organizational structures will be adopted for reasons of economic efficiency alone. Given that coordination inputs are costly and that these costs differ among resource owners and settings, a variety of efficient modes of coordination can exist simultaneously. Organizational structures are dependent on relative costs of producing each realizable obligation. If coordination inputs are costly, and if these costs differ among individuals, circumstances, and places, insistence on employing one mode of coordination in environmental quality problems appears inappropriate. The decade-long debate over the economic efficacy of effluent charges versus direct regulation in environmental quality control seems more an academic exercise than a serious discussion of real policy alternatives. It seems far-fetched to assert that a regulatory body can perform efficiently without using any criteria other than observable price, particularly when private markets are unable to do this most of the time. A sustained effort to discover a decision rule capable of pointing to efficient combinations of realizable property right obligations is more likely to yield useful results.

Figure 1 also makes it clear that if coordination costs are sufficiently great no obligations whatever will be adopted. If relative prices of coordination inputs remain constant but severity of the budget constraint increases, the increase will be reflected in a scaler reduction in the transformation function. That is, the function will maintain its form but it will shift back toward the origin. If the scaler reduction is great enough, neither of the obligations will be adopted. Something similar appears to have dominated the environmental aspects of water resources until the last ten or fifteen years. In effect, no user of water resources had any obligations to anyone else.

Frequently the obligations that a regulatory authority is able to consider are limited by the mandate of the authority. Thus it could be that the regulatory authority whose isocost function for obligations is depicted in Figure 1 is unable to consider employing combinations of effluent standards and charges lying outside the AD interval. Apart from its budget constraint and the cost of coordination inputs, the authority would face no effective limitation on the size of effluent charge it could impose. However, the legislative mandate of the authority could set the maximum severity of effluent standard at D. Given the isorevenue surface, it is legally impossible for the authority to adopt the most economic institutional structure for managing the river basin. In environmental quality problems, this phenomenon is most often observed with respect to the limited geographic jurisdictions of control agencies.

A carefully studied case of restrictions upon the combinations of obligations from which authorities can select is available in Robert K. Davis' study (1969) of the efforts of the U.S. Army Corps of Engineers to improve water quality in the Potomac River by employing low-flow augmentation. Davis found that the same water pollution control objective could be achieved by a combination of mechanical reoxygenation and low-flow augmentation at approximately one-fifth of the cost of the augmentation alone. Davis argues that "a large part of the failure to consider alternatives is attributable to institutional factors." The Corps had a right to improve water quality through low-flow augmentation, but it did not have the right to achieve this objective through treatment of wastes. Authority for the latter resided with local and state governments and the Federal Water Quality Control Administration. Any coordination of the Corps' activities with these agencies would have required each agency to forego some self-discretion and expend some costly coordination inputs. At the existing relative prices for coordination inputs, it was not worthwhile apparently for the separate agencies to make the necessary efforts. In effect, the Corps had the authority to dissolve interdependencies by altering the environment, but it was unable to resolve these interdependencies by altering behavior of relevant economic agents.

Even though prices of coordination inputs may have contributed to failure of the agencies to coordinate their activities, this coordination might have been achieved by altering incentive structures under which different agency managers operated. It is by now widely recognized that there can exist substantial discrepancies between the objectives of managers of an organization and objectives of the organization's owners. It is possible that as a consequence of its past history the Corps had developed a strong capability in, and orientation toward, structural alternatives. Therefore it had a strong vested interest in avoiding serious consideration of nonstructural alternatives such as reoxygenation. Less cynically, it was highly likely that Corps personnel did not have the background and training to make them consider nonstructural means as serious alternatives for improvement of water quality.

Finally, relative prices of various alternatives as they were confronted by the Corps managers made the low-flow augmentation alternative look particularly appealing. Under the Water Quality Act of 1951, if low-flow augmentation is used for purposes of improvements in water quality, it is financed 100 per cent from the federal treasury. Alternatives, including nonstructural ones, receive no federal subsidy. The Water Quality Act of 1965 did provide reimbursement to municipalities for waste treatment in amounts up to 55 per cent of the total cost. However, the augmentation system, despite the fact that it was five times more costly, was still the low cost alternative in the view of the Corps and the local communities involved. This is because the Corps required political support in the Congress from the local communities in order to undertake the project. A benefit that has no cost attached is preferred to an identical benefit that is costly.

At least two conclusions can be drawn from the preceding paragraphs. First, in a great many "externality" problems, relatively minor changes in the feasible set of obligations can have a powerful effect upon the pattern of economic activities. In particular, the degree of coordination attainable for any given expenditure can be substantially altered. Second, it should be recognized that the incentive structure of agency managers may be perverse so that the marginal rate at which they are willing to substitute one obligation for another differs from that of owners of the resource.

Thus, if the isorevenue surface of Figure 1 is that of the owners, the managers may have another surface. The latter surface is likely to be operative. Therefore, the combination of obligations adopted for users of the water resource will be inefficient in maximizing the extent to which the owner's objectives are met. The reason is simply because the returns from one activity relative to another differ between managers and owners.

Finally, it should be emphasized that the previous analysis implies that the institutional structures a society adopts are not independent of the initial distribution of endowments of coordination inputs. Those who have the coordination inputs possessing the greatest productivity are likely to have adopted the institutional structures they favor. A change in initial endowments of coordination inputs, given production functions for realizable obligations, can change the institutional structure that will be adopted. This point is important to environmental questions if society makes the judgment that coordination inputs have been excessively available to polluters relative to sufferers.[2]

**REFERENCES**

Alchian, A., and H. Demsetz. "Production, Information Costs, and Economic Organization," *Amer. Econ. Rev.* **62**:777 (1972).

Arrow, K. J., and F. Hahn. *General Competitive Analysis* (Reading, Mass.: Holden-Day, Inc., 1972).

Bain, J. W., et al. *Northern California's Water Industry* (Baltimore: The Johns Hopkins Press, 1966) p. 343.

Baumol, W. J., and T. Fabian. "Decomposition, Pricing for Decentralization and External Economies," *Management Sci.* **11**:1 (1964).

Crocker, T. D. "Externalities, Property Rights, and Transactions Costs: An Empirical Study," *J. Law Econ.* **14**:451 (1971).

Crocker, T. D. "Contractural Choice," *Natural Res. J.* (forthcoming).

Davis, R. K. *The Range of Choice in Water Management* (Baltimore: The Johns Hopkins Press, 1969).

---

2. Warren Samuels describes a real case involving apple growers and owners of cedar trees that served as hosts to an apple fungus. In essence he concludes that the greater relative productivity of the coordination inputs available to the apple growers enabled them to procure a set of laws favorable to their interests and unfavorable to the owners of cedar trees. (Samuels, 1971). However, it should be noted that the authorities could have arrived at their decision because the cost of coordination was less and the value of the social output was greater when the interests of apple growers rather than cedar tree owners were favored. For an empirical example supporting this explanation, see Crocker (1971).

Knight, R. H. *Risk, Uncertainty and Profit* (New York: Harper Torchbooks, 1965).

Niskanen, W. *Bureaucracy and Representative Government* (Chicago: Aldine Publishing Co., 1971).

Peltzman, S. "Pricing in Public and Private Enterprises: Electric Utilities in the United States," *J. Law Econ.* 14:109 (1971).

Radner, R. "Competitive Equilibrium Under Uncertainty," *Econometrica* **36**:31 (1968).

Samuels, W. J. "Interrelations Between Legal and Economic Processes," *J. Law Econ.* 14:435 (1971).

Stigum, B. P. "Competitive Equilibria Under Uncertainty," *Quart. J. Econ.* 83:533 (1969).

Williamson, O.E. *Corporate Control and Business Behavior* (Englewood Cliffs, N.J.: Prentice-Hall, Inc., 1970).

# 14. The Three Fixes: Technological, Cognitive, and Structural

### THOMAS A. HEBERLEIN

The losses that accompany flood, drought, hail and snow may be reduced by modifying the physical world to change the amount or form of water, to reduce water levels, to increase rainfall, to disperse hailstorms and to suppress snow in urban areas. Changing human behavior will also reduce losses. Limits on certain types of flood plain encroachment, drought-resistant farm practices, hail and flood insurance, and urban mass transit are actions in the social system that would yield the same outcomes.

The effectiveness of these strategies depends on the social context. The goal of this paper is to point out some of the sociological and psychological factors that modify the effectiveness of these actions.

## THE TECHNOLOGICAL FIX

Although there are a number of ways to reduce variability in the physical environment (especially when the variation itself is related to human behavior), the most popular choice appears to be the application of technology. Variability in water has been modified for centuries via this application. River level and velocity have been modified by dams, levees, and channelization. Water available in arid areas has been increased by irrigation projects. Recently rainfall has been augmented, hail suppressed, and wind velocity of hurricanes reduced by weather modification techniques.

Salt and polluted water have been purified by treatment.

Technological applications have often been spectacularly effective, and this, in part, accounts for their attractiveness. Modern industrial societies have hurled men to the moon, increased agricultural production at a geometric rate, revolutionized communications and transportation. Great dams have generated hydroelectric power, reduced floods (if not flood losses) and provided recreation sites. Irrigation projects have made deserts bloom (if one ignores the cost). In short, if all else were equal, such applications of technology have a long history of being effective and demonstrate a kind of visible, flashy success.

Perhaps because of such past successes, the technological fix enjoys strong institutional support, which also accounts for its adoption. Although some changes are occurring, The Army Corps of Engineers, The Bureau of Reclamation, and National Oceanic and Aeronautics Administration all rely heavily on the technological fix. Over the years they have accumulated personnel and experience in this domain to the exclusion of alternatives. The technological fix has institutional advocates, with on-line budgets and relatively long-time horizons. This allows a strong case to be made for environmental modifications.

The technological fix is also appealing because it largely by-passes the human element. Trying to reduce losses by modifying people or social structure is a difficult process. It is much easier to simply build a dam or seed clouds than to change land use or other behavior patterns. One may be sure that the river itself or a phalanx of cumulous clouds will not storm a public hearing, or write congressmen as will those people who are driven off the floodplain by zoning ordinances. Because we do not take an animistic view of nature, it is of no consequence to manipulate rivers, rainfall, or water composition (White, 1967). This is not to ignore the growing group of citizens who recently have been trying with some success to represent the physical environment. However their general plea is usually based on negative impacts to the human system, rather than on inherent rights of rivers, trees, and air.

Of course all is not well with the technological fix. One problem that has been given much attention lately involves the second order unplanned effects. Cloud seeding may create more rainfall in one area, but what are the downwind effects? Will it produce less rainfall somewhere else? A process that reduces water pollution may increase air pollution. These sorts of outcomes have been investigated under the rubric of technology assessment. While everyone agrees such assessment is important, no very clear methodology has evolved for such evaluation.

A more circumscribed problem involves the actual implementation of the technological fix. This fix may successfully modify the physical environment but fail to reduce losses because some aspect of the social system has been changed as well. A well-documented case in the area of water resources is the past thirty years of federal investment in flood control works (U.S. House of Representatives, 1966). While it is clear that the frequency and magnitude of floods have been reduced by flood control structures, actual losses have increased! These appear not to be due solely to population increase and inflation, but because modification of the flood potential made people feel that flood plains were safe and this land was developed with structures that were not floodproofed. Although fewer floods occurred after the technological fix, there was greater damage and loss of life. This suggests that one of the appeals of the technological fix is also its Achilles' heel. Modification of the physical environment is appealing because it largely bypasses the human and social system. However, it risks missing its ultimate goal of reducing losses (rather than modifying the environment) by making only the simplest assumptions about human behavior. These assumptions often have great intuitive appeal, but a general lack of empirical support in the behavioral science literature. Two that are relevant here are that man attempts to optimize his outcomes (*i.e.*, minimize his losses and maximize his gains) in his interactions with environmental variation, and that an individual's attitudes are relatively good predictors of his behavior. The pitfalls of these assumptions will be spelled out later.

## REDUCING VARIABILITY IN THE HUMAN SYSTEM

Sometimes it is simply not technologically possible to modify the variation in the physical environment, or while technologically possible, a modification may be economically unjustifiable. Until recently, variations in the weather were an example of the former. The current problem of high water levels in the Great Lakes involves both. Water projects with cost benefit ratios of less than 1.0 are examples of the latter. In these situations reductions in losses are sought by modifying the behavior of man rather than the behavior of the environment. Two related strategies for changing human behavior may be identified.

**The Cognitive Fix**

The cognitive fix views man as a rational, consistent actor who will modify his internally controlled behavior on the basis of new information. The cognitive fix always involves the transfer of information, often under the rubric of educational programs, information campaigns, or advertising, that tries to modify beliefs, attitudes, values or motivation. The target of this information is generally the individual whose own behavior seems to be associated most closely with losses. In the case of water resources, flood warnings directed at flood plain dwellers, pollution control information to individual polluters, and weather reports disseminated to those who may be adversely affected by rainfall are all examples of the cognitive fix.

**The Structural Fix**

The essence of the structural fix is to modify individual behavior by modifying the physical structure or social setting in which the action takes place. Unlike the cognitive fix, which must assume some model of personality, the structural fix concentrates on behavior. (This is not to imply that there is no information transfer in the structural fix. Indeed the actor must have information about the change in structure. However, it is the change in structure rather than the information itself that influences behavior.) It assumes that the future behavior of an individual will be much like his past behavior. The model of man, if you will, which is the basis of the structural fix, is very much like that used in behavioral psychology, and tends to be descriptive rather than normative. This can be better illustrated by example.

**The Cognitive and Structural Fixes: Comparisons**

Suppose that the manager of a water recreation area wished to eliminate powerboating on the lake. A very effective way to do this would be to remove all the boat launching spots on the lake, since his past experience suggests that almost all such boats are brought by cars and trailers. With no ramps, most powerboating will be kept from the lake. This is an example of a structural fix where behavior was modified by changing the physical structure in which the act took place. It is based on the past behavior of the boater.

Suppose the manager did not have control of all boat ramps or felt that taking them out would eliminate desirable forms of boating recreation. He might then go to a cognitive fix where he posted signs, ran ads in the newspaper, sent letters to boat owners telling them the reasons why it was bad to powerboat in the lake. Perhaps stumps destroyed motors or injured water skiers, or perhaps sport fishermen were disturbed. Trying to change behavior by changing the beliefs and attitudes of the boater with informational techniques is the classic case of the cognitive fix. It is important to note that the target of the information is the boater himself.

The manager may also use information techniques to bring about changes in social structure. Although this may appear similar to a cognitive fix, it differs in the target of the information because information influences boaters only indirectly through some structural change. Suppose the manager felt some state law were necessary to limit boating on the lake. He would have to use an informational campaign to convince legislators to introduce and approve such a law. He would be applying the rules of the cognitive fix to get legislators to create a social structure that would in turn influence boater behavior. The great difference between the cognitive and structural fixes here is the notion of role. The cognitive fix goes for each individual boater, while the informational aspect of the structural fix is directed at those who, because of their special role, are in a position to modify social structure. In general, the motivations of these two groups will be vastly different. Once a law is passed, its publication and subsequent enforcement is the new structure that influences behavior.

Outside the specific case of water resources, one can illustrate the application of these fixes to a classic natural resource problem discussed by Hardin (1969) in "The Tragedy of the Commons." When everyone uses a commons area to graze his cattle, it is economically rational for each person to add cattle since he realizes a great deal of the gain at little personal cost. The tragedy is that if everyone acts economically rational, the commons area will be overgrazed and the land destroyed. The psychological fix to this problem is to try to change peoples' attitudes so they act in ways that lead to the common good. Through persuasion and information the cognitive fix tries to change the motivational base of behavior from economic self-interest to altruism. The structural fix involves setting up a new institution, which makes each individual liable for the consequences of adding cattle. The institution of private property made it economically rational for each individual to not overgraze. It was not necessary to change the motivational basis for action (*i.e.*, maximizing personal gain).

Returning to the kinds of issues of man's interaction with variation in water, the cognitive and the structural fixes have both been used as alternatives to reduce flood losses. One explanation for human floodplain occupancy in spite of the high risks involved was that people were simply unaware of the floodplain location. If this information were provided, one would expect individuals who live in, or anticipate living in the area, to make some sort of adjustment.

To bring about the cognitive fix the USGS was encouraged to produce floodplain maps that showed the extent of probable floods. It was hoped that by making these maps available, a change in both attitudes and behavior would result. Unfortunately this was not very effective. After investigating the program, White (1966) concluded: "The U.S. Geological Survey map of Topeka in 1959 did not have a prompt, significant effect upon the thinking of the people in Topeka."

Dismayed by this failure of the cognitive fix, University of Chicago investigators began to explore the social structural aspects of building a home. The process of obtaining mortgages and appraisals were necessary conditions for the construction of new homes. By modifying this social structure, advances were made. "We have learned, for example," White (1966) suggests, "that while the flood hazard map alone may have little influence upon the decision of a property owner to build in a flood-plain, it becomes powerful when placed in the hands of a professional appraiser who has been instructed in its use, and even more powerful when mortgage insurance officers in The Federal Housing Administration are instructed to look for it and use it."

*Appeals of the Cognitive Fix*

The cognitive fix has both practical and ideological appeals. It certainly will often be cheaper than massive technological enterprises, and it is applicable when the physical environment is not susceptible to change. Moreover, in U.S. society this approach has ideological appeals. Individuals are seen as responsible for their own fate. Making information available to them is consistent with notions of free choice. The apparent absence of coercion that is part of the cognitive fix also fits well with notions of freedom and responsibility.

*Problems of the Cognitive Fix*

In general, the cognitive fix is less likely than either the technological or structural fix to reduce losses. It doesn't work because it is very difficult to change an individual's beliefs or attitudes and, even if these are modified, there is little reason to believe that changes in behavior will follow. Unfortunately this is not conjecture, but rather is backed up by years of social psychological research. Before mentioning some of the most general trends in these investigations, I wish to deal with one qualification to these sweeping assertions about attitude change and behavioral response.

Of course, attitudes change and with these changes we see that actions change as well. Most recently we have been able to document general changes in public attitudes toward pollution and the environment. As Erskine reports in what she calls a "Miracle of Public Opinion," from May, 1965, to June, 1970, the proportion of people viewing air pollution as a serious problem jumped from 28 to 69 per cent. Water pollution showed a similar increase with 35 to 74 per cent increase (Erskine, 1972). With these changes have come new programs and billions of dollars and man hours directed at reducing the problem. In the context of a fix however, this example of public attitude and behavior change is quite irrelevant and does not refute my basic point. The question of a fix, cognitive, structural, or technological, is one of engineering. Can man willfully bring about change? We can often implement technological fixes. Although it is a bit more difficult, we can engineer social systems to bring about changes such as floodplain zoning. However, it appears extremely difficult to *engineer* widespread cognitive change that effectively modifies behavior. Although I have penned an explanation for the environmental crisis (Heberlein, 1972), I am sure that my explanation is not sufficient to either create (by identifying the important variables to manipulate) or predict general shifts in attitudes.

Social psychologists over the past half-century have devoted substantial amounts of time and energy to studies of attitudes and the dynamics of change (McGuire, 1968; Kiesler, Collins, and Miller, 1969). Usually these studies have been conducted in tightly controlled laboratory situations and have shown that single attitudes or beliefs are influenced by all sorts of independent variables, such as content of the message, characteristics of the communicator, fear arousal, and degree of dissonance, to name a few. It also appears that attitudes revert back to their former state with great rapidity. Even when investigators have a captive audience in an unusual setting, long-term changes in attitude are seldom observed.

In the real world one finds less than an ideal setting for engineering a cognitive fix. Usually educational or informational programs are carried out in the field, rather than the laboratory. The target population is ill-defined and hardly captive. Those who need the information most will be those most likely to ignore the input. This selective exposure is one explanation for the generally dismal findings of mass communication studies (Hovland, 1959). Unlike laboratory experiments where the investigator selects a single attitude or belief that he feels is likely to change, mass communication efforts often involve whole clusters of beliefs and attitudes that are imbedded in the cognitive structure and solidified by past behavior and choices. Moving these calls for a massive psychological reorganization, a reorganization that a functioning organism will avoid if at all possible. To the degree that a man's interaction with water resources has a long history and is an integral part of his psychology and his behavior, the more difficult it will be to modify his attitudes and beliefs.

*Attitudes and Behavior*

Even if one were successful in changing attitudes, to be effective the cognitive fix must lead to behavior change. In a recent review of thirty years of research examining the relationship between attitudes and behavior Wicker (1969) concluded, "Only rarely can as much as 10 per cent of the variance in overt behavioral measure be accounted for by attitude." This suggests that even if public attitudes about water use, floods, cropping practices, and land use could be changed, one would not be successful at reducing the population in the interaction cell because behavior would be unlikely to change. Social psychologists have acknowledged this gap between attitudes and behavior, and have directed their attention to exploring intervening variables that act to surpass the relationship (Ehrlich, 1969). These are briefly reported below.

Before an actor can behave consistently with his attitudes and beliefs, he must have knowledge of the appropriate behavior. People may already feel that they shouldn't pollute and risk their lives and property to environmental variation, but they don't associate their behaviors with these outcomes. A manager may simply not know that certain crop practices yield water pollution or increase his risk of hail damage, or he may have no idea where the floodplain is located.

Knowledge alone is not enough. The actor must have the ability to take an action. He may not have the economic resources available to do so. He may know what should be done and have the resources to pay for it but may not have command of the technology necessary to bring it about. Limitations of ability are a very serious stumbling block to the quick and easy translation of attitudes into behavior.

The actor may have the knowledge and ability to take actions but be constrained by social and psychological factors. Social norms tend to define appropriate or inappropriate behavior. A reasonable proposal may be rejected because "that's not the way we do it around here," or because one would lose favor with or be ostracized by one's neighbors. Role requirements and constraints also reduce the attitude-behavior relationship. An individual may not take action because he feels that the responsibility lies in some other sector.

Psychological factors also account for some of the attitude-behavior slippage. The individual's cognitive structure may contain many competing attitudes and beliefs, some of which may serve to inhibit the behavior that might logically follow from a given attitude. In my own research I have found that it is not attitudes toward littering that influence littering behavior (once opportunity has been controlled experimentally), but rather one's disposition to ascribe responsibility to himself and one's awareness of the negative interpersonal consequences of the act (Heberlein, 1971). Modifications of these tendencies will be more fruitful than trying to change attitudes about litter.

## Motivation, Role and Information

I have stated the case against the cognitive fix as strongly as possible because it is overworked as a simple and unproductive solution to complex problems. It is important to abandon the cognitive fix for structural fixes that are more likely to change human behavior. However, sometimes the cognitive fix is the only one available or, because of its low costs, it may be used in conjunction with other fixes. From experience I do have some suggestions about the conditions under which the cognitive fix may be less than hopeless. I have not reviewed the literature in an attempt to document or complicate these hunches.

The mainstay of the cognitive fix is to transmit information. This information is likely to be effective when it helps the person realize the goals he is already motivated to achieve, rather than to change old motivations or to create new motives. For example, if a person's prime concern in purchasing a new home is to avoid flood losses, he will seek out and be influenced by flood relevant information. If the purchaser has more usual concerns of price, style, location, and appeal to other family members, flood relevant information will be unlikely to have an effect. This is consistent with Kates' (1962) finding that those communities that have more regular or recurrent floods develop a wider range and more effective adaptive mechanisms. The flooding frequency creates the motivation and people appear to seek out both information and technology. In our example of the control of power boats, it is easy to see why the cognitive fix would be unlikely to work. A person who owns a large boat and has just towed it to a lake for an outing clearly has a great deal of motivation to powerboat. Informing him that his action disturbs others and harms fishing is not likely to keep him off the lake. If, however, by playing on his motivations, we can show him an even better lake nearby on which to powerboat, the information will lead to behavior change.

Accurately assessing each individual's motivation is an impossible task. However, by employing the sociological concept of role, one can go beyond personality and be more effective in bringing about a fix. In the case of effective use of flood plain maps, it was necessary to locate the particular role where the incumbent would be motivated to reduce low probability loss to the property. Only with someone who has this motivation would the map be effective. The potential owner has many other stronger motivations than this one. However, this is the prime motivation for those people who grant loans, and for them the floodplain maps produced a change in behavior. To bring about a cognitive fix, one has to be quite canny about both roles and motivation to be cognizant of the information role incumbents need to realize goals or to realize these goals by some different means.

**Decision Theory and the Cognitive Fix**

Another assumption behind the cognitive fix is that man is an optimizer, that he behaves in a way that maximizes gains and minimizes losses. Thus, to reduce losses due to the interaction between man and environment, one only needs to show floodplain dwellers that they live in a floodplain and that they have a non-zero probability of losing their homes and possessions. Given that man is economically rational, he will move, floodproof, or buy flood insurance. To account for the strange finding that most people won't move, floodproof, or buy flood insurance, theorists have been moving toward an alternative model called "bounded rationality." This has been discussed in terms of water resources and natural hazards by Kates (1962) and Slovic, Kunreuther, and White (1973). It stems from earlier work by Simon (1956, 1957, 1959, and 1972) in the area of microeconomic decision-making and has been extended by Cyert and March (1963) to organizations. The bounded rationality model appears to fit quite well with the work of social psychologists in the attitude behavior investigations. While no attempt is made in this paper to integrate these two approaches, such an integration would benefit both areas.

Bounded rationality asserts that the cognitive limitations of the decision-maker force him to construct a simplified model of the world in order to deal with it. The key principle is satisfying rather than optimizing. Man is viewed as striving to attain some satisfactory, though not necessary, optimal level of achievement. The principles of the BR model may be discussed in terms of an optimization model. Given environmental variation and a number of alternative actions, man the optimizer can be expected to take actions that maximize his utilities. A simplified version of this paradigm can be expressed in terms of a utility matrix illustrated in Table I. Given three states of nature and a number of alterna-

**Table I**
Utilities Matrix for Probabilistic States of Nature and Several Alternative Actions

| Alternatives | State of Nature | | |
|---|---|---|---|
| | $S_1$ $p = 0.60$ | $S_2$ $p = 0.35$ | $S$ $p = 0.05$ |
| $A_1$ | $u_{11}$ | $u_{12}$ | $u_{13}$ |
| $A_2$ | $u_{21}$ | $u_{22}$ | $u_{23}$ |
| $A_3$ | $u_{31}$ | $u_{32}$ | $u_{33}$ |
| $A_n$ | $u_{n1}$ | $u_{n2}$ | $u_{n3}$ |

tives, it is assumed that the alternative chosen will be that where $\sum_{j=1}^{3} u_{ij} p_i$ is greatest. One implication of this is that the choice of great losses in the event of low probability states $S_3$ (*e.g.*, floods, droughts, hailstorms) would lead to low or negative values of $\sum_{j=1}^{3} u_{ij} p_i$ and that such alternatives ought to be avoided. When behavior is actually observed, it often appears that some suboptimal choice is selected; the bounded rationality literature suggests the following reasons why this may happen.

Economists can correctly argue that the bounded rationality model views man as rational, as does the optimization model, but merely specifies a priori, that the decision setting is constrained in various ways. Constraints are certainly no news to standard economic theory. However, the nature of the constraints considered by the B.R. theorists are psychologically based and revolve around the decision process. Bounded rationality assumptions are much more descriptive than normative. In that sense they are less general but tend to be more accurate, where data is available, than normative economic analysis. Because of the nature and importance of these assumptions, it would be helpful to spell them out.

The first kind of cognitive limitation of the decision-maker in the B.R. model deals with the probabilities associated with the states of nature. Kates (1962, chapter 4) discusses the scientific and technical difficulties of establishing probabilities associated with various states of nature. Slovic, *et al.* (1973) reviewed a broad literature showing that when objective probabilities are available or computable, decision-makers make substantial distortions. If these are inaccurate, $\sum_{j=1}^{3} u_{ij} p_i$ can lead to an appropriate ordering of alternatives. One generalization about the cognitive distortions of probabilities that can be made is that people tend to simplify the matrix by zeroing out low probability events. This simplifies the decision, but ignores the cells in the utility matrix with the largest negative values.

A second way that the matrix is simplified is by limiting the range of alternatives. If one has no alternatives, then choice is simple. The more the alternatives, the more things must be considered, and the more complicated and exasperating the decision becomes. The full range of potential alternatives may be limited by prior experience, knowledge, or ability. They may also be limited by norms and roles.

Kates (1962) concluded that those people who had repeated experience with floods showed a wider range of adaptation than those with little experience. Given a low probability event that occurs when physical phenomena range to the tails of their probability distribution, it is axiomatic that one will have little experience as a consequence. Such limitations may well lead to suboptimal behavior.

A third bound to rationality involves the utilities themselves. Having limited experience with low probability events handicaps one's evaluation of the joint effect of that state with given alternatives. It is difficult for the decision-maker to know what his utilities will be in advance of his experience of the events. Outcomes are undoubtedly multidimensional, and the mass of information needed to assess utilities will never be close at hand. To reduce this uncertainty, it is likely that the decision-maker will use only a single dimension to estimate utilities or will ignore some cells altogether. These limits to rationality might be a bit clearer if you think about the process of buying your last automobile.

The characteristics of an automobile may be viewed as states of nature, some probablistic (repair record), some not (price). Not all cars were comparable, tradeoffs in the face of uncertain information could not be made, many alternatives (car models, styles, bicycles, mass transit, etc.) were not fully evaluated. And remember how good it felt to finally make some decision. It is this dimension of the utility of a decision itself, any decision, and the idea that people select some satisfactory rather than optimal outcome that characterizes the B.R. model.

Since it is descriptive, rather than normative, the B.R. model is difficult to use in policy situations. Theorists have yet to work out sets of rules that describe how bounded rationality works. Even if it is usually wrong, the optimization model makes clear specifications about action, and allows clear predictions. Since one knows little about how people simplify the decision across situations or what levels of outcome are satisfactory, one needs a great deal of data to suggest how people might react to some new policy, assuming that rationality is bounded. Without such data, as is usually the case in discussions of new policies, those who assume bounded rationality are perpetual "nay-sayers." They can only suggest that the obvious solution which assumes optimization will not work, but can seldom suggest a cognitive fix that works under the B.R. assumptions.

*Individual vs. Collective Action*

A final problem of the cognitive fix is that by focusing on individual action it misses those important problems that are due to the collective action of men. In fact, it may exacerbate these problems. In Hardin's (1969) discussion, the commons was in danger precisely because if every *individual* would behave rationally, it would lead to *collective losses*. The cognitive fix ignores the system properties of human action. Any action exists in a social context and to ignore that context involves serious risks.

*Appeals of the Structural Fix*

Given the general ineffectiveness of the cognitive fix and the high costs and polluting effects of the technological fix, the structural fix is an appealing alternative. Flood losses can be reduced by floodplain zoning much more efficiently than by either dams or appeals to self-interest. Water use can be drastically altered by changes in the productivity sector, by changes from agriculture to industry in locales where water is short. If a man's total wheat holdings were separated by several miles, he would avoid severe hail losses. Mass transit is less affected by urban snow than individual autos. Moreover, structural change may lead to a sort of cognitive fix. Recent social psychological evidence (Bem, 1970) suggests that attitudes *follow* behavior. If behavior can be changed through structural means, it is possible that the appropriate attitudes will develop.

*Problems of the Structural Fix*

There are three sorts of problems with this approach, all three serious. While the technological fix has great institutional support, the structural fix has little. I am unfamiliar with any research program that investigates modifications of the sociocultural system that would reduce losses due to the interaction with the physical environment. Not only does it lack institutional support, but it is thwarted by institutional inertia. Changes in social structure must be deliberated and approved by many separate political units, both formal and informal. The process itself is slow, and the compromise produced by pluralistic societies may make such measures ineffective. Given the effectiveness of the structural fix, it should have the same institutional status as the technological fix. However uncomfortable in the short run, the institutional inertia, review and deliberation are things we would not wish to see eliminated. Rather, the technological fix should receive the same kind of review and public deliberation that the structural fix receives, for indeed its consequences are equally important.

Another problem with the structural fix is that traditionally we have pretty much ignored social evaluation. In the case of the technological fix experimentation and evaluation of the first order effects, *i.e.*, that the technology produces significant observable modification in the physical environment, is part of standard operating procedure. The Army Corps of Engineers routinely evaluates complex models, and investigators in the experimental meteorological labs in the National Oceanic and Aeronautics Administration conduct both laboratory and field experiments to determine the effect of seeding on the physical environment. While those who implement technological fixes may be faulted for not looking much beyond the direct impacts of their modifications (*i.e.*, flood levels rather than losses), implementation of the structural fix is usually void of the most basic evaluation procedures. Recently we have begun to seriously evaluate social programs (Coleman, *et al.*, 1966; Weiss, 1972), but such events are still rare.

Campbell (1969) has discussed reasons for the political inertia toward evaluation. Important among these is program rather than solution orientation toward problems taken by politicians. Rather than saying we have a serious problem, we are going to try program A, and if that doesn't work, we will try B, political strategy focuses on a single program. In this case evaluation can only show the failure of a program, and it is not advantageous to have it evaluated.

Besides this political inertia, there are problems inherent in social experimentation. These include cost, time lags, reactivity, and ethical issues. If new data must be collected or the community itself (rather than individuals) is the unit of analysis, social research is extremely costly. Single experiments may cost at least hundreds of thousands of dollars. While laboratory and field experiments evaluating the effects of a technological fix can be done in hours or weeks, social experiments take months or years. The information may simply not be worth these costs or delays. Moreover, humans who believe they are in an experiment may behave uniquely because of this, and the findings may not generalize to program implementation. Finally, there are ethical problems. If the program is to bring benefits to those in the experimental group, agencies may find it difficult to justify a control group. If the opposite is hypothesized, then inclusion into the experimental group may be successfully opposed by certain groups, making the findings nonrepresentative. In addition to these problems are the normal analytic problems of quasi-experiments (Campbell and Stanley, 1966).

A final problem of the structural fix is our nearly complete ignorance of the second order effects. Lately a great deal of discussion has been devoted to technology assessment. The unanticipated consequences of technology have been seen as an important area of research. While it is clear that we have a long way to go in this area, many of the secondary effects, such as the effect of air pollution on people and plants, can be anticipated and measured. Well-known theories of chemistry, physics and biology help us to anticipate and evaluate these effects. Our theories of society are much less precise, and will not allow even guesses at the nature of these consequences. Does floodplain zoning weaken other governmental structures, change basic patterns of industrialization and economic development, modify communication systems, or change the social structure of the community? Who knows? What might be the unanticipated sociological consequences of changing land tenure on the great plains, such that a single man's holdings were not contiguous?

In light of these ponderous unknowns, the caution with which the sociological fix is viewed may have some strong justification. However, this suggests that research effort on sociological fixes would be well directed. A mere typology of consequences would be helpful to consider alternatives among the three fixes.

## CONCLUSION

The tone of this paper is pessimistic. My hope is that it might temper some enthusiasm for any particular fix by pointing out the assumptions and problems with the fix. I tend to be quite an advocate of the structural fix. I think it is efficient, effective, and tends to reduce losses rather than merely change the environment. However, I'm pretty scared about the unknown secondary effects that may be brought about by structural change. Some day I may learn that while some solution I proposed reduced losses, it also widened the gap between rich and poor, changed some aspect of the community that most people enjoyed, and weakened feelings of individual autonomy. In face of such risks, I feel some humility when I criticize engineers for not anticipating and checking all the side effects of the technological fix. The psychological fix usually does not work and ought to be avoided. It often appears to me that there is an inverse relationship between one's training in social psychology and one's enthusiasm for the cognitive fix. The limited utility of the cognitive fix for policy doesn't much bother me as a social psychologist. I see the role of the scientist to help policymakers. Often it's just as helpful to be able to say what won't work as it is to say what will.

The upshot of this paper, it seems to me, is to suggest we focus on problems themselves rather than fixes. Our institutions are now roughly organized around fixes, with many focusing on technological fixes, some on structural fixes, a few on cognitive fixes. I'd like to see all three fixes for water problems happening in the same shop—the mixing and combining of fixes to solve the problem. This would be the combination of active ingredients that doctors have been known to recommend.

## ACKNOWLEDGMENT

I would like to thank Gilbert White, Robert Kates, and Irving Fox for their helpful comments on earlier drafts. This revision also benefitted from the seminar discussion by the staff of the West Water Research Centre of the University of British Columbia.

## REFERENCES

Bem, D. *Beliefs, Attitudes and Human Affairs* (Belmont, Calif.: Brooks/Cole, 1970).

Burton, I., R. W. Kates, and G. F. White. "The Human Ecology of Extreme Geographical Events," Working paper No. 1, Natural Hazard Research, Dept. of Geography, University of Toronto (1968).

Campbell, D. T. "Reforms as Experiments," *Amer. Psychol.* 24 (4), 409 (1969).

Campbell, D. T. and J. C. Stanley. *Experimental and Quasi Experimental Designs for Research* (Chicago: Rand McNally, 1966).

Coleman, J. S., E. Q. Campbell, C. F. Hobson, J. McPartland and A. Mood, et al. *Equality of Educational Opportunity* (Washington: U.S. Office of Education, 1966).

Cyert, R. M. and J. G. March. *A Behavioral Theory of the Firm* (Englewood Cliffs: Prentice-Hall, 1963).

Ehrlich, H. J. "Attitudes, Behavior, and the Intervening Variables," *Amer. Sociol.* **4**, 29 (1969).
Erskine, H. "The Polls: Pollution and Its Cost," *Public Opinion Quart. Spring:* 120 (1972).
Hardin, G. "The Tragedy of the Commons," *Science* **162** (1969).
Heberlein, T. A. "The Land Ethic Realized: Some Social Psychological Explanations for Changing Environmental Attitudes," *J. Soc. Issues.* **28** (4), 79 (1972).
Heberlein, T. A. "Moral Norms, Threatened Sanctions, and Littering Behavior," Madison: University of Wisconsin, unpublished Ph.D. dissertation (1971).
Hovland, C. I. "Reconciling Conflicting Results Derived from Experimental and Survey Studies of Attitude Change," *Amer. Psychol.* **14**, 8 (1959).
Kates, R. W. "Hazard and Choice Perception in Flood Plain Management," Department of Geography Research Paper #78, University of Chicago (1962).
Kiesler, C. A., B. E. Collins and N. Miller. *Attitude Change* (New York: John Wiley and Sons, 1969).
McGuire, W. J. "The Nature of Attitudes and Attitude Change," in *The Handbook of Social Psychology*, Vol. III, G. Lindzey and E. Aronson, Eds., (Reading, Mass.: Addison-Wesley, 1968).
Simon, H. A. "Rational Choice and the Structure of the Environment," *Psychol. Rev.* **63**, 129 (1956).
Simon, H. A. *Models of Man* (New York: Wiley, 1957).
Simon, H. A., "Theories of Decision Making in Economics and Behavioral Sciences," *Amer. Econ. Rev.* **49**, 253 (1959).
Simon, H. A. *Theories of Bounded Rationality in Decision and Organization,* C. B. McGuire and R. Rudner, Eds., New York: American Elsevier Publishing Co., 1972).
Slovic, P., H. Kunreuther, and G. F. White. "Decision Process, Rationality and Adjustment to Natural Hazards," in *Natural Hazards: Local, Regional & Global.* G. F. White, Ed. (Oxford University Press, New Jersey, 1974).
U.S. House of Representatives. Second Session Task Force on Federal Flood Control Policy, House Document No. 465 (1966).
Weiss, C. H. *Evaluating Action Programs* (Boston: Allyn and Bacon, Inc., 1972).
White, G. F. "Optimal Flood Damage Management: Retrospect and Prospect," in *Water Research,* A. V. Kneese and S. C. Smith, Eds., (Baltimore: Johns Hopkins Press, 1966), pp. 258-261.
White, L. "The Historical Roots of Our Ecological Crisis," *Science* **155**, 1203 (1967).
Wicker, A. W. "Attitudes vs. Actions: The Relationship of Verbal and Overt Behavioral Responses to Attitude Objects," *J. Soc. Issues* **25**, 41 (1969).

# Index

Activists, 159, 160
Activity clusters, 204, 229
Activity substitution, 207, 218, 219
Advocates, 159, 160
Agglomeration, 67
Air pollution, 17, 18, 20, 281, 285
Alchian, A., 265
Allee, D. J., 127
Allocating resources, 7
American Great Plains, 48
Analysis of variance, 22
Analytic pluralism, 82
Andrews, R. B., 33
Andrews, W. H., 50
Appalachia, 170
Arid regions, 44
Arizona, 43
Army Corps of Engineers, 28, 30, 84, 91, 93, 97, 107, 125, 128-130, 134, 135, 138, 145, 146, 154, 169, 170, 177, 179, 274, 280, 293
Arrow, K. J., 262
Attitudes, 17, 19, 171, 282, 283, 285, 286
Atomic Energy Commission, 96

Back, W. B., 34
Bain, J. W., 262
Bank protection, 155
Barkley Dam, 169
Barrows, R. L., 88, 99
Barth, F., 47
Baskin, D., 82
Baumol, W. J., 266
Beattie, B. R., 88
Bear Lake Region, 50
Becker, C. J., 171, 172
Behan, R. W., 126
Beliefs, 282, 283, 286
Bem, D., 292
Ben-David, S., 62

Bend Ranger District, 238
Benefit/cost, 7, 32, 113, 128, 144
Benoit-Smullyan, E., 41
Bentham, Jeremy, 31
Benstock, M., 93
Berger, B. M., 207
Bilinski, R., 86, 87
Boggs, K. S., 138
Bohrnstedt, G. W., 225
Bolle, A., 126
Bonner, E. J., 138
Bonneville Power Administration, 90, 154
Borton, T. E., 97
Boulding, K., 11, 236
Bounded rationality, 289-291
Brémaud, O., 46
Brewer, M. F., 115
Bromley, D. W., 89, 127
Burch, W. R., 202, 203, 205, 208
Burdge, Rabel, 171, 176, 197
Bureau of Land Management, 125
Bureau of Reclamation, 32, 33, 62, 89, 90, 125, 154, 280
Burton, T. L., 220, 223
Butcher, W. R., 118

California, 35
California Public Outdoor Recreation Plan, 199
Campbell, D. T., 293, 294
Carr Fork Reservoir, 176
Cave Run Reservoir, 176, 178, 184
Central Africa, 43
Central America, 43
Central Valley Project, 108
Cheek, N. H., 202, 203, 205
Ciriacy-Wantrup, S. C., 110
Citizen involvement, 126, 127, 132, 136, 137, 139, 144

297

## 298   WATER AND COMMUNITY DEVELOPMENT

Citizens for a Clean Environment, 156, 157, 163
Clark, V., 152
Clark, R. N., 219
Cognitive fix, 282-289, 292, 295
Cognitive structure, 287
Coleman, J. S., 293
Collective action, 292
Collective choice, 21
Collective optimum, 269
Collins, B. E., 285
Columbia Basin, 35, 36, 63, 108
Communities, 8, 15, 42, 195, 217, 219, 229, 235, 238, 244, 247, 252
Communities of interest, 18, 113
Community adaptation, 165
Community development, 1-8, 13, 41-47, 81, 88, 98-113, 211, 212, 236
Community life, 184
Competition-location models, 67
Conner, J. R., 251
Conservation, 7
Conservation groups, 20
Coordination costs, 263-266, 271, 273
Coordination inputs, 268, 274
Cost/benefit, 8, 170, 184, 185
Cost sharing, 98, 100, 102
Cottrell, W. F., 48
Council on Environmental Quality, 96
Crocker, T. D., 270, 276
Cronbach, L. J., 225
Cultural Patterns, 2, 8, 19
Cultural organization, 16
Cyert, R. M., 289

Darwin, C., 164
Davis, Arthur P., 153
Davis, Robert K., 274
Decision criteria, 270
Decision rule, 273
Delaware River Basin, 108
Demsetz, H., 265
Department of Housing and Urban Development, 92
Derogates, 160, 162
Direct regulation, 273
Discount rate, 32, 39
Disequilibrium, 65
Douglas, W., 129
Drainage, 155
Drew, E., 129
Earth Week, 156
Easter, K. W., 62
Eckstein, Otto, 32, 34

Economic analysis, 15
Economic base, 33, 36
Economic constraints, 20
Economic damage, 15
Economic efficiency, 273
Economic growth, 8, 9, 17, 20, 34, 57, 61, 161
Economic structure models, 68, 266
Economic theory, 14, 17, 42
Economies of scale, 67, 69
Ecosystem, 8
Edwards, J. A., 243
Efficiency, 27, 30
Effluent charges, 273, 274
Ehrlich, H. J., 286
Elasticity of demand, 241
Eminent domain, 177
Employment, 19
Energy, 3, 89
Environmental ethic, 7
Environmental impact statement, 100, 102, 250
Environmental impact studies, 235, 249
Environmental objectives, 262
Environmental Policy Act, 83, 259
Environmentalists, 19
Equilibrium, 37, 38
Equity, 27
Erskine, H., 285
Eskimo, 43
Expertise model, 126, 127
Export-base model, 68
Externalities, 7, 8, 17, 18, 113, 185, 275

Fabian, T., 266
Farb, P., 45
Farmers Home Administration, 92
Federal Housing Administration, 284
Federal Power Commission, 154, 155
Federal Water Pollution Control Act, 93
Federal Water Quality Control Administration, 274
Ferriss, A. L., 219
Fesler, J. W., 115
Field, Donald, 200, 203, 204
Firey, Walter, 28
Fish and wildlife maintenance, 155
Flood control, 2, 30, 83, 84, 89, 91, 92, 97, 129, 136, 156, 184, 280, 281, 288
Flood Control Act of 1936, 32, 112, 154
Flood plain insurance, 91
Flood plain regulation, 84
Flood plain zoning, 91, 157

INDEX 299

Folz, W. E., 32
Forrester, J. W., 75
Foss, P., 127
Fried, M., 176
Friesma, H. P., 126
Fuguitt, G. V., 196

Garrison, C. B., 61
Geersten, D. C., 50
General equilibrium approach, 64
Geographic theory, 14
Gillette, R., 95, 96
Gilpin, William, 49
Gleicher, P., 176
Gobi Desert, 44
Goebel, E. R., 178
Ground water, 112
Group decision-making, 17, 21
Grubb, H. W., 35
Guedry, L. J., 238

Haas, J. E., 138
Habitat, 42
Hahn, F., 262
Hallberg, M. C., 37
Hamburg, D., 164
Hargrove, M. B., 185
Hardin, G., 283, 292
Harmon, H. H., 223
Haroldsen, A., 246
Haurin, D. R., 35, 36
Haveman, R., 130
Heady, E. D., 94
Heard, Dwight B., 153
Heberlein, T. A., 285, 287
Hendee, J., 197
Henning, D., 125, 127
Hetch-Hetchy complex, 29
Hite, J. C., 249
Hogg, T. C., 81, 87, 127, 130
Holje, H. C., 34
Holme, A., 220
Hovland, C. I., 286
Howe, Charles, 61, 62
Huang River, 44
Human adaptation, 164-166
Human behavior, 13, 14, 16, 21-23, 282
Human communities, 16
Human rationality, 17
Human system, 281
Hutchins, W. A., 109, 111
Hydraulic civilizations, 44
Hydroelectric power, 2, 83, 84, 89, 90, 96, 98, 100, 108, 280

Idaho, 50
Income distribution, 27
Indirect benefits, 84
Indus River, 44
Industrial water supply, 83, 85, 89, 92, 97, 98, 100, 102
Ingram, H., 82, 115, 127
Input-output model, 20, 21, 36, 68, 72, 75, 247
Institution, 9, 41, 269, 284
Institutional change, 259
Institutional design, 261
Institutional development, 8
Institutional reorganization, 110, 112, 115
Institutional structure, 1, 269, 273, 276
Institutionalism, 28
Instream uses, 109, 116, 117
Integrated research, 13
Integrative systems, 11
Interbasin transfer, 62
Interchangeability, 207
Interdisciplinary research, 9, 12-14, 23
Interest groups, 82, 83, 86, 99, 128, 129, 146
Interindustry analysis, 17
Interindustry models, 20, 246
Internalizing externalities, 18
Iowa Conservation Commission, 131
Iranian Desert, 44
Irrigation, 2, 3, 31-34, 62, 69, 77, 83, 84, 89, 92, 100, 108, 155
Irrigation projects, 63, 94, 96, 98, 151, 279, 280
Isard, W., 68, 249

Jansma, J. D., 34
Jefferson Reservoir Project, 129, 134, 146

Kates, R. W., 288-291
Kelso, M. M., 34
Khalahari Desert, 43
Kiesler, C. A., 285
Klamath Lake study, 238, 242, 253
Knetsch, J. L., 197, 251
Knight, R. H., 263
Korsching, P. F., 172
Kung Bushmen, 44, 45
Kunreuther, H., 289

Lamphear, S. C., 219, 223
Land use planning, 99, 100
Lapland, 43

# 300 WATER AND COMMUNITY DEVELOPMENT

Laurent, E. A., 249
League of Women Voters, 156
Lee, R., 45, 46
Legal constraints, 20
Legitimizers, 160
Leisure behavior, 16, 221
Leisure participation, 196, 197, 202, 204, 208, 211
Leisure setting, 204
Lenski, G., 41
Leontief, W. W., 36, 38, 246, 249
Leven, C. L., 64, 88
Lewis, W. C., 64
Lime, D. W., 218, 219
Linear programming, 20
Lord, W. B., 83, 127
Low-flow augmentation, 274, 275
Lucas, R. C., 219
Ludtke, R., 171, 176
Lund, F., 164

March, J. G., 289
Market society, 50
Market system, 18
Markets, 65, 110
Marshall, Hubert, 127, 145
Marts, Marion, 33
Massie, P., 220
Mather, E. C., 48
Maxwell, George H., 153
Mayer, L. V., 94
McEvoy, J., 125
McGuire, W. J., 285
McKinley, C., 115
Meadows, D. H., 252
Meigs, P., 43
Meyersohn, R., 202
Miller, N., 285
Mills, C. W., 169
Mississippi River, 91
Missouri Basin Account, 108
Missouri Outdoor Recreation Plan, 199
Mode of coordination, 267, 269
Molotch, H., 126
Monitoring data, 266
Moore, H., 152
Moss, W. T., 219, 223
Motivation, 287
Multiple regression, 22
Multiplier, 33, 246
Municipal water supply, 83, 85, 89, 92, 97, 98, 100, 102

National Environmental Policy Act (NEPA), 95, 97, 100, 235

National Irrigation Act of 1902, 151, 153
National Oceanic and Aeronautics Administration, 280, 293
National Park Service, 125, 200
National Reclamation Association, 153, 154
National Water Commission, 3, 91, 92, 94, 96, 108, 109, 112, 114, 259
Natural resources, 2, 7, 8, 13, 14, 127, 144
Navigation projects, 63, 92, 96, 155
New Mexico, 43
Nile River, 4, 45
Niskanen, W., 263
Nomadic groups, 46
North Cascades National Park, 196
Nuclear energy, 90, 98
Nunnally, J. C., 223

Objective function, 273
Obligations, 268-273
Ohio River Valley Water Sanitation Commission, 118
O'Leary, J. T., 203
Opportunity costs, 17-19
Oregon Environmental Council, 156, 157, 160, 163
Outdoor recreation, 236, 237
Owens Valley, 29, 30

Pagot, J., 46
Paintsville Dam, 184
Pecuniary interdependence, 264, 265
Peltzman, S., 263
Pima Indians, 153
Planned obsolescence, 35
Plutchik, R., 164
Pollution, 15, 19, 285
Pollution abatement, 19, 155
Pollution damage, 22
Population aggregates, 198
Population control, 3
Powell, John Wesley, 49
Power generation, 155
Preferences, 22
Premigration stress, 175
Principal component analysis, 201
Private costs, 18
Process approach, 87
Proctor, C., 220, 223
Property rights, 24, 110
Pseudo-systems, 11
Psychological fix, 283, 295

Public awareness, 134
Public choice, 21, 22
Public goods, 28, 39
Public interest, 125, 157
Public involvement, 16, 127, 138, 144
Public Law 566, 32
Public participation, 83, 97, 98, 101, 102, 185
Public policy, 15

Quality environment, 20

Raccoon River, 129
Radner, R., 264
Reagan, M. J., 130
Reclamation Act, 31, 32
Recreation, 83, 85, 89, 100, 136
Recreation demand, 197
Recreation expenditures, 245, 246
Recreation types, 219, 223, 227
Recreational benefits, 129, 131, 184, 185, 237, 238
Recreational development, 212, 217
Recreational facilities, 2, 280
Recreational projects, 85, 102
Recreational uses, 3
Red River Gorge Reservoir, 184
Red Rock Reservoir, 220, 230
Regional development, 57
Reich, C., 125
Reiling, S. D., 238
Reservoir projects, 128
Resource constraints, 8
Resource management, 229
Roberts, K. J., 249
Rogers, E., 171
Roos, L. L., 125
Roosevelt, Theodore, 153
Roosevelt Dam, 154
Rural planning, 99

Sahara Desert, 43, 48
Sahlins, M. O., 45
Salt River Valley, 151-153, 159-161
Samuels, Warren, 276
Schmid, A. A., 127
Schutjer, W. H., 37
Secondary effects, 39
Self-interest groups, 157, 159, 160, 163, 164
Selznic, P., 127
Senate Document 97, 155
Shadegg, S., 152
Shoemaker, F. F., 171

Sierra Club, 131, 156, 157, 163
Simon, H. A., 289
Simulation model, 75
Slovic, P., 289, 290
Smith, S. C., 83, 109, 112, 113
Smith, C. L., 127, 130, 152
Snake River Valley, 63
Snell, 203
Social costs, 18
Social experiments, 293
Social group, 16, 17, 19, 20, 197, 199, 202, 203
Social honor, 41, 49-51
Social interaction, 14
Social norms, 287
Social organization, 16, 41, 164
Social overhead capital, 35
Social person, 203
Social power, 22
Social science research, 23
Social status, 9, 41
Social structure, 8, 9, 110, 111, 280, 283, 284, 292
Social system, 20, 21, 281
Social welfare function, 18, 88
Socialization patterns, 208
Socialization process, 19-21
Sociological fix, 294
Sociological theory, 11, 14
Soil Conservation Service, 84, 154
South Santiam River, 156
Southeast Asia, 43
Special interest groups, 126, 127, 157
Stanley, J. C., 294
Statistical methods, 17, 22
Stankey, G. H., 219
Stigum, B. P., 264
Stroevener, H. H., 238
Structural fix, 282-287, 292-294
Sweet, L. E., 46

Task-oriented approach, 87
Taylor, Henry, 118
Taylorsville Reservoir, 175
Technological fix, 279-281, 285, 292, 293, 295
Tempe Canal, 153
Tennessee-Tombigbee Waterway, 96
Tennessee Valley Authority, 61, 108
Texas High Plains, 35
Thar Desert, 44
Tiger, Lionell, 205
Tigris-Euphrates, 44
Tolley, G. S., 35, 36

Traditional community, 107, 114-117
Train, Russell E., 95
Transhumance cycle, 46
Trop, C., 125
Turkestan, 44
Tweeten, L. G., 94

Unemployment, 19
Urban congestion, 17
U.S. Forest Service, 125
U.S. Geological Survey, 153, 284
User charges, 96
Utah, 50
Utilitarians, 31

Values, 7, 15, 17, 19, 22, 282

Warren, R., 86, 225
Washington, 36
Washington Statewide Outdoor Recreation and Open Space Plan, 199
Washington Water Research Center, 69
Wastewater management, 89, 93, 96, 99, 102
Water and community, 8, 23, 28, 30-39, 52
Water and economic growth, 27, 60, 75
Water-based recreation, 36
Water development, 2, 3, 29, 57, 151
Water policy, 3, 9, 107
Water pollution, 17, 18, 20, 280, 285
Water projects, 59, 60, 62, 66, 67, 81, 83, 86, 89
Water quality, 3, 20, 129, 136
Water Quality Act of 1951, 275
Water Quality Act of 1965, 275
Water resource development, 2, 8, 23, 25, 37, 39

Water resource investments, 89, 91, 98, 99
Water resource planning, 2, 14
Water Resources Council, 60, 90, 92, 97
Water resources management, 2, 107-110, 115
Water rights, 109, 111
Water transport, 2
Weather modification, 279
Weiss, C. H., 293
Welfare economics, 15
Wengert, N., 125, 126
Western Agricultural Economics Research Council, 28
Western Environmental Trade Association, 161, 165
White, Gilbert, 51, 127, 284, 289
White, L., 280
Wicker, A., 139, 286
Wilkinson, K. P., 81
Willamette Basin Project Committee, 156
Willamette Basin Task Force Study, 154-156, 161
Willamette Valley, 151, 154
Willamette Valley Project Committee, 156, 157
Williamson, O. E., 271
Wisconsin River, 91
Wittfogel, K. A., 45

Yakima River Basin, 69, 71, 76
Yancey, 203
Yanggen, D. A., 91
Yaquina Bay Study, 238, 241, 252
Yoesting, D., 208
Youmens, R., 246

Zwick, D., 93